Thomas Hawkins

The Origin of the English Drama

Vol. 2

Thomas Hawkins

The Origin of the English Drama
Vol. 2

ISBN/EAN: 9783337303174

Printed in Europe, USA, Canada, Australia, Japan

Cover: Foto ©Thomas Meinert / pixelio.de

More available books at **www.hansebooks.com**

OF

THE ENGLISH D[RAMA]

ILLUSTRATED IN ITS VARIOUS [SPECIES]

VIZ.

MYSTERY, MORALITY, T[RAGEDY]
AND COMEDY,

BY SPECIMENS FROM OUR EARLIEST [WRITERS]

WITH

EXPLANATORY NO[TES]
By THOMAS HAWKI[NS]
OF MAGDALENE COLLEGE,

VOLUME THE SEC[OND]

——— *Res antiquæ laudis et artis*
Ingredior, sanctos ausus recludere fontes.

OXFORD,
PRINTED AT THE CLAREND[ON PRESS]
For S. LEACROFT, CHARING-CR[OSS]
And Sold by D. PRINCE at OXFORD,
at CAMBRIDGE.
M. DCC. LXX. I[X.]

THE
SPANISH TRAGEDY,

CONTAINING

THE LAMENTABLE END OF

DON HORATIO,

AND

BEL-IMPERIA,

WITH THE PITIFUL DEATH OF

OLD HIERONIMO.

THE SPANISH TRAGEDY,
Or,
HIERONIMO IS MAD AGAIN,

— *has ever been an admired play.* Phillips *and* Winstanley *ascribe it to* William Smith, *but erroneously:* Heywood *tells us in his* Actor's Vindication, *page* 14 *of book* 2d, *that it was written by* Thomas Kyd; "*Therefore,*" *says he, (treating of the ancient dignity of Actors)* "M. Kyd *in* The Spanish "Tragedy, *upon occasion presenting itself, writes thus:*

> *Why* Nero *thought it no disparagement,*
> *And kings and emperors have ta'en delight*
> *To make experience of their wits in plays.*"

He is enumerated among the best tragick writers of his times by Fra. Meres. Ben Jonson *ranks him with* Lyly *and* Marloe; *see his verses in memory of* Shakespeare:

> *And tell how far thou didst our* Lyly *outshine;*
> *Or sporting* Kyd, *or* Marloe's *mighty line.*

And another writer, speaking of Kyd, *says,* "Cornelia's "Tragedy, *however not respected, was excellently well done* "*by him.*" Polimanteia &c. *by* W. C. 4°. Camb. 1595.

Mr. Dodsley *printed* The Spanish Tragedy *in the second volume of his collection; but from a very incorrect copy: of which there were many: viz.* 1618, 23, 33. *The present edition is given from the second impression,* "*printed by* "Edward Allde, *amended of such gross blunders as passed in* "*the first,*" *compared with those of* 1618, 23, *and* 33. Allde's *edition has no date; we cannot therefore ascertain the year when it was printed: but it appears in the* Induction *to* Ben Jonson's Bartholomew Fair *to have been acted before the year* 1590.

A 2

DRAMATIS PERSONÆ.

THE Ghost of ANDREA.
Revenge.
King of Spain.
Viceroy of Portingale.
DON CYPRIAN, *Duke of* Castile.
HIERONIMO, *Marshal of* Portingale.
BALTHAZAR, *the Viceroy's Son, in Love with*
BEL-IMPERIA.
LORENZO, *Duke of* Castile's *Son.*
HORATIO, HIERONIMO'S *Son.*
ALEXANDRO
VILLUPPO.
PEDRINGANO.
SERBERINE.
Old Man.
Painter.
Page.
Hangman.
Citizens, Soldiers, Attendants.

ISABELLA, HIERONIMO'S *Wife.*
BEL-IMPERIA, LORENZO'S *Sister.*

THE
SPANISH TRAGEDY, &c.

ACT I.

Enter the Ghost of Andrea, *and with him* Revenge.

Ghost.

WHEN this eternal substance of my soul
Did live imprison'd in my wanton 1 flesh,
Each in their function serving other's need,
I was a courtier in the *Spanish* court:
My name was *Don Andrea*; my descent,
Though not ignoble, yet inferiour far
To gracious fortunes of my tender youth:
For there in prime and pride 2 of all my years,
By duteous service, and deserving love,
In secret I possess'd a worthy dame,
Which hight sweet *Bel-imperia* by name.
But, in the harvest of my summer 3 joys,
Death's winter nip'd the blossoms of my bliss,
Forcing divorce betwixt my love and me;
For in the late conflict with *Portingale*,
My valour drew me into danger's mouth,

1 *wonted* 1618, 23, 33.
2 *There in the pride and prime* — ditto.
3 *summer's* 1623, 33.

Till

Till life to death made passage through my wounds.
When I was slain, my soul descended straight
To pass the flowing stream of *Acheron*;
But churlish *Charon*, only boatman there,
Said, that, my rites of burial not perform'd,
I might not sit amongst his passengers.
Ere *Sol* had slept three nights in *Thetis*' lap,
And slak'd [1] his smoking chariot in her flood,
By *Don Horatio*, our knight marshal's son,
My funerals and obsequies were done:
Then was the ferryman of hell content
To pass me over to the slimy strond,
That leads to fell *Avernus*' ugly waves;
There, pleasing *Cerberus* with honied speech,
I pass'd the perils of the foremost porch.
Not far from hence, amidst ten thousand souls,
Sat *Minos*, *Æacus*, and *Rhadamant*;
To whom no sooner 'gan I make approach,
To crave a passport for my wand'ring ghost,
But *Minos*, in graven leaves of lottery,
Drew forth the manner of my life and death.
This knight, quoth he, both liv'd and dy'd in love;
And, for his love, try'd fortune of the wars;
And by war's fortune lost both love and life.
Why then, said *Æacus*, convey him hence,
To walk with lovers in our fields of love,
And spend the course of everlasting time
Under green myrtle trees, and cypress shades.
No, no, said *Rhadamant*, it were not well,
With loving souls to place a martialist:
He dy'd in war, and must to martial fields,
Where wounded *Hector* lives in lasting pain,
And *Achilles*' myrmidons do scour the plain.
Then *Minos*, mildest censor [2] of the three,
Made this device, to end the difference:
Send him, quoth he, to our infernal king,

[1] *slackt* 1618.   [2] *censurer* 1618, 23, 33.

THE SPANISH TRAGEDY.

To doom him as beſt ſeems his majeſty.
To this effect my paſſport ſtraight was drawn.
In keeping on my way to *Pluto's* court,
Through dreadful ſhades 1 of ever-glooming night,
I ſaw more ſights than thouſand tongues can tell,
Or pens can write, or mortal hearts can think.
Three ways there were; that on the right hand ſide
Was ready way unto the 'foreſaid fields, 2
Where lovers live, and bloody martialiſts;
But either ſort contain'd within his bounds.
The left hand path, declining fearfully,
Was ready downfal 3 to the deepeſt hell,
Where bloody furies ſhake their whips of ſteel,
And poor *Ixion* turns an endleſs wheel;
Where uſurers are chok'd with melting gold,
And wantons are embrac'd with ugly ſnakes;
And murderers grone 4 with never-killing wounds,
And perjur'd wights, ſcalded in boiling lead,
And all foul ſins with torments overwhelm'd.
'Twixt theſe two ways I trod the middle path,
Which brought me to the fair *Elyſian* green;
In midſt whereof there ſtands a ſtately tower,
The walls of braſs, the gates of adamant:
Here finding *Pluto* with his *Proſerpine*,
I ſhow'd my paſſport, humbled on my knee;
Whereat fair *Proſerpine* began to ſmile, 5
And begg'd that only ſhe might give my doom:
Pluto was pleas'd, and ſeal'd it with a kiſs.
Forthwith, *Revenge*, ſhe rounded thee in th' ear,
And bade thee lead me through the gates of horn, *

1 *ſhapes of ever-blooming night:* 1618.
 ſhades of ever-blooming night: 1623, 33.
2 *field* 1618, 23, 33.   3 *fall down* ditto.
4 *murderers greeve* 1618. *murderers greene* 1623, 33.
5 — *ſmile.* | *I begg'd* 1618, 23, 33.

* of *Hor*: ſecond edit. of *Horror,* 1618, 23, 33. For, — the gates of *horn*, ſee Virgil. B. v. I. *Sunt geminæ ſomni portæ*: &c.

Where

Where dreams have paſſage in the ſilent night.
No ſooner had ſhe ſpoke, but we were here,
I wot not how, in twinkling of an eye.
     Revenge.
 Then know, *Andrea*, that thou art arriv'd
Where thou ſhalt ſee the author of thy death,
Don Balthazar, the prince of *Portingale*,
Depriv'd of life by *Bel-imperia*.
Here ſit we down to ſee the myſtery,
And ſerve for *Chorus* in this tragedy.

Enter Spaniſh *King, General,* Caſtile, *and* Hieronimo.
     King.
 Now ſay, lord *General*, how fares our camp?
     General.
 All well, my ſovereign liege, except ſome few
That are deceas'd by fortune of the war.
     King.
 But what portends [1] thy cheerful countenance,
And poſting to our preſence thus in haſte?
Speak, man, hath fortune given us victory?
     General.
 Victory, my liege, and that with little loſs.
     King.
 Our *Portingals* will pay us tribute then?
     General.
 Tribute and wonted homage therewithal.
     King.
 Then bleſt be heav'n, and guider of the heavens,
From whoſe fair influence ſuch juſtice flows.
     Caſtile.
 O multum dilecte Deo, tibi militat æther,
 Et conjuratæ curvato poplite gentes
 Succumbunt: recti-ſoror eſt victoria juris.

   1 *pretends* 1618, 23, 33.
           King.

THE SPANISH TRAGEDY.

King.
Thanks to my loving brother of *Caſtile*,—
But, *General*, unfold in brief diſcourſe
Your form of battle, and your war's ſucceſs;
That, adding all the pleaſure of thy news
Unto the height of former happineſs,
With deeper wage, and greater dignity,
We may [1] reward thy bliſsful chivalry.
General.
Where *Spain* and *Portingale* do jointly knit
Their frontiers, leaning on each other's bound, [2]
There met our armies in their proud array;
Both furniſh'd well, both full of hope and fear,
Both menacing alike with daring ſhows,
Both vaunting ſundry colours of device,
Both cheerly ſounding trumpets, drums, and fifes,
Both raiſing dreadful clamours to the ſkie, [3]
That vallies, hills, and rivers made rebound,
And heav'n itſelf was frighted with the ſound.
Our battles both were pitch'd in ſquadron form,
Each corner ſtrongly fenc'd with wings of ſhot;
But ere we join'd, and came to puſh of pike,
I brought a ſquadron of our readieſt ſhot,
From out our rearward, to begin the fight:
They brought another wing t' encounter us:
Mean while, our ordnance play'd on either ſide,
And captains ſtrove to have their valours [4] try'd.
Don Pedro, their chief horſemen's colonel,
Did, with his cornet, [5] bravely make attempt
To break the order of our battle ranks;
But *Don Rogero*, worthy man of war,
March'd forth againſt him with our muſketeers,
And ſtop'd the malice of his fell approach.
While they maintain hot ſkirmiſh to and fro,
Both battles join, and fall to handy-blows;

1 *will* 1633.   2 *bounds* 1623, 33.   3 ſkies 1633.
4 *valour* 1618, 23, 33.   5 *coronet*, ditto.

Their

Their violent shot resembling the ocean's rage,
When, roaring loud and with a swelling tide,
It beats upon the rampires of huge rocks,
And gapes to swallow neighbour bounding lands.
Now while [1] *Bellona* rageth here and there,
Thick storms of bullets ran like winter's hail,
And shiver'd lances dark [2] the troubled air.

Pede pes, & cuspide cuspis,
Arma sonant armis, vir petiturque viro.

On every side drop [3] captains to the ground,
And soldiers some ill-maim'd, [4] some slain outright:
Here falls a body, sunder'd from his head,
There legs and arms lie bleeding on the grass,
Mingled with weapons, and unbowel'd [5] steeds,
That scattering overspread the purple plain.
In all this turmoil three long hours and more,
The victory to neither part inclin'd;
Till *Don Andrea*, with his brave lanciers,
In their [6] main battle made so great a breach,
That, half dismay'd, the multitude retir'd:
But *Balthazar*, the *Portingale's* young prince,
Brought rescue, and encourag'd them to stay.
Here-hence the fight was eagerly renew'd,
And in that conflict was *Andrea* slain;
Brave man at arms, but weak to *Balthazar*:
Yet while the prince, insulting over him,
Breath'd out proud vaunts, sounding to our reproach,
Friendship and hardy valour join'd in one,
Prick'd [7] forth *Horatio*, our knight marshal's son,
To challenge forth that prince to single fight:
Not long between these twain the fight endur'd,
But straight the prince was beaten from his horse,
And forc'd to yield him prisoner to his foe.

1. *when* 1618, 23, 33.   2 *dark'd* ditto.
3 *dropt* ditto.   4 *And soldiers lie maim'd* ditto.
5 *unbowed* ditto.   6 *his* 1618.   7 *pickt* ditto.

When

THE SPANISH TRAGEDY.

When he was taken, all the reft they fled,
And our carbines purfu'd them to the death;
Till *Phœbus* waving to the weftern deep,
Our trumpeters were charg'd to found retreat.
    King.
Thanks, good lord *General*, for thefe good news;
And for fome argument of more to come,
Take this, and wear it for thy fovereign's fake.
    [*Gives him his chain.*
But tell me now, haft thou confirm'd a peace?
    General.
No peace, my liege, but peace conditional,
That if, with homage, tribute be well pay'd, 1
The fury of your 2 forces will be ftay'd:
And to this 3 peace their viceroy hath fubfcrib'd,
    [*Gives the King a paper.*
And made a folemn vow, that during life
His 4 tribute fhall be truly pay'd to *Spain*.
    King.
Thefe words, thefe deeds, become thy perfon well.—
But now, knight marfhal, frolick with thy 5 king,
For 'tis thy fon that wins this 6 battle's prize.
    Hieronimo.
Long may he live to ferve my fovereign liege,
And foon decay, unlefs he ferve my liege.
    King.
Nor thou, nor he, fhall die without reward.
    [*A tucket* 7 *afar off.*
What means this warning of the trumpet's found?
    General.
This tells me, that your grace's men of war,
Such as war's fortune hath referv'd from death,
Come marching on towards your royal feat,

1 *tribute may be paid,* 1618, 23, 33.   2 *our* ditto.
3 *that* ditto.   4 *this* ditto.   5 *the* ditto.
6 *that* 1618, 23.   7 *trumpet* 1618, 23, 33.

                                        To

To show themselves before your majesty,
For so I gave in ¹ charge at my depart;
Whereby, by demonstration shall appear,
That all, except three hundred, or few more,
Are safe return'd, and by their foes enrich'd.

The army enters. ² Balthazar, *between* Lorenzo *and*
Horatio, *captive.*

King.
A gladsome sight! I long to see them here.
      [*They enter, and pass by.*
Was that the warlike prince of *Portingale*,
That by our nephew was in triumph led?

General.
It was, my liege, the prince of *Portingale*.

King.
But what was he, that on the other side
Held him by th' arm, as partner of the prize?

Hieronimo.
That was my son, my gracious sovereign;
Of whom, though from his tender infancy
My loving thoughts did never hope but well,
He never pleas'd his father's eyes till now,
Nor fill'd my heart with over-cloying joys.

King.
Go, let them march once more about these walls,
That, staying them, we may confer and talk
With our brave prisoner and his double guard.—
Hieronimo, it greatly pleaseth us
That in our victory thou have a share,
By virtue of thy worthy son's exploit.
      [*Enter again.*
Bring hither the young prince of *Portingale*.—
The rest march on; but ere they be dismiss'd,
We will bestow on every soldier two ducats,

---

¹ *gave them charge* 1618, 23, 33.   ² *meets* ditto.

And

THE SPANISH TRAGEDY.

And on every leader ten, that they may know
Our largefs welcomes them. —
　　　　　　　[*Exeunt all but* Bal. Lor. *and* Hor.
Welcome *Don Balthazar*,— welcome, nephew;—
And thou, *Horatio*, thou art welcome too. —
Young prince, although thy father's hard mifdeeds,
In keeping back the tribute that he owes,
Deferve but evil meafure at our hands,
Yet fhalt thou know that *Spain* is honourable.
　　　　　　　Balthazar.
　The trefpafs, that my father made in peace,
Is now control'd by fortune of the wars;
And cards once dealt, it boots not afk why fo:
His men are flain, a weak'ning to his [1] realm;
His colours feiz'd, a blot unto his name;
His fon diftrefs'd, a cor'five to his heart:
Thefe punifhments may clear his late offence.
　　　　　　　King.
　Ay, *Balthazar*, if he obferve [2] this truce,
Our peace will grow the ftronger for thefe wars:
Mean while live thou, though [3] not in liberty,
Yet free [4] from bearing any fervile yoke;
For, in our hearing, thy deferts were great,
And in our fight thyfelf art gracious.
　　　　　　　Balthazar.
　And I fhall ftudy to deferve this grace.
　　　　　　　King.
　But tell me, (for their holding makes me doubt)
To which of thefe twain art thou prifoner?
　　　　　　　Lorenzo.
　To me, my liege. [5]
　　　　　　　Horatio.
　To me, my fovereign.

1 *the* 1618, 23, 33.　　2 *obferves* ditto.
3 *as though* 1618.　　4 *free* omitted ditto.
5 *lord.* 1618, 23, 33.

　　　　　　　　　　　　　　　Lorenzo.

Lorenzo.
This hand first took his¹ courser by the reins.
Horatio.
But first my lance did put him from his horse.
Lorenzo.
I seiz'd his weapon, and enjoy'd it first.
Horatio.
But first I forc'd him lay his weapons down.
King.
Let go his arm, upon our privilege.—

[*They let him go.*
Say,² worthy prince, to whether didst thou yield?
Balthazar.
To him in courtesy, to this perforce;
He spake me fair, this other gave me strokes;
He promis'd life, this other threaten'd death;
He won my love, this other conquer'd me :
And truth to say, I yield myself to both.
Hieronimo.
But that I know your grace for just and wise,
And might seem partial in this difference,
Enforc'd by nature, and by law of arms,
My tongue should plead for young *Horatio's* right.
He hunted well, that was a lion's death ;
Not he that in a garment wore his skin :
So hares may pull dead lions by the beard.
King.
Content thee, marshal, thou shalt have no wrong;
And, for thy sake, thy son shall want no right.—
Will both abide the censure of my doom?
Lorenzo.
I crave no better than your grace awards.
Horatio.
Nor I, although I sit beside my right.
King.
Then, by my judgment, thus your strife shall end:

1 *the* 1618, 23, 33.   2 *So,* ditto.

You

You both deserve, and both shall have reward.—
Nephew, thou took'st his weapons and his horse;
His weapons and his horse are thy reward.—
Horatio, thou didst force him first to yield;
His ransome therefore is thy valour's fee:
Appoint the sum as you shall both agree.—
But, nephew, thou shalt have the prince in guard;
For thine estate best fitteth such a guest.
Horatio's house were small for all his train;
Yet in regard thy substance passeth his,
And that just guerdon may befall desert,
To him we yield the armour of the prince.—
How likes *Don Balthazar* of this device?
     Balthazar.
Right well, my liege, if this proviso were,
That *Don Horatio* bear us company,
Whom I admire and love for chivalry.
     King.
Horatio, leave him not that loves thee so.—
Now let us hence to see our soldiers pay'd,
And feast our prisoner as our friendly guest. [*Exeunt.*

Enter Viceroy, Alexandro, *and* Villuppo.
     Viceroy.
Is our ambassador despatch'd for *Spain?*
     Alexandro.
Two days, my liege, are pass'd since his depart.
     Viceroy.
And tribute payment gone along with him?
     Alexandro.
Ay, my good lord.
     Viceroy.
Then rest we here a while in our unrest,
And feed our sorrows with some inward sighs;
For deepest cares break never into tears.

But

But wherefore fit I in a ¹ regal throne?
This ² better fits a wretch's endless moan.
                                [Falls to the ground.
Yet this is higher than my fortunes reach,
And therefore better than my state deserves.
Ay, ay, this earth, image of melancholy,
Seeks him whom fates adjudge ³ to misery.
Here let me lie, now am I ⁴ at the lowest.

        Qui jacet in terra, non habet unde cadat.
        In me consumpsit vires fortuna nocendo:
        Nil ⁵ superest ut jam possit obesse magis.

Yes, fortune may bereave me of my crown:
Here, take it now; let fortune do her worst,
She will not rob me of this sable weed:
O no, she envies none but pleasant things;
Such is the folly of despiteful chance!
Fortune is blind, and sees not my deserts:
So is she deaf, and hears not my laments:
And could she hear, yet is she wilful mad,
And therefore will not pity my distress.
Suppose that she could pity me; what then?
What help can be expected at her hands,
Whose foot is standing on a rolling stone,
And mind more mutable than fickle winds?
Why wail I then, where's hope of no redress?
O, yes; complaining makes my grief seem less.
My late ambition hath distain'd my faith;
My breach of faith occasion'd bloody wars;
Those ⁶ bloody wars have spent my treasure;
And with my treasure my people's blood;
And with their blood, my joy and best belov'd,
My best belov'd, my sweet and only son.
O wherefore went I not to war myself?

   1 *this* 1618, 23, 33.   2 *It* 1618.
   3 *adjudged* 1618, 23, 33.   4 *I am* 1633.
   5 *Nihil* 1633.   6 *These* 1623, 33.

The caufe was mine; I might have died for both:
My years were mellow, his but ¹ young and green;
My death were natural, but his was forced.
Alexandro.
No doubt, my liege, but ftill the prince furvives.
Viceroy.
Survives! ay, where? ²
Alexandro.
In *Spain*, a prifoner, by mifchance of war.
Viceroy.
Then they have flain him for his father's fault.
Alexandro.
That were a breach to common law of arms.
Viceroy.
They reck no laws that meditate revenge.
Alexandro.
His ranfome's worth will ftay from foul revenge.
Viceroy.
No; if he liv'd, the news would foon be here.
Alexandro.
Nay, evil news fly ³ fafter ftill than good.
Viceroy.
Tell me no more of news, for he is dead.
Villuppo.
My fovereign, pardon the author of ill news,
And I'll bewray the fortune of thy fon.
Viceroy.
Speak on, I'll guerdon thee, whate'er it be:
Mine ear is ready to receive ill news;
My heart grown hard 'gainft mifchief's battery.
Stand up, I fay, and tell thy tale at large.
Villuppo.
Then hear that ⁴ truth, which thefe mine eyes have feen:
When both the armies were in battle join'd,

1 *but his* 1623, 33. 2 *but where?* 1618, 23, 33.
3 *will fly* ditto. 4 *the* ditto.

Don Balthazar, amidst the thickest troops,
To win renown, did wondrous feats of arms:
Amongst the rest I saw him, hand to hand,
In single fight with their lord general;
Till *Alexandro*, that here counterfeits
Under the colour of a duteous friend,
Discharg'd his pistol at the prince's back,
As though he would have slain their general:
But therewithal *Don Balthazar* fell down;
And when he fell, then we began to fly:
But, had he liv'd, the day had sure been ours.
    Alexandro.
 O wicked forgery! O trait'rous miscreant!
    Viceroy.
 Hold thou thy peace: — But now, *Villuppo*, say,
Where then became the carcase of my son?
    Villuppo.
 I saw them drag it to the *Spanish* tents.
    Viceroy.
 Ay, ay; my nightly dreams have told me this. —
Thou false, unkind, unthankful, trait'rous beast,
Wherein had *Balthazar* offended thee,
That thou shouldst thus betray him to our foes?
Was't *Spanish* gold that bleared so thine eyes,
That thou couldst see no part of our deserts?
Perchance, because thou art *Tersera's* lord,
Thou hadst [1] some hope to wear this diadem,
If first my son, and then myself were slain;
But thy ambitious thought [2] shall break thy neck:
Ay, this was it that made thee spill his blood.
   [*He takes the crown, and puts it on agai*.
But I'll now [3] wear it, till thy blood be spilt.
    Alexandro.
 Vouchsafe, dread [4] sovereign, to hear me speak.

 1 *hast* 1623, 33.   2 *thoughts* 1618, 23, 33.
 3 *now Ile* ditto.   4 *deare* ditto.

THE SPANISH TRAGEDY.

Viceroy.
Away with him; his fight is fecond hell:
Keep him, till we determine of his death.
If *Balthazar* be dead, he fhall not live.—
Villuppo, follow us for thy reward.   [*Exit Vice.*
Villuppo.
Thus have I, with an envious forged tale,
Deceiv'd the king, betray'd mine enemy,
And hope for guerdon of my villany.   [*Exit.*

Enter Horatio, *and* Bel-imperia.
Bel-imperia.
Signior *Horatio*, this is the place and hour
Wherein I muſt entreat thee to relate
The circumſtance of *Don Andrea*'s death,
Who, living, was my garland's ſweeteſt [1] flower,
And in his death hath buried my delights.
Horatio.
For love of him, and ſervice to yourſelf,
I nill refuſe this heavy doleful [2] charge;
Yet tears and ſighs, I fear, will hinder me.
When both our armies were enjoin'd in [3] fight,
Your worthy chivalier amidſt the thickeſt,
For glorious cauſe, ſtill aiming at the faireſt,
Was at the laſt by young *Don Balthazar*
Encounter'd hand to hand: their fight was long;
Their hearts were great; their clamours menacing;
Their ſtrength alike; their ſtrokes both dangerous:
But wrathful *Nemeſis*, that wicked power,
Envying at *Andrea's* praiſe and worth,
Cut ſhort his life, to end his praiſe and worth:
She, ſhe herſelf, diſguis'd in armour's maſk,
(As *Pallas* was before proud *Pergamus*)
Brought in a [4] freſh ſupply of halberdiers,

1 *chiefeſt* 1623, 33.
2 *Ile not refuſe this doleful heavy* 1618, 23, 33.
3 *to* ditto.   4 *a* omitted 1618, 23.   Which

Which paunch'd his horse, and ding'd him to the ground;
Then young *Don Balthazar*, with ruthless rage,
Taking advantage of his foe's distress,
Did finish what his halberdiers begun,
And left not, till *Andrea's* life was done.
Then, though too late, incens'd with just remorse,
I, with my band, set forth against the prince,
And brought him prisoner from his halberdiers.

Bel-imperia.
'Would thou hadst slain him that so [1] slew my love!
But then, was *Don Andrea's* carcase lost?

Horatio.
No, that was it for which I chiefly strove,
Nor step'd I back till I recover'd him:
I took him up, and wound him in mine arms;
And welding him unto my private tent,
There lay'd him down, and dew'd him with my tears,
And sigh'd and sorrow'd as became a friend:
But neither friendly sorrow, [2] sighs, nor tears,
Could win pale death from his usurped right.
Yet this I did, and less I could not do;
I saw him honour'd with due funeral:
This scarf I pluck'd from off [3] his lifeless arm,
And wear it in remembrance of my friend.

Bel-imperia.
I know the scarf: 'would he had kept it still;
For had he liv'd, he would have kept it still,
And worn it for his *Bel-imperia's* sake:
For 'twas my favour at his last depart.
But now, wear thou [4] it, both for him and me;
For, after him, thou hast deserv'd it best:
But for thy kindness in his life and death,
Be sure, while *Bel-imperia's* life endures,
She will be *Don Horatio's* thankful friend.

1 *so* omitted, 1618, 23, 33.   2 *sorrowes* ditto.
3 *This scarfe pluckt off from* — ditto.
4 *thou* omitted, ditto.

Horatio,

THE SPANISH TRAGEDY. 21

Horatio.
And, madam, *Don Horatio* will not flack
Humbly to ferve fair *Bel-imperia*.
But now, if your good liking ftand thereto,
I'll crave your pardon to go feek the prince;
For fo the duke your father gave me charge.
Bel-imperia.
Ay, go *Horatio*, leave me here alone;
For folitude beft fits my cheerlefs mood.
[*Exit* Horatio.
Yet, what avails to wail *Andrea's* death,
From whence *Horatio* proves my fecond love?
Had he not lov'd *Andrea* as he did,
He could not fit in *Bel-imperia's* thoughts.
But how can love find harbour in my breaft,
Till I revenge the death of my belov'd?
Yes, fecond love fhall further my revenge:
I'll love *Horatio*, my *Andrea's* friend,
The more to fpite the prince that wrought his end.
And where *Don Balthazar* that flew my love,
Himfelf now pleads for favour at my hands,
He fhall in rigour of my juft difdain,
Reap long repentance for [1] his murd'rous deed;
For what waft elfe but murd'rous cowardife,
So many to opprefs one valiant knight,
Without refpect of honour in the fight?
And here he comes that murder'd my delight.

Enter Lorenzo, *and* Balthazar.

Lorenzo.
Sifter, what means this melancholy walk?
Bel-imperia.
That for a while I wifh no company.
Lorenzo.
But here the prince is come to vifit you.

[1] *of* 1618, 23, 33.

Bel-imperia.
That argues, that he lives in [1] liberty.
Balthazar.
No, madam, but in pleasing servitude.
Bel-imperia.
Your prison then, belike, is your conceit.
Balthazar.
Ay, by conceit my freedom is inthrall'd.
Bel-imperia.
Then with conceit enlarge yourself again.
Balthazar.
What if conceit have lay'd my heart to gage?
Bel-imperia.
Pay that you borrow'd, and recover it.
Balthazar.
I die, if it return from whence it lies.
Bel-imperia.
A heartless man, and live? [2] a miracle!
Balthazar.
Ay, lady, love can work such miracles.
Lorenzo.
Tush, tush! my lord, let go these ambages,
And in plain terms acquaint her with your love.
Bel-imperia.
What boots complaint, when there's no remedy?
Balthazar.
Yes, to your gracious self must I complain,
In whose fair answer lies my remedy;
On whose perfection all my thoughts attend;
On whose aspect mine eyes find beauty's bower;
In whose translucent breast my heart is lodg'd.
Bel-imperia.
Alas, my lord, these are but words of course,
And but device [3] to drive me from this place.
[*She in going in, lets fall her glove, which* Horatio,
coming out, takes up.

[1] *at* 1618, 23, 33.   [2] *lives!* ditto.
[3] *devis'd* ditto.
Horatio.

THE SPANISH TRAGEDY. 23

Horatio.
Madam, your glove.
Bel-imperia.
Thanks, good *Horatio*; take it for thy pains.
Balthazar.
Signior *Horatio* ſtoop'd in happy time.
Horatio.
I reap'd more grace than I deferv'd, or hop'd.
Lorenzo.
My lord, be not difmay'd for what is paſt;
You know, that women oft are humorous:
Theſe clouds will overblow with little wind;
Let me alone, I'll ſcatter them myſelf.
Mean while, let us deviſe to ſpend the time
In ſome delightful¹ ſports and revelling.²
Horatio.
The king, my lords,³ is coming hither ſtraight,
To feaſt the *Portingale* ambaſſador:
Things were in readineſs before I came.
Balthazar.
Then here it fits us to attend the king,
To welcome hither our ambaſſador,
And learn my father and my country's health.

Enter the Banquet, Trumpets, the King, *and* Ambaſſador.
King.
See, lord *Ambaſſador*, how *Spain* entreats
Their priſoner *Balthazar*, thy viceroy's ſon:
We pleaſure more in kindneſs than in wars.
Ambaſſador.
Sad is our king, and *Portingale* laments,
Suppoſing that *Don Balthazar* is ſlain.
Balthazar.
So am I ſlain by beauty's tyranny.—
You ſee, my lord, how *Balthazar* is ſlain:

1 *delightſome* 1618, 12, 33.	2 *revellings.* ditto.
3 *lord*, ditto.	I frolick

I frolick with the duke of *Castile's* son,
Wrap'd every hour in pleasures of the court,
And grac'd with favours of his majesty.
              King.
  Put off your greetings till our feast be done;
Now come and sit with us, and taste our cheer.
                        [*Sit to the banquet.*
Sit down, young prince, you are our second guest:
Brother, sit down; — and, nephew, take your place: —
Signior *Horatio*, wait thou upon our cup,
For well thou hast deserved to be honour'd. —
Now, lordings, fall to, *Spain* is *Portingale*,
And *Portingale* is *Spain*; we both are friends;
Tribute is pay'd, and we enjoy our right.
But where is old *Hieronimo*, our marshal?
He promis'd us, in honour of our guest,
To grace our banquet with some pompous jest.

Enter Hieronimo *with a drum, three knights, each his 'scutcheon: then he fetches three kings, they take their crowns and them captive.*

Hieronimo, this mask contents mine eye,
Although I found not well the mystery.
              Hieronimo.
  The first arm'd knight, that hung his 'scutcheon up,
     [*He takes the 'scutcheon, and gives it to the King.*
Was *English Robert*, earl of *Glocester*,
Who, when king *Stephen* bore sway in *Albion*,
Arriv'd with five and 1 twenty thousand men
In *Portingale*, and by success of war,
Enforc'd the king, then but a *Saracen*,
To bear the yoke of th' *English* monarchy.
              King.
  My lord of *Portingale*, by this you see,
That which may comfort both your king and you,

       1 *five and* omitted 1623, 33.

And make your late difcomfort feem the lefs.—
But fay, *Hieronimo*, what was the next?
  Hieronimo.
The fecond knight that hung his 'fcutcheon up,
  [*He doth as he did before.*
Was *Edmond* earl of *Kent* in *Albion*,
When *Englifh Richard* wore the diadem :
He came likewife and razed *Lifbon* walls,
And took the king of *Portingale* in fight;
For which, and other fuch like fervice done,
He after was created duke of *York*.
  King.
This is another fpecial argument,
That *Portingale* may deign to bear our yoke,
When it by little *England* hath been yok'd.—
But now, *Hieronimo*, what were the laft?
  Hieronimo.
The third and laft, not leaft in our account,
  [*Doing as he did before.*
Was, as the reft, a valiant *Englifhman*,
Brave *John* of *Gaunt*, the duke of *Lancafter*,
As by his 'fcutcheon plainly may appear :
He with a puiffant army came to *Spain*,
And took our king of *Caftile* prifoner.
  Ambaffador.
This is an argument for our viceroy,
That *Spain* may not infult for her fuccefs,
Since *Englifh* warriours likewife conquer'd *Spain*,
And made them bow their knees to *Albion*.
  King.
Hieronimo, I drink to thee for this device,
Which hath pleas'd both the ambaffador and me :
Pledge me, *Hieronimo*, if thou love the king.—
  [*Takes the cup of* Horatio.
My lord, I fear we fit but over-long,
Unlefs our dainties were more delicate :
But welcome are you to the beft we have.

Now

Now let us in, that you ¹ may be defpatch'd;
I think, our council is already fet.   [*Exeunt omnes.*

Andrea.
Come we for this from depth of under ground,
To fee him feaft that gave me my death's wound?
Thefe pleafant fights are forrow to my foul;
Nothing but league, and love, and banqueting?

Revenge.
Be ftill, *Andrea*; ere we go from hence,
I'll turn their friendfhip into fell defpite;
Their love to mortal hate, their day to night;
Their hope into defpair, their peace to war;
Their joys to pain, their blifs to mifery.

ACT II.

Enter Lorenzo, *and* Balthazar.

Lorenzo.
MY lord, though *Bel-imperia* feem thus coy,
Let reafon hold you in your wonted joy:
In time the favage bull fuftains the yoke;
In time all haggard hawks will ftoop to lure;
In time fmall wedges cleave the hardeft oak;
In time the flint ² is pierc'd with fofteft fhower;
And fhe in time will fall from her difdain,
And rue ³ the fufferance of your friendly pain.

Balthazar.
No, fhe is wilder, and more hard withal,
Than beaft, or bird, or tree, or ftony wall:

1 *we* 1618, 23, 33.
2 *In time the hardeft flint* &c. ditto.
3 *rule* ditto.

But

THE SPANISH TRAGEDY.

But wherefore blot I *Bel-imperia's* name?
It is my fault, not fhe that merits blame.
My feature is not to content her fight;
My words are rude, and work her no delight:
The lines I fend her are but harfh and ill,
Such as do drop from *Pan* and *Marfia's* [1] quill.
My prefents are not of fufficient coft,
And being worthlefs, all my labour's loft.
Yet might fhe love me for my valiancy:
Ay, but that's flander'd by captivity.
Yet might fhe love me to content her fire:
Ay, but her reafon mafters his [2] defire.
Yet might fhe love me, as her brother's friend:
Ay, but her hopes aim at fome other end.
Yet might fhe love me to uprear her ftate:
Ay, but perhaps fhe hopes [3] fome nobler mate.
Yet might fhe love me as her beauty's thrall:
Ay, but I fear fhe cannot love at all.
          Lorenzo.
My lord, for my fake leave thefe extafies,
And doubt not but we'll find fome remedy.
Some caufe there is, that lets you not be lov'd;
Firft that muft needs be known, and then remov'd.
What if my fifter love fome other knight?
          Balthazar.
My fummer's day will turn to winter's night.
          Lorenzo.
I have already found a ftratagem,
To found the bottom of this doubtful theme.
My lord, for once you fhall be rul'd by me;
Hinder me not, whate'er you hear or fee:
By force, or fair means, will I caft about,
To find the truth of all this queftion out.
Ho, *Pedringano!*

1 *Marfes* 1618, 23, 33.   2 *her* ditto.
3 *hves* 1623, 33.

Enter Pedringano.

Pedringano.
Signior!

Lorenzo.
Vien que presto.

Pedringano.
Hath your lordship any service to command me?

Lorenzo.
Ay, *Pedringano*, service of import;
And, not to spend the time in trifling words,
Thus stands the case: It is not long, thou know'st,
Since I did shield thee from my father's wrath,
For thy conveyance in *Andrea's* love:
For which thou wert adjudg'd to punishment:
I stood betwixt thee and thy punishment.
And since, thou know'st how I have favour'd thee.
Now to these favours will I add reward,
Not with fair words, but store of golden coin,
And lands and living¹ join'd with dignities,
If thou but satisfy my just demand:
Tell truth, and have me for thy lasting friend.

Pedringano.
Whate'er it be your lordship shall demand,
My bounden duty bids me tell the truth,
If case it lie in me² to tell the truth.

Lorenzo.
Then, *Pedringano*, this is my demand:
Whom loves my sister *Bel-imperia*?
For she reposeth all her trust in thee;
Speak, man, and gain both friendship and reward:
I mean, whom loves she in *Andrea's* place?

Pedringano.
Alas, my lord, since *Don Andrea's* death,
I have no credit with her as before;
And therefore know not if she love or no.

---

1 *livings* 1618, 23, 33.   2 *in me in lies* — ditto.

Lorenzo.

THE SPANISH TRAGEDY. 29

Lorenzo.
Nay if thou dally, then I am thy foe,
[*Draws his sword.*
And fear shall force what friendship cannot win:
Thy death shall bury what thy life conceals;
Thou dy'st for more esteeming her than me.
Pedringano.
O, stay, my lord.
Lorenzo.
Yet speak the truth, and I will guerdon thee,
And shield thee from whatever can ensue;
And will conceal whate'er proceeds from thee:
But if thou dally once again, thou dy'st.
Pedringano.
If madam *Bel-imperia* be in love,—
Lorenzo.
What, villain? ifs and ands?
Pedringano.
O, stay, my lord; she loves *Horatio*.
[Balthazar *starts back.*
Lorenzo.
What *Don Horatio*, our knight marshal's son?
Pedringano.
Even him, my lord.
Lorenzo.
Now say but how know'st thou he¹ is her love,
And thou shalt find me kind and liberal:
Stand up, I say, and fearless tell the truth.
Pedringano.
She sent him letters, which myself perus'd,
Full fraught with lines, and arguments of love,
Preferring him before prince *Balthazar*.
Lorenzo.
Swear on this cross,* that what thou say'st is true;
And that thou wilt conceal what thou hast told.

1 *how knowest thou that be* — ditto.
* — *the cross at the hilt of the sword: in times of chivalry a most sacred oath.* See Hamlet, *A.* 1. *S.* 9.

Pedringano.

Pedringano.
I swear to both, by him that made us all.
Lorenzo.
In hope thine oath is true, here's thy reward!
But if I prove thee perjur'd and unjust,
This very sword whereon thou took'st thine oath,
Shall be the worker of thy tragedy.
Pedringano.
What I have said is true, and shall for me
Be still conceal'd from *Bel-imperia:*
Besides, your honour's liberality
Deserves my duteous service ev'n till death.
Lorenzo.
Let this be all that thou shalt do for me:
Be watchful when, and where these lovers meet,
And give me notice in some secret sort.
Pedringano.
I will, my lord.
Lorenzo.
Then shalt thou find that I am liberal:
Thou know'st, that I can more advance thy state
Than she; be therefore wise, and fail me not:
Go and attend her, as thy custom is,
Lest absence make her think thou dost amiss.
[*Exit Ped*
Why so: *tam armis, quam ingenio:*
Where words prevail not, violence prevails;
But gold doth more than either of them both.
How likes prince *Balthazar* this [1] stratagem?
Balthazar.
Both well and ill; it makes me glad and sad:
Glad, that I know the hinderer of my love;
Sad, that I fear she hates me whom I love;
Glad, that I know on whom to be reveng'd;
Sad, that she'll fly me if I take revenge;
Yet must I take revenge, to die myself,
For love resisted, grows impatient.

a *of this* 1618, 23, 33. I thin

I think, *Horatio* be my deſtin'd plague:
Firſt, in his hand he brandiſhed a ſword,
And with that ſword he fiercely waged war,
And in that war, he gave me dang'rous wounds,
And by thoſe wounds, he forced me to yield,
And by my yielding, I became his ſlave:
Now in his mouth he carries pleaſing words,
Which pleaſing words do harbour ſweet conceits;
Which ſweet conceits are lim'd with ſly deceits, 1
Which ſly deceits 2 ſmooth *Bel-imperia's* ears;
And through her ears, dive down into her heart,
And in her heart ſet 3 him, where I ſhould ſtand.
Thus hath he ta'en my body by his force,
And now by flight would captivate my ſoul:
But in his fall, I'll tempt the deſtinies,
And either loſe my life, or win my love.
     Lorenzo.
 Let's go, my lord, your 4 ſtaying ſtays revenge:
Do you but follow me, and gain your love,
Her favour muſt be won by his remove. [*Exeunt.*

   Enter Horatio, *and* Bel-imperia.
     Horatio.
Now, madam, ſince by favour of your love,
Our hidden ſmoke is turn'd to open flame,
And that with looks and words we feed our thoughts,
(Two chief contents) where more cannot be had;
Thus in the midſt of love's fair blandiſhments,
Why ſhow you ſign of inward languiſhments?
  [*Pedringano ſhows all to the prince and* Lorenzo,
   placing them in ſecret.
     Bel-imperia.
 My heart, ſweet friend, is like a ſhip at ſea,
She wiſheth port; where riding all at eaſe,

---

1 this line omitted 1618, 23, 33.   2 *ſweet* ditto.
3 *ſets* ditto.   4 *our* 1633.

              She

She may repair what stormy times have worn:
And leaning on the shore, may sing with joy,
That pleasure follows pain; and bliss, annoy.
Possession of thy love is the only port,
Wherein my heart, with fears and hopes long toss'd,
Each hour doth wish and long to make resort,
There to repair ¹ the joys that it hath lost:
And sitting safe, to sing in *Cupid's* quire,
That sweetest bliss is crown of love's desire.

[Balthazar, *and* Lorenzo *aside.*
Balthazar.

O, sleep, mine eyes, see not my love profan'd;
Be deaf mine ears, hear not my discontent;
Die, heart, another 'joys what thou deserv'st.

Lorenzo.

Watch still, mine eyes, to see this ² love disjoin'd:
Hear still, mine ears, to hear them both lament:
Live,³ heart, to joy at fond *Horatio's* fall.

Bel-imperia.

Why stands *Horatio* speechless all this while?

Horatio.

The less I speak, the more I meditate.

Bel-imperia.

But whereon dost thou chiefly ⁴ meditate?

Horatio.

On dangers past, and pleasures to ensue.

Balthazar.

On pleasures past, and dangers to ensue.

Bel-imperia.

What dangers, and what pleasures dost thou mean?

Horatio.

Dangers of war, and pleasures of our love.

Lorenzo.

Dangers of death, but pleasures none at all.

1 *There on repair* 1618, 23, 33.
2 *the* ditto.   3 *Leave* ditto.
4 *chiefly dost thou* 1618, 23, 33.

Bel-imperia.

Bel-imperia.
Let dangers go, thy war shall be with me:
But such a warring, as breaks no bond of peace.
Speak thou fair words, I'll cross them with fair words;
Send thou sweet looks, I'll meet them with sweet looks:
Write loving lines, I'll answer loving lines;
Give me a kiss, I'll countercheck thy kiss:
Be this our warring peace, or peaceful war.
Horatio.
But, gracious madam, then appoint the field,
Where trial of this war shall first be made.
Balthazar.
Ambitious villain, how his boldness grows!
Bel-imperia.
Then be ¹ thy father's pleasant bow'r, the field
Where first we vow'd a ² mutual amity;
The court were dangerous, that place is safe:
Our hour shall be, when *Vesper* 'gins to rise,
That summons home distressful 3 travellers:
There none shall hear us but the harmless birds;
Happily the gentle nightingale
Shall carol us asleep ere we be ware,
And singing with the prickle at her breast,
Tell our delight and mirthful 4 dalliance:
Till then, each hour will seem a year and more.
Horatio.
But, honey sweet, and honourable love,
Return we now into your father's sight,
Dangerous suspicion waits on our delight.
Lorenzo.
Ay, danger mixed with jealous despite,
Shall send thy soul into eternal night. [*Exeunt.*

1 *by* 1618, 23, 33.
2 *our* ditto.
3 *distressed* 1623, 33.
4 *sportfull* ditto.

Vol. II. C *Enter*

Enter king of Spain, Portingale *Ambassador,*
Don Cyprian, &c.

King.

Brother of *Castile,* to the prince's love
What says your daughter *Bel-imperia?*

Cyprian.

Although she coy it, as becomes her kind,
And yet dissemble that she loves the prince;
I doubt not I, but she will stoop in time:
And were she froward, which she will not be,
Yet herein shall she follow my advice;
Which is to love him, or forego my love.

King.

Then, lord ambassador of *Portingale,*
Advise thy king to make this marriage up,
For strength'ning of our late confirmed league;
I know no better means to make us friends.
Her dowry shall be large and liberal;
Besides that she is daughter and half heir
Unto our brother here, *Don Cyprian,*
And shall enjoy the moiety of his land,
I'll grace her marriage with an uncle's gift:
And this it is, (in case the match go forward)
The tribute which you pay, shall be releas'd:
And if by *Balthazar* she have a son,
He shall enjoy the kingdom after us.

Ambassador.

I'll make the motion to my [1] sovereign liege,
And work it, if my counsel may prevail.

King.

Do so, my lord, and if he give consent,
I hope his presence here will honour us,
In celebration of the nuptial day;
And let himself [2] determine of the time.

1 *our* 1618.   2 *let him* 1633.

Ambassador.
Will't please your grace command¹ me aught beside?
King.
Commend me to the king; and so farewel.
But where's prince *Balthazar* to take his leave?
Ambassador.
That is perform'd already, my good lord.
King.
Amongst the rest of what you have in charge,
The prince's ransome must not be forgot:
That's none of mine, but his that took him prisoner;
And well his forwardness deserves reward:
It was *Horatio*, our knight marshal's son,
Ambassador.
Between us there's a price already pitch'd,
And shall be sent with all convenient speed.
King.
Then once again farewel, my lord.
Ambassador.
Farewel, my lord of *Castile*, and the rest. [*Exit.*
King.
Now, brother, you must take some little pains, ²
To win fair *Bel-imperia* from her will;
Young virgins must be ruled by their friends:
The prince is amiable, and loves her well:
If she neglect him and forego his love,
She both will wrong her own estate and ours;
Therefore whiles I do entertain the prince,
With greatest pleasure ³ that our court affords,
Endeavour you to win your daughter's thought:
If she give back, all this will come to nought. [*Exeunt.*

Enter Horatio, Bel-imperia, *and* Pedringano.
Horatio.
Now that the night begins with sable wings,

1 *to command* 1618.   2 *paine* 1618, 23, 33.
3 *pleasures* ditto.

To over-cloud the brightnefs of the fun,
And that in darknefs pleafures may be done;
Come, *Bel-imperia*, let us to the bower,
And there in fafety pafs a pleafant hour.
Bel-imperia.
I follow thee, my love, and will not back,
Although my fainting heart controls my foul.
Horatio.
Why, make you doubt of *Pedringano's* faith?
Bel-imperia.
No, he is as trufty as my fecond felf.—
Go, *Pedringano*, watch without the gate,
And let us know if any make approach.
Pedringano.
Inftead of watching, I'll deferve more gold,
By fetching *Don Lorenzo* to this match. [*Exit Ped.*
Horatio.
What means my love?
Bel-imperia.
I know not what myfelf:
And yet my heart foretels me fome mifchance.
Horatio.
Sweet, fay not fo; fair fortune is our friend,
And heav'ns have [1] fhut up day, to pleafure us.
The ftars, thou feeft, hold back their twinkling fhine,
And *Luna* hides herfelf to pleafure us.
Bel-imperia.
Thou haft prevail'd, I'll conquer my mifdoubt,
And in thy love and counfel drown my fear:
I fear no more, love now is all my thoughts.
Why fit we not? for pleafure afketh eafe.
Horatio.
The more thou fit'ft within thefe leafy bow'rs,
The more will *Flora* deck it with her flow'rs.
Bel-imperia.
Ay, but if *Flora* fpy *Horatio* here,
Her jealous eye will think I fit too near.

---

[1] *heaven hath* 1618, 23, 33.   *Horatio.*

Horatio.
Hark, madam, how the birds record by night,
For joy that *Bel-imperia* sits in sight.
Bel-imperia.
No, *Cupid* counterfeits the nightingale,
To frame sweet musick to *Horatio's* tale.
Horatio.
If *Cupid* sing, then *Venus* is not far:
Ay, thou art *Venus*, or some fairer star.
Bel-imperia.
If I be *Venus*, thou must needs be *Mars*;
And where *Mars* reigneth, there must needs be wars.
Horatio.
Then thus begin our wars; put forth thy hand,
That it may combat with my ruder hand.
Bel-imperia.
Set forth thy foot, to try the push of mine.
Horatio.
But first my looks shall combat against thine.
Bel-imperia.
Then ward thyself, I dart this kiss at thee.
Horatio.
Thus I retort ¹ the dart thou threw'st at me.
Bel-imperia.
Nay, then to gain the glory of the field,
My twining arms shall yoke, and make thee yield.
Horatio.
Nay, then my arms are large and strong withal:
Thus elms by vines are compass'd till they fall.
Bel-imperia.
O let me go, for in my troubled eyes
Now may'st thou read, that life in passion dies.
Horatio.
O stay a while, and I will die with thee,
So shalt thou yield, and yet have conquer'd me.
Bel-imperia.
Who's there, *Pedringano?* we are betray'd.

¹ *return* 1618, 23, 33. *Enter*

Enter Lorenzo, Balthazar, Cerberine, *and* Pedringano, *difguifed*.

Lorenzo.
My lord, away with her, take her afide. — †
O, fir, forbear, your valour is already try'd. —
Quickly defpatch, my mafters.
[*They hang him in the arbour.*
Horatio.
What, will ye murder me?
Lorenzo.
Ay thus, and thus; thefe are the fruits of love.
[*They ftab him.*
Bel-imperia.
O fave his life, and let me die for him:
O fave him, brother, fave him, *Balthazar*;
I lov'd *Horatio*, but he lov'd not me.
Balthazar.
But *Balthazar* loves *Bel-imperia.*
Lorenzo.
Although his life were ftill [1] ambitious, proud,
Yet is he at the higheft now he is dead.
Bel-imperia.
Murder! murder! help, *Hieronimo,* help.
Lorenzo.
Come, ftop her mouth, away with her. [*Exeunt.*

Enter Hieronimo *in his fhirt* &c.

Hieronimo.
What outcries pluck [2] me from my naked bed,
And chill [3] my throbbing heart with trembling fear,
Which never danger yet could daunt before?
Who calls *Hieronimo?* fpeak, here I am.

1 *ftill* omitted 1618, 23, 33.
2 *outcry calls* ditto.   3 *chills* ditto.
† *Take her afide* is printed as a marginal direction 1618, 23, 33.

I did

I did not slumber; therefore 'twas no dream.
No, no, it was some woman cry'd for help;
And here within this ¹ garden did she cry;
And in this garden must I rescue her.
But stay, what murd'rous spectacle is this?
A man hang'd up, and all the murderers gone!
And in my bower, to lay the guilt on me!
This place was made for pleasure, not for death.
                    [*He cuts him down.*
Those garments that he wears I oft have seen:
Alas, it is *Horatio,* my sweet son!
O no, but he that ² whilome was my son!
O, was it thou that call'dst me from my bed?
O speak, if any spark of life remain:
I am thy father; who hath slain my son?
What savage monster, not of human kind,
Hath here ³ been glutted with thy harmless blood,
And left thy bloody corps dishonour'd here,
For me amidst these dark and deathful shades,
To drown thee with an ocean of my tears?
O heav'ns, why made you night to cover sin?
By day, this deed of darkness had not been.
O earth, why didst thou not in time devour
The vilde ⁴ profaner of this sacred bow'r?
O poor *Horatio!* what hadst thou misdone,
To leese thy life, ere life was new begun?
O wicked butcher! whatsoe'er thou wert,
How couldst thou strangle virtue and desert?
Ay me most wretched, that have lost my joy,
In leesing my *Horatio,* my sweet boy!

Enter Isabella.

Isabella.
My husband's absence makes my heart to throb:—
Hieronimo!

1 *the* 1618, 23, 33.   2 *that who whilome* 1618.
3 *Here hath* 1618, 23, 33.   4 *vile* ditto.
                                        Hieronimo.

Hieronimo.
Here, *Isabella*, help me to lament;
For sighs are stop'd, and all my tears are spent.
Isabella.
What world of grief! my son *Horatio*!
O where's the author of this endless wo?
Hieronimo.
To know the author were some ease of grief,
For in revenge, my heart would find relief.
Isabella.
Then is he gone? and is my son gone too?
O gush out tears, fountains and floods of tears;
Blow sighs, and raise an everlasting storm;
For outrage fits our cursed wretchedness. *⁂*

Hieronimo.

⁂ The following scene seems to have been foisted in by the players, it being omitted in the second edition.

Aye me, *Hieronimo*, sweet husband, speak!
Hieronimo.
He supp'd with us to-night, frolick and merry,
And said, he would go visit *Balthazar*,
At the duke's palace: there the prince doth lodge.
He had no custom to stay out so late,
He may be in his chamber; some go see — *Roderigo*, ho.

Enter Pedro, *and* Jaques.

Isabella.
Aye me, he raves! sweet *Hieronimo*!
Hieronimo.
True, all *Spain* takes note of it.
Besides, he is so generally belov'd,
His majesty the other day did grace him
With waiting on his cup: these be favours,
Which do assure me that he cannot be short liv'd.
Isabella.
Sweet *Hieronimo*!
Hieronimo.
I wonder, how this fellow got his cloths:
Sirrah, sirrah, I'll know the truth of all:
Jaques, run to the duke of *Castile*'s presently,
And bid my son *Horatio* to come home,

I, and

THE SPANISH TRAGEDY. 41

Hieronimo.
Sweet lovely rose, ill pluck'd before thy time,
Fair worthy son, not conquer'd, but betray'd,
I'll kiss thee now, for words with tears are stay'd.
Isabella.

I, and his mother have had strange dreams to-night:
Do you hear me, sir?
Jaques.
Ay, sir,
Hieronimo.
Well, sir, be gone. — *Pedro,* come hither;
Know'st thou who this is!
Pedro.
Too well, sir.
Hieronimo.
Too well! who? who is it? Peace, *Isabella,*
Nay, blush not, man.
Pedro.
It is my lord *Horatio.*
Hieronimo.
Ha, ha, St. *James;* but this doth make me laugh,
That there are more deluded than myself.
Pedro.
Deluded?
Hieronimo.
Ay, I would have sworn myself, within this hour,
That this had been my son *Horatio,*
His garments are so like: ha, are they not great persuasions?
Isabella.
O, would to God it were not so!
Hieronimo.
Were not, *Isabella?* dost thou dream it is?
Can thy soft bosom entertain a thought,
That such a black deed of mischief should be done
On one so pure and spotless as our son?
Away, I am asham'd.
Isabella.
Dear *Hieronimo,*
Cast a more serious eye upon thy grief,
Weak apprehension gives but weak belief.
Hieronimo.
It was a man, sure, that was hang'd up here,
A youth, as I remember: I cut him down.
If it should prove my son now after all,
Say you, say you: light, lend me a taper;

Let

Isabella.
And I'll clofe up the glaffes of his fight,
For once thefe eyes were only [1] my delight.
Hieronimo.
Seeft thou this handkerchief befmear'd with blood?
It fhall not from me, till I take revenge:
Seeft thou thofe wounds, that yet are bleeding frefh?
I'll not intomb them till I have reveng'd: [2]
Then will I joy amidft my difcontent;
Till then, my forrow [3] never fhall be fpent.
Isabella.
The heav'ns are juft, murder cannot be hid:
Time is the author both of truth and right,
And time will bring this treachery to light.
Hieronimo.
Mean while, good *Isabella*, ceafe thy plaints,
Or, at the leaft, diffemble them awhile:
So fhall we fooner find the practife out,
And learn by whom all this was brought about.
Come, *Isabel*, now let us take him up,
[*They take him up.*

[1] *chiefly* 1623, 33.   [2] *revenge* ditto.
[3] *forrowes* 1618, 23, 33.

And

Let me look again.
O God! confufion, mifchief, torment, death and hell,
Drop all your ftings at once in my cold bofom,
That now is ftiff with horror; kill me quickly:
Be gracious to me, thou infective night,
And drop this deed of murder down on me;
Gird in my wafte of grief with thy large darknefs,
And let me not furvive to fee the light,
May put me in the mind I had a fon.
Isabella.
O fweet *Horatio!* O my deareft fon!
Hieronimo.
How ftrangely had I loft my way to grief!

And bear him in from out this curfed place:
I'll fay his dirge, finging fits not this cafe.

   O aliquis mihi quas pulchrum ver educat herbas,
        [Hieronimo *fets his breaft unto his fword.*
Mifceat, et noftro detur medicina dolori:
Aut fi qui faciunt annorum oblivia fuccos
Præbeat, ipfe metam magnum quæcunque per orbem
Gramina fol pulchras ejecit lucis in oras;
Ipfe bibam quicquid meditatur faga veneni,
Quicquid et irarum vi cæca nenia nectit.
Omnia perpetiar, lethum quoque, dum femel omnis
Nofter in extincto moriatur pectore fenfus:
Ergo tuos oculos nunquam, mea vita, videbo,
Et tua perpetuus fepelivit lumina fomnus?
Emoriar tecum fic, fic juvat ire fub umbras.
Attamen abfiftam properato cedere letho,
Ne mortem vindicta tuam tum nulla fequatur.
[*Here he throws it from him,* ¹ *and bears the body away.*

            Andrea.
Brought'ft thou me hither to increafe my pain?
I look'd, that *Balthazar* fhould have been flain;
But 'tis my friend *Horatio* that is flain:
And they abufe fair *Bel-imperia,*
On whom I doted more than all the world,
Becaufe fhe lov'd me more than all the world.
            Revenge.
   Thou talk'ft of harveft ¹ when the corn is green;
The end is crown ² of every work well done:
The fickle comes not till the corn be ripe.
Be ftill; and ere I lead thee from this place,
I'll fhow thee *Balthazar* in heavy cafe.

  1 *thee harveft* 1618, 23, 33.   2 *growne* ditto.

  6 *faciunt annum oblimia*   7 *metum magnum quicunque*
  8 *pulchras effecit in luminis oras,* 10 *et iravi evecæca*
menia   Sic.

                                    A C T

ACT III.

Enter the Viceroy of Portingale, *Nobles,* Alexandro, Villuppo.

Viceroy.

INfortunate condition of kings,
Seated amidſt 1 ſo many helpleſs doubts!
Firſt, we are plac'd upon extremeſt height,
And oft ſupplanted with exceeding hate;
But ever ſubject to the wheel of chance;
And at our higheſt, never joy we ſo,
As we both doubt and dread our overthrow.
So ſtriveth not the waves with ſundry winds,
As fortune toileth in th' affairs of kings,
That would be fear'd, yet fear to be belov'd,
Sith fear, or love, to kings is flattery:
For inſtance, lordings, look upon your king,
By hate deprived of his deareſt ſon;
The only hope of our ſucceſſive line. 2

Nobles.

I had not thought, that *Alexandro's* heart
Had been envenom'd with ſuch extreme hate:
But now I ſee, that words have ſeveral works,
And there's no credit in the countenance.

Villuppo.

No; for, my lord, had you beheld the train,
That fained love had colour'd in his looks,
When he in camp conſorted *Balthazar,*
Far more inconſtant had you thought the ſun,
That hourly coaſts the centre of the earth,
Than *Alexandro's* purpoſe to the prince.

1 *among* 1623, 33.   2 *lives.* 1618, 23, 33.

Viceroy.

THE SPANISH TRAGEDY. 45

Viceroy.
No, more, *Villuppo:* thou haſt ſaid enough,
And with thy words, thou ſlay'ſt our wounded thoughts;
Nor ſhall I longer dally with the world,
Procraſtinating *Alexandro's* death:
Go, ſome of you, and fetch the traitor forth,
That as he is condemned, he may die.

Enter Alexandro, *with a Nobleman, and halberts.*
Nobleman.
In ſuch extremes, will nought but patience ſerve.
Alexandro.
But in extremes, what patience ſhall I uſe?
Nor diſcontents it me to leave the world,
With whom there nothing can prevail but wrong.
Nobleman.
Yet hope the beſt.
Alexandro.
'Tis heaven is my hope;
As for the earth, it is too much infect, [1]
To yield me hope of any of her mould.
Viceroy.
Why linger ye? bring forth that daring fiend,
And let him die for his accurſed deed.
Alexandro.
Not that I fear the extremity of death,
(For nobles cannot ſtoop to ſervile fear)
Do I, o king, thus diſcontented live.
But this, o, this torments my labouring ſoul,
That thus I die ſuſpected of a ſin,
Whereof, as heav'ns have known my ſecret thoughts,
So am I free from this ſuggeſtion.
Viceroy.
No more, I ſay; to the tortures, when?
Bind him, and burn his body in thoſe flames,
[*They bind him to the ſtake.*

1 *infeſted* 1618, 23, 33.

That

That shall prefigure those unquenched fires
Of *Phlegethon*, prepared for his soul.
     Alexandro.
My guiltless death will be aveng'd on thee,
On thee, *Villuppo*, that hath malic'd thus;
Or for [1] thy meed hast falsely me accus'd.
     Villuppo.
Nay, *Alexandro*, if thou menace me,
I'll lend a hand to send thee to the lake,
Where those thy words shall perish with thy works:
Injurious traitor! monstrous homicide!

    Enter Ambassador.
     Ambassador.
Stay, hold a while; and here (with pardon of
His majesty) lay hands upon *Villuppo*.
     Viceroy.
Ambassador, what news hath urg'd this sudden entrance?
     Ambassador.
Know, sovereign lord, [2] that *Balthazar* doth live.
     Viceroy.
What say'st thou? liveth *Balthazar* our son?
     Ambassador.
Your highness' son lord *Balthazar* doth live;
And, well entreated in the court of *Spain*,
Humbly commends him to your majesty:
These eyes beheld, and these my followers,
With these the letters of the king's commends, [3]
       [*Gives him letters.*
Are happy witness of his highness' health.
   [*The king looks on the letters, and proceeds.*

[1] *of* 1618, 23, 33.
[2] *Know sovereign: I. that* — 1618.
 Know my soveraigne, that — 1623, 33.
[3] *commend* 1618, 23, 33.

         Viceroy.

Viceroy.
Thy son doth live, your tribute is receiv'd:
Thy peace is made, and we are satisfied:
The rest resolve upon as things propos'd
For both our honours, and thy benefit.
   Ambassador.
Thefe are his highnefs' farther articles.
   [*Gives him more letters.*
   Viceroy.
Accurfed wretch, to intimate thefe ills
Againft the life and reputation
Of noble *Alexandro!* — Come, my lord, unbind him:
Let him unbind thee, that is bound to death,
To make a quital for thy difcontent. [*They unbind him.*
   Alexandro.
Dread lord, in kindnefs you could do no lefs,
Upon report of fuch a damned fact;
But, thus we fee our innocence hath fav'd
The hopelefs life which thou, *Villuppo*, fought
By thy fuggeftions to have maffacred.
   Viceroy.
Say, falfe *Villuppo*, wherefore didft thou thus
Falfely betray lord *Alexandro's* life?
Him, whom thou know'ft that no unkindnefs elfe,
But ev'n the flaughter of our deareft fon,
Could once have mov'd 1 us to have mifconceiv'd.
   Alexandro.
Say, treacherous *Villuppo*, tell the king:
Or wherein hath *Alexandro* us'd thee ill?
   Villuppo.
Rent with remembrance of fo foul a deed,
My guilty foul 2 fubmits me to thy doom:
For, not for *Alexandro's* injuries,
But for reward, and hope to be prefer'd,
Thus have I fhamelefsly hazarded his life.

1 *Could never once mov'd* — 1633.
2 *guiltful* 1618, 23, 33.

Viceroy.

Viceroy.
Which, villain, shall be ransom'd with thy death;
And not so mean a torment as we here
Devis'd for him, who, thou said'st, slew our son:
But with the bitter'st torments and extremes,
Thay may be yet invented for thine end.
[*Alex. seems to entreat.*
Entreat me not;— go take the traitor hence:—
[*Exit Villuppo.*
And, *Alexandro*, let us honour thee
With publick notice of thy loyalty.
To end those things articulated here,
By our great lord, the mighty king of *Spain*,
We with our council will deliberate:
Come, *Alexandro*, keep us company. [*Exeunt.*

Enter Hieronimo.
Hieronimo.
O eyes! no eyes, but fountains fraught with tears:
O life! no life, but lively form of death:
O world! no world, but mass of publick wrongs,
Confus'd and fill'd with murder and misdeeds:
O sacred heav'ns! if this unhallow'd deed,
If this inhuman, and barbarous attempt;
If this incomparable murder thus,
Of mine, but now no more my son,
Shall unreveal'd, and unrevenged pass,
How should we term your dealings to be just,
If you unjustly deal with those that in your justice trust?
The night, sad secretary to my moans,
With direful visions wake my vexed soul,
And with the wounds of my distressful son,
Solicit me for notice of his death.
The ugly fiends do sally forth of hell,
And frame my steps to unfrequented paths,
And fear my heart with fierce inflamed thoughts.
The cloudy day my discontents 1 records,

---

1 *discontent* 1618, 23, 33.   Early

THE SPANISH TRAGEDY. 49

Early begins to regifter my dreams,
And drive me forth to feek the murderer.
Eyes, life, world, heav'ns, hell, night, and day,
See, fearch, fhow, fend fome man,
Some mean, that may —   [*A letter falleth.*
What's here? a letter? tufh! it is not fo:
A letter written to *Hieronimo*.   [*Red ink.*

> *For want of ink, receive this bloody writ;*
> *Me hath my haplefs brother hid from thee:*
> *Revenge thyfelf on* Balthazar *and him;*
> *For thefe were they that murdered thy fon.*
> Hieronimo, *revenge* Horatio's *death,*
> *And better far than* Bel-imperia *doth.*

What means this unexpected miracle?
My fon flain by *Lorenzo*, and the prince!
What caufe had they *Horatio* to malign?
Or what might move thee, *Bel-imperia*,
To accufe thy brother, had he been the mean?
Hieronimo, beware, thou art betray'd,
And to entrap thy life, this train is lay'd:
Advife thee therefore, be not credulous;
This is devifed to endanger thee,
That thou by this *Lorenzo* fhouldft accufe;
And he, for thy difhonour done, fhould draw
Thy life in queftion, and thy name in hate.
Dear was the life of my beloved fon,
And of his death behooves me be reveng'd:
Then hazard not thine own, *Hieronimo*;
But live to effect thy refolution.
I therefore will by circumftances try,
What I can gather to confirm this writ;
And, heark'ning¹ near the duke of *Caftile's* houfe,
Clofe, if I can, with *Bel-imperia*,
To liften more; but nothing to bewray.

¹ *hęarken* 1618, 23, 33.

VOL. II.   D   *Enter*

Enter Pedringano.

Hieronimo.
Now, *Pedringano!*
Pedringano.
Now, *Hieronimo!*
Hieronimo.
Where's thy lady?
Pedringano.
I know not: here's my lord.

Enter Lorenzo.
Lorenzo.
How now, who's this, *Hieronimo?*
Hieronimo.
My lord.
Pedringano.
He asketh for my lady *Bel-imperia.*
Lorenzo.
What to do, *Hieronimo?* the duke my father hath
Upon some disgrace, a while remov'd her hence;
But if it be aught I may inform her of,
Tell me, *Hieronimo,* and I'll let her know it.
Hieronimo.
Nay, nay, my lord, I thank you, it shall not need;
I had a suit unto her, but too late,
And her disgrace makes me unfortunate.
Lorenzo. 1
Why so, *Hieronimo?* use me. *Hieronimo.*

---

1 *Lorenzo.*
Why so, *Hieronimo?* use me.
Hieronimo.
Who you, my lord?
I reserve your favour for a greater honour:
This is a very toy, my lord, a toy.
Lorenzo.
All's one, Hieronimo, *acquaint me with it.*
Hieronimo.

THE SPANISH TRAGEDY. 51

Hieronimo.
O, no, my lord; I dare not, it muſt not be:
I humbly thank your lordſhip.
Lorenzo.
Why then, farewel.
Hieronimo.
My grief no heart, my thoughts no tongue can tell.
Exit.
Lorenzo.
Come hither, *Pedringano*; ſee'ſt thou this?
Pedringano.
My lord, I ſee it, and ſuſpect it too.
Lorenzo.
This is that damned villain, *Serberine*,
That hath, I-fear, reveal'd *Horatio's* death.
Pedringano.
My lord, he could not, 'twas ſo lately done;
And ſince, he hath not left my company.
Lorenzo.
Admit he have not, his condition's ſuch,
As fear or flattering words may make him falſe.
I know his humour; and therewith repent,
That ere I us'd him in this enterpriſe.
But, *Pedringano*, to prevent the worſt,
And 'cauſe I know thee ſecret as my ſoul,
Here, for thy further ſatisfaction, take thou ¹ this,
[*Gives him more gold.*

¹ *thee* 1623, 33.

And

Hieronimo.
*I'faith, my lord, 'tis an idle thing, I muſt confeſs,
I ha' been too ſlack, too tardy, too remiſs unto your honour.*
Lorenzo.
How new, Hieronimo?
Hieronimo.
*In troth, my lord, it is a thing of nothing;
The murder of a ſon, or ſo:
A thing of nothing, my lord.*
Lorenzo.
Why then farewel. 1618, 23, 33.

And hearken to me; thus it is devis'd,[1]
This night thou muſt, (and, pr'ythee, ſo reſolve)
Meet *Serberine* at St. *Liugis'* park:
Thou know'ſt, 'tis here hard by behind the houſe;
There take thy ſtand, and ſee thou ſtrike him ſure:
For die he muſt, if we do mean to live.

Pedringano.
But how ſhall *Serberine* be there, my lord?

Lorenzo.
Let me alone, I'll ſend to him to meet
The prince and me, where thou muſt do this deed.

Pedringano.
It ſhall be done, my lord, it ſhall be done;
And I'll go arm myſelf to meet him there.

Lorenzo.
When things ſhall alter, as I hope they will,
Then ſhalt thou mount for this; thou know'ſt my mind.
Che le Jeron! [*Exit* Pedringano.

Enter Page.

Page.
My lord?

Lorenzo.
Go, ſirrah, to *Serberine*, and bid him forthwith
Meet the prince and me at St. *Liugis'* park,
Behind the houſe, this evening, boy.

Page.
I go, my lord.

Lorenzo.
But, ſirrah, let the hour be eight o'clock:
Bid him not fail.

Page.
I fly, my lord. [*Exit.*

Lorenzo.
Now to confirm the complot thou haſt caſt,
Of all theſe practiſes, I'll ſpread the watch,

[1] —*thus it is: diſguis'd,* 1618, 23, 33.

Upon

THE SPANISH TRAGEDY.

Upon precife commandment from the king,
Strongly to guard the place where *Pedringano*
This night fhall murder haplefs *Serberine*.
Thus muft we work, that will avoid diftruft,
Thus muft we practife to prevent mifhap:
And thus one ill another muft expulfe.
This fly inquiry of *Hieronimo*
For *Bel-imperia* breeds fufpicion,
And this fufpicion bodes a further ill.
As for myfelf, I know my fecret fault,
And fo do they; but I have dealt for them.
They that for coin their fouls endangered,
To fave my life, for coin fhall venture theirs:
And better 'tis, that bafe companions die,
Than by their life to hazard our good haps;
Nor fhall they live, for me to fear their faith:
I'll truft myfelf, myfelf fhall be my friend;
For die they fhall, flaves are ordain'd to [1] no other end.
[*Exit.*

Enter Pedringano, *with a piftol.*

Pedringano.
Now, *Pedringano*, bid thy piftol hold;
And hold on, fortune, once more favour me,
Give but fuccefs to mine attempting fpirit,
And let me fhift for taking of mine aim.
Here is the gold, this is the gold propos'd,
It is no dream that I adventure for,
But *Pedringano* is poffefs'd thereof;
And he that would not ftrain his confcience
For him, that thus his liberal purfe hath ftretch'd,
Unworthy fuch a favour may he fail;
And, wifhing, want, when fuch as I prevail:
As for the fear of apprehenfion,
I know, if need fhould be, my noble lord
Will ftand between me and enfuing harms:

[1] *for* 1618, 23, 33.

Befides

Besides this place is free from all suspect.
Here therefore will I stay, and take my stand.

Enter the Watch.

1 *Watch.*
I wonder much to what intent it is,
That we are thus expressly charg'd to watch.
2 *Watch.*
'Tis by commandment in the king's own name.
3 *Watch.*
But we were never wont to watch and [1] ward
So near the duke his brother's [2] house before.
2 *Watch.*
Content yourself, stand close, there's somewhat in't.

Enter Serberine.

Serberine.
Here, *Serberine*, attend and stay thy pace;
For here did *Don Lorenzo's* page appoint,
That thou by his command shouldst meet with him:
How fit a place, if one were so dispos'd,
Methinks this corner is to close with one.
Pedringano.
Here comes the bird that I must seize upon:
Now, *Pedringano*, or never, play the man.
Serberine.
I wonder, that his lordship stays so long,
Or wherefore should he send for me so late?
Pedringano.
For this, *Serberine*, and thou shalt ha't.
  [*Shoots the* Dag.
So, there he lies; my promise is perform'd.

[1] *nor* 1618, 23, 33.
[2] *brother's* om. ditto.

1 *Watch.*

1 Watch.
Hark, gentlemen, this is a piftol fhot.
2 Watch.
And here's one flain; ftay the murderer.
Pedringano.
Now by the forrows of the fouls in hell,
[*He ftrives with the Watch.*
Who firft lays hand on me, I'll be his prieft.
3 Watch.
Sirrah, confefs, and therein play the prieft,
Why haft thou thus unkindly kill'd the man?
Pedringano.
Why? becaufe he walk'd abroad fo late.
3 Watch.
Come, fir, you had been better kept your bed,
Than have committed this mifdeed fo late.
2 Watch.
Come to the marfhal's [1] with the murderer.
1 Watch.
On to *Hieronimo's*: [2] help me here
To bring the murder'd body with us too.
Pedringano.
Hieronimo? carry me before whom you will,
Whate'er he be, I'll anfwer him and you;
And do your worft, for I defy you all.   [*Exeunt.*

Enter Lorenzo, *and* Balthazar.

Balthazar.
How now, my lord, what makes you rife fo foon?
Lorenzo.
Fear of preventing our mifhaps too late.
Balthazar.
What mifchief is it that we not miftruft?

[1] *marfhall* 1618, 23, 33.
[2] *Hieronimo:* ditto.

Lorenzo.

Lorenzo.
Our greatest ills we least mistrust, my lord,
And inexpected harms do hurt us most.
Balthazar.
Why, tell me, *Don Lorenzo*, tell me, man,
If aught concerns our honour, and your own?
Lorenzo.
Nor [1] you, nor me, my lord, but both in one:
For I suspect, and the presumption's great,
That by those base confederates in our fault,
Touching the death of *Don Horatio*,
We are betray'd to old *Hieronimo*.
Balthazar.
Betray'd, *Lorenzo?* tush! it cannot be.
Lorenzo.
A guilty conscience, urged with the thought
Of former evils, easily cannot err:
I am persuaded, and dissuade me not,
That all's revealed to *Hieronimo*,
And therefore know, that I have cast it thus.

Enter Page.

But here's the *Page*:— How now? what news with thee?
Page.
My lord, *Serberine* is slain.
Balthazar.
Who, *Serberine* my man?
Page.
Your highness' man, my lord.
Lorenzo.
Speak, *Page*, who murder'd him?
Page.
He that is apprehended for the fact.
Lorenzo.
Who?
Page.
Pedringano.

[1] *Not* 1618, 23, 33.   *Balthazar.*

Balthazar.
Is [1] *Serberine* slain, that lov'd his lord so well?
Injurious villain! murderer of his friend!
Lorenzo.
Hath *Pedringano* murder'd *Serberine?*
My lord, let me entreat you to take the pains
To exasperate and hasten his revenge,
With your complaints unto my lord the king:
This their dissension breeds a greater doubt.
Balthazar.
Assure thee, *Don Lorenzo*, he shall die,
Or else his highness hardly shall deny.
Mean while I'll haste the marshal sessions:
For die he shall for this his damned deed.
[*Exit* Balthazar.
Lorenzo.
Why so, this fits our former policy,
And thus experience bids the wise to deal:
I lay the plot, he prosecutes the point;
I set the trap, he breaks the worthless twigs,
And sees not that wherewith the bird was lim'd.
Thus hopeful men, that mean to hold their own,
Must look like fowlers to their dearest friends;
He runs to kill, whom I have holp [2] to catch,
And no man knows it was my reaching fetch.
'Tis hard to trust unto a multitude,
Or any one, in mine opinion,
When men themselves their secrets will reveal.

Enter a Messenger, with a letter.
Boy,—
Page.
My lord?

[1] *I, Serberine* 1618, 23, 33.
[2] *hope* 1623, 33.

Lorenzo.
What's he?
Messenger.
I have a letter to your lordship.
Lorenzo.
From whence?
Messenger.
From *Pedringano*, that's imprison'd.
Lorenzo.
So, he is in prison [1] then?
Messenger.
Ay, my good lord.
Lorenzo.
What would he with us?
He writes us here, *To stand good L. and help him in distress.*
Tell him, I have his letters, know his mind;
And what we may, let him assure him of.
Fellow, be gone; my boy shall follow thee.
[*Exit Messenger.*
This works like wax; yet once more try thy wits.—
Boy, go, convey this purse to *Pedringano*;
Thou know'st the prison, closely give it him,
And be advis'd that none be there about:
Bid him be merry still, but secret;
And though the marshal [2] sessions be to day,
Bid him not doubt of his delivery;
Tell him, his pardon is already sign'd:
And thereon bid him boldly be resolv'd;
For were he ready to be turned off,
(As 'tis my will the uttermost be try'd)
Thou with his pardon shalt attend him still:
Show him this box, tell him his pardon's in't;
But open't not, and if thou lov'st thy life:
But let him wisely keep his hopes unknown,
He shall not want while *Don Lorenzo* lives: away.

[1] *imprison'd* 1618, 23, 33.
[2] *marshals* ditto.

Page.

Page.
I go, my lord, I run. [*Exit* Page.
Lorenzo.
But, sirrah, see that this be cleanly done.
Now stands our fortune on a tickle point,
And now or never, ends *Lorenzo's* doubts:
One only thing is uneffected yet,
And that's to see the executioner;
But to what end? I [1] list not trust the air
With utterance of our pretence therein;
For fear the privy whispering of the wind
Convey our words amongst unfriendly ears,
That lie too open to advantages.
 E quel che voglio io, nessun lo sa,
 Intendo io quel mi bastara.

Enter Boy, with the box.
Boy.
My master hath forbidden me to look in this box; and, by my troth,[2] 'tis likely, if he had not warned me, I should not have had so much idle time: for we menskind[3] in our minority, are like women in their uncertainty; that they are most forbidden, they will soonest attempt: so I now. — By my bare honesty,[4] here's nothing but the bare empty box: were it not sin against secrecy, I would say it were a piece of gentleman-like knavery. I must go to *Pedringano,* and tell him his pardon is in this box; nay, I would have sworn it, had I not seen the contrary. I cannot choose but smile, to think how the villain will flout the gallows, scorn the audience, and descant on the hangman; and all presuming of his pardon from hence. Will't not be an odd jest, for me to

1 *I* om. 1618, 23, 33. 2 *honesty* ditto.
3 *men-kind* ditto. 4 *credit.* ditto.

12 *Et quel que voglio, Il nessun le sa,*
 Intendo io quel mi bassara. Sic

stand

stand and grace every jest he makes, pointing my finger at this box, as who would [1] say, mock on, here's thy warrant? Is't not a scurvy jest, that a man should jest himself to death? Alas! poor *Pedringano*, I am in a sort sorry for thee; but if I should be hang'd with thee, I cannot [2] weep. [*Exit*.

Enter Hieronimo, *and the Deputy*.
 Hieronimo.
Thus must we toil in other men's extremes,
That know not how to remedy our own;
And do them justice, when unjustly we,
For all our wrongs, can compass no redress.
But shall I never live to see the day,
That I may come, by justice of the heav'ns,
To know the cause that may my cares allay?
This toils my body, this consumeth age,
That only I, to all men just must be,
And neither gods nor men be just to me.
 Deputy.
Worthy *Hieronimo*, your office asks
A care to punish such as do transgress.
 Hieronimo.
So is't my duty to regard his death,
Who, when he liv'd, deserv'd my dearest blood.
But come, for that we came for: let's begin,
For here lies that, which bids me to be gone.

Enter Officers, Boy, and Pedringano, *with a letter in his hand, bound.*
 Deputy.
Bring forth the prisoner, for the court is set.
 Pedringano.
Gramercy, boy, but it was time to come;
For I had written to my lord anew,

[1] *should* 1618, 23, 33.   [2] *could not* ditto.

A nearer

A nearer matter that concerneth him,
For fear his lordship had forgotten me:
But sith he hath remember'd me so well,—
Come, come, come on, when shall we to this gear?
     Hieronimo.
Stand forth, thou monster, murderer of men,
And here for satisfaction of the world,
Confess thy folly, and repent thy fault;
For there's thy¹ place of execution.
     Pedringano.
This is short work: well, to your marshalship.
First, I confess, nor fear I death therefore,
I am the man, 'twas I slew *Serberine*.
But, sir, then you think this shall be the place,
Where we shall satisfy you for this gear?
     Deputy.
Ay, *Pedringano*.
     Pedringano.
Now², I think not so.
     Hieronimo.
Peace, impudent; for thou shalt find it so:
For blood with blood, shall (while I sit as judge)
Be satisfied, and the law discharg'd.
And though myself cannot receive the like,
Yet will I see that others have their right.
Despatch, the fault's approved, and confess'd;
And by our law, he is condemn'd to die.

     Enter Hangman.
     Hangman.
Come on, sir; are you ready?
     Pedringano.
To do what, my fine officious knave?
     Hangman.
To go to this gear.

1 *the* 1618, 23, 33.   2 *No,* ditto.
          Pedringano.

Pedringano.

O sir, you are too forward; thou wouldst fain furnish me with a halter, to disfurnish me of my habit:

So I should go out of this gear my raiment, into that gear the rope:

But, hangman, now I spy your knavery; I'll not change without boot, that's flat.

Hangman.

Come, sir.

Pedringano.

So then, I must up?

Hangman.

No remedy.

Pedringano.

Yes, but there shall be for my [1] coming down.

Hangman.

Indeed here's a remedy for that.

Pedringano.

How? be turn'd off?

Hangman.

Ay, truly; come, are you ready? I pray you, sir, despatch; the day goes away.

Pedringano.

What, do you hang by the hour? If you do, I may chance to break your old custom.

Hangman.

'Faith, you have [2] reason; for I am like to break your young neck.

Pedringano.

Dost thou mock me, hangman? pray God, I be not preserv'd to break your knave's pate for this.

Hangman.

Alas! sir, you are a foot too low to reach it: and, I hope, you will never grow so high, while I am in the office.

[1] *my* omitted ditto.
[2] *no reason* 1618, 23, 33.

Pedringano.

Pedringano.
Sirrah, doſt ſee yonder boy with the box in his hand ?
Hangman.
What, he that points to it with his finger ?
Pedringano.
Ay, that companion.
Hangman.
I know him not, but what of him ?
Pedringano.
Doſt thou think to live till his old doublet will make thee a new truſs ?
Hangman.
Ay, and many a fair year after, to truſs up many an honeſter man, than either thou, or he.
Pedringano.
What hath he in his box, as thou thinkeſt ?
Hangman.
'Faith, I cannot tell, nor I care not greatly;
Methinks, you ſhould rather hearken to your ſoul's health.
Pedringano.
Why, ſirrah hangman, I take it, that that is good for the body, is likewiſe good for the ſoul : and it may be, in that box is balm for both.
Hangman.
Well, thou art even the merrieſt piece of man's fleſh, that ever groan'd at my office door.
Pedringano.
Is your roguery become an office with a knave's name ?
Hangman.
Ay, and that ſhall all they witneſs, that ſee you ſeal it with a thief's name.
Pedringano.
I pr'ythee, requeſt this good company to pray with me.
Hangman.
Ay, marry, ſir, this is a good motion. — My maſters, you ſee here's a good fellow.

for 1618, 23, 3?.
Pedringano.

Pedringano.
Nay, nay, now I remember me, let them alone till
some other time; for now I have no great need.
Hieronimo.
I have not seen a wretch so impudent.
O monstrous times! where murder's set so light,
And where the soul, that should be shrin'd in heav'n,
Solely delights in interdicted things,
Still wand'ring in the thorny passages,
That intercepts itself of happiness.
Murder? o bloody monster! God forbid,
A fault so foul should 'scape unpunished.
Despatch, and see this ¹ execution done:
This makes me to remember thee, my son.   [*Exit* Hier.
Pedringano.
Nay, soft, no haste.
Deputy.
Why, wherefore stay you? Have you hope of life?
Pedringano.
Why, ay.
Hangman.
As how?
Pedringano.
Why, rascal, by my pardon from the king.
Hangman.
Stand you on that? then you shall off with this.
            [*He turns him off.*
Deputy.
So, executioner; convey him hence:
But let his body be unburied;
Let not the earth be choked or infect
With that which heaven contemns, and men neglect.
                [*Exeunt.*

Enter Hieronimo.

Hieronimo.
Where shall I run to breathe abroad my woes,

¹ *the* 1611, 23, 33.   My

THE SPANISH TRAGEDY. 65

My woes, whose weight hath wearied the earth?
Or mine exclaims, that have surcharg'd the air
With ceaseless plaints for my deceased son?
The blust'ring winds, conspiring with my words,
At my lament, have mov'd the leafless trees,
Disrob'd the meadows of their flower'd green,
Made mountains marsh, with spring-tides¹ of my tears,
And broken through the brazen gates of hell.
Yet still tormented is my tortur'd soul
With broken sighs and restless passions,
That, winged, mount; and, hovering in the air,
Beat² at the windows of the brightest heavens,
Soliciting for justice and revenge:
But they are plac'd in those imperial heights,
Where, countermur'd with walls of diamond,
I find the place impregnable; and they
Resist my woes, and give my words no way.

Enter Hangman, with a letter.

Hangman.
O lord, sir, God bless you, sir; the man, sir, *Petergad,*
sir, he that was so full of merry conceits—
Hieronimo.
Well, what of him?
Hangman.
O lord, sir, he went the wrong way; the fellow had a fair commission to the contrary. Sir, here is his passport; I pray you, sir, we have done him wrong.
Hieronimo.
I warrant thee, give it me.
Hangman.
You will stand between the gallows and me?
Hieronimo.
Ay, ay.
Hangman.
I thank your lord worship. [*Exit* Hang.

1 *spring-tide* 1618, 23, 33. 2 *But* ditto.
Vol. II. E *Hieronimo.*

Hieronimo.
And yet, though somewhat nearer me concerns,
I will, to ease the grief that I sustain,
Take truce with sorrow while I read on this.

> *My lord, I write as mine extremes require,*
> *That you would labour my delivery:*
> *If you neglect, my life is desperate;*
> *And in my death, I shall reveal the troth.*
> *You know, my lord, I slew him for your sake,*
> *And was confederate with the prince and you:*
> *Won by rewards and hopeful promises,*
> *I holp to murder Don Horatio too.*

Holp he to murder mine *Horatio?*
And actors in the accursed tragedy
Wast thou, *Lorenzo, Balthazar* and thou,
Of whom my son, my son deserv'd so well?
What have I heard? what have mine eyes beheld?
O sacred heavens! may it come to pass
That such a monstrous and detested deed,
So closely smother'd, and so long conceal'd,
Shall thus by this be venged 1, or reveal'd?
Now see I what I durst not then suspect,
That *Bel-imperia's* letter was not feign'd;
Nor feigned she, though falsely they have wrong'd
Both her, myself, *Horatio,* and themselves.
Now may I make compare 'twixt her's and this,
Of every accident I ne'er could find
Till now, and now I feelingly perceive
They did what heaven unpunish'd would 2 not leave.
O false *Lorenzo!* are these thy flattering looks?
Is this the honour that thou didst my son?
And *Balthazar,* bane to thy soul and me,

1 *shall thus be this revenged,* 1618.
 shall thus be thus revenged, 1623, 33.
2 *should* 1618, 23, 33.

THE SPANISH TRAGEDY.

Was this the ranſome he reſerv'd thee for ? [1]
Wo to the cauſe of theſe conſtrained wars!
Wo to thy baſeneſs and captivity!
Wo to thy birth, thy body, and thy ſoul,
Thy curſed father, and thy conquer'd ſelf!
And ban'd with bitter execrations be,
The day and place where he did pity thee!
But wherefore waſte I mine unfruitful words,
When nought but blood will ſatisfy my woes?
I will go plain me to my lord the king,
And cry aloud for juſtice through the court,
Wearing the flints with theſe my wither'd feet;
And either purchaſe juſtice by entreats,
Or tire them all with my revenging threats. [*Exit.*

† ACT IV.

Enter Iſabella, *and her maid.*

Iſabella.

SO that you ſay this herb will purge the eye, [2]
And this the head.—Ah, but none of them will purge
the heart!
No, there's no medicine left for my diſeaſe,
Nor any phyſick to recure the dead.—
[*She runs lunatick.*
Horatio! O where's Horatio?

1 *for thee* 1618, 23, 33.   2 *eyes* ditto.

† *Hitherto this play has been made to conſiſt of four acts; but, ſurely, through miſtake: the third act containing more pages than any two beſides. The preſent editor has therefore ventured, againſt the authority of the printed copies, to divide the third into two; and ſubmits the propriety of the arrangement to the judgment of the reader.*

E 2   *Maid.*

Maid.
Good madam, affright not thus yourself
With outrage for your son *Horatio*;
He sleeps in quiet in the *Elysian* fields.
Isabella.
Why, did I not give you gowns, and goodly things?
Bought you a whistle, and a whipstalk too,
To be revenged on their villanies?
Maid.
Madam, these humours do torment my soul.
Isabella.
My soul, poor soul; thou talk'st of things
Thou know'st not what: my soul hath silver wings,
That mount me up unto the highest heavens:
To heaven, ay, there sits my *Horatio*,
Back'd with a troop of fiery cherubims,
Dancing about his newly healed wounds,
Singing sweet hymns, and chanting heavenly notes:
Rare harmony to greet his innocence, 1
That died, 2 ay, died a mirror in our days.
But say, where shall I find the men, the murderers,
That slew *Horatio?* Whither shall I run,
To find them out that murdered my son? [*Exeunt.*

Bel-imperia at a window.

Bel-imperia.
What means this outrage that is offer'd me?
Why am I thus sequester'd from the court?
No notice! shall I not know the cause
Of these my secret and suspicious ills!
Accursed brother, unkind murderer,
Why bend'st thou thus thy mind to martyr me?
Hieronimo, why writ 3 I of thy wrongs?
Or why art thou so slack in thy revenge?

1 *innocency* 1618, 23, 33.   2 *ay'd* ditto.
3 *write* ditto.

Andrea

Andrea, O *Andrea!* that thou saw'st
Me for thy friend *Horatio* handled thus;
And him for me, thus causeless murdered!
Well, force perforce, I must constrain myself
To patience, and apply me to the time,
Till heav'n, as I have hop'd, shall set me free.

Enter Christophil.

Christophil.
Come, madam *Bel-imperia*, this may¹ not be.
[*Exeunt.*

Enter Lorenzo, Balthazar, *and the Page.*
Lorenzo.
Boy, talk no further. Thus far things go well.
Thou art assured that thou saw'st him dead?
Page.
Or else, my lord, I live not.
Lorenzo.
That's enough.
As for his resolution in his end,
Leave that to him with whom he sojourns now.
Here, take my ring, and give it *Christophil*,
And bid him let my sister be enlarg'd,
And bring her hither straight. — *Exit* Page.²
This that I did was for a policy,
To smooth and keep the murder secret,
Which, as a nine-days wonder, being o'er-blown,
My gentle sister will I now enlarge.
Balthazar.
And time, *Lorenzo*; for my lord the duke,
You heard, inquired for her yester-night,
Lorenzo.
Why, and my lord, I hope, you heard me say,

¹ *must* 1618, 23, 33.
² *Exit Page,* omitted ditto.

E 3   Sufficient

Sufficient reason why she kept away:
But that's all one. My lord, you love her?
Balthazar.
Ay.
Lorenzo.
Then in your love beware; deal cunningly;
Salve all suspicions, only sooth me up;
And if she hap to stand on terms with us,
As for her sweetheart, and concealment so,
Jest with her gently: under feigned jest
Are things conceal'd, that else would breed unrest.
But here she comes.

Enter Bel-imperia.

Lorenzo.
Now, sister?
Bel-imperia.
Sister! no, thou art no brother, but an enemy;
Else wouldst thou not have us'd thy sister so:
First, to affright me with thy weapons drawn,
And with extremes abuse my company;
And then to hurry me, like whirlwind's rage,
Amidst a crew of thy confederates,
And clap me up where none might come at me,
Nor I at any, to reveal my wrongs.
What madding fury did possess thy wits? [1]
Or wherein is't that I offended thee?
Lorenzo.
Advise you better, *Bel-imperia*,
For I have done you no disparagement;
Unless, by more discretion than deserv'd,
I sought to save your honour and mine own.
Bel-imperia.
Mine honour! why, *Lorenzo*, wherein is't
That I neglect my reputation so,
As you or any need to rescue it?

--- [1] *edit* 1618, 23, 33.   *Lorenzo.*

THE SPANISH TRAGEDY.

Lorenzo.
His highnefs, and my father, were refolv'd
To come confer with old *Hieronimo*,
Concerning certain matters of eftate,
That by the viceroy was determined.
Bel-imperia.
And wherein was mine honour touch'd in that?
Balthazar.
Have patience, *Bel-imperia*, hear the reft.
Lorenzo.
Me (next in fight) as meffenger they fent,
To give him notice that they were fo nigh:
Now when I came, conforted with the prince,
And, unexpected, in an arbour there,
Found *Bel-imperia* with *Horatio*.
Bel-imperia.
How then?
Lorenzo.
Why then, remembering that old difgrace
Which you for *Don Andrea* had endur'd,
And now were likely longer to fuftain,
By being found fo meanly accompanied,
Thought rather, for I knew ¹ no readier mean,
To thruft *Horatio* forth my father's way.
Balthazar.
And carry you obfcurely fomewhere elfe,
Left that his highnefs fhould have found you there.
Bel-imperia.
Even fo, my lord? and you are witnefs
That this is true which he entreateth of? —
You, gentle brother, forg'd this for my fake;
And you, my lord, were made his inftrument:
A work of worth, worthy the noting too!
But what's the caufe that you conceal'd me fince?
Lorenzo.
Your melancholy, fifter, fince the news

¹ *know* 1618, 23, 33.

Of your first favourite *Don Andrea's* death,
My father's old wrath hath exasperate.
            Balthazar.
  And better was't for you, being in disgrace,
To absent yourself, and give his fury place.
            Bel-imperia.
  But why had I no notice of his ire?
            Lorenzo.
  That were to add more fuel to your [1] fire,
Who burnt like *Ætna* for *Andrea's* loss.
            Bel-imperia.
  Hath not my father then inquir'd for me?
            Lorenzo.
  Sister, he hath, and thus excus'd I thee.
                    [*He whispereth in her ear.*
But, *Bel-imperia*, see the gentle prince,
Look on thy love, behold young *Balthazar*,
Whose passions by thy presence are increas'd;
And in whose melancholy thou may'st see
Thy hate, his [2] love, thy flight, his following thee.
            Bel-imperia.
  Brother, you are become an orator,
I know not I, by what experience,
Too politick for me past all compare,
Since last I saw you; but content yourself,
The prince is meditating higher things.
            Balthazar.
  'Tis of thy beauty then, that conquers kings;
Of those thy tresses, *Ariadne's* twines, [3]
Wherewith my liberty thou hast surpriz'd:
Of that thine ivory front, my sorrow's map,
Wherein I see no haven to rest my hope.
            Bel-imperia.
  To love, and fear, and both at once, my lord,
In my conceit are things of more import

[1] *the* 1618, 23, 33.   [2] *Thy hate is love:* 1618.
[3] *twinnes* 1618, 23, 33.
                                    Than

THE SPANISH TRAGEDY. 73
Than women's wits are to be bufied with.
    Balthazar.
'Tis I that love.
    Bel-imperia.
Whom?
    Balthazar.
Bel-imperia.
    Bel-imperia.
But I, that fear.
    Balthazar.
Whom?
    Bel-imperia.
Bel-imperia.
    Lorenzo.
Fear yourfelf?
    Bel-imperia.
Ay, brother.
    Lorenzo.
How?
    Bel-imperia.
As thofe that, what [1] they love, are loath and fear to lofe.
    Balthazar.
Then, fair, let *Balthazar* your keeper be.
    Bel-imperia.
No, [2] *Balthazar* doth fear as well as we:
 Et tremulo metui pavidum junxere timorem,
 Et vanum ſtolidæ proditionis opus.   [*Exit.*
    Lorenzo.
Nay, an' you argue things fo cunningly,
We'll go continue this difcourfe at court.
    Balthazar.
Led by the loadftar of her heavenly looks,
Wends poor oppreffed *Balthazar,*
As o'er the mountains walks the wanderer,
Incertain to effect his pilgrimage.   [*Exeunt.*

[1] *when* 1618, 23, 33.
[2] *No*, omitted ditto.   Enter

Enter two Portingales, *and* Hieronimo *meets them.*

1 *Portingale.*

By your leave, fir. *⁎*

Hieronimo.

⁎ *See note, page* 40.

Hieronimo.

'Tis neither as you think, nor as you think,
Nor as you think: you are wide all:
These flippers are not mine, they were my fon *Horatio's*.
My fon! and what's a fon?
A thing begot within a pair of minutes, thereabout:
A lump bred up in darkness, and doth ferve
To balance those light creatures we call women;
And, at nine months end, creeps forth to light.
What is there yet in a fon,
To make a father dote, rave, or run mad?
Being born, it pouts, cries, and breeds teeth.
What is there yet in a fon?
He muft be fed, be taught to go, and fpeak:
Ay, or yet; why might not a man love a calf as well?
Or melt in paffion o'er a frifking kid, as for a fon?
Methinks, a young bacon,
Or a fine little fmooth horfe colt,
Should move a man as much as doth a fon;
For one of thefe, in very little time,
Will grow to fome good ufe; whereas a fon,
The more he grows in ftature and in years,
The more unfquar'd, unbeveled 1 he appears,
Reckons his parents among the rank of fools,
Strikes care 2 upon their heads with his mad riots,
Makes them look old before they meet with age:
This is a fon; and what a lofs were this, confider'd truly?
O, but my *Horatio* grew out of reach of thofe
Infatiate humours: he lov'd his loving parents;
He was my comfort, and his mother's joy,
The very arm that did hold up our houfe:
Our hopes were ftored up in him.
None but a damned murderer could hate him:
He had not feen the back of nineteen years,
When his ftrong arm unhors'd the proud prince *Balthazar*;
And his great mind, too full of honour,
Took him us to mercy that valiant but ignoble *Portingale*.

1 *unleavell'd* 1623, 33.   2 *cares* ditto.   Well

THE SPANISH TRAGEDY. 75

Hieronimo.
Good leave have you; nay, I pray you, go,
For I'll leave you, if you can leave me so.
    2 Portingale.
Pray you, which is the next [1] way to my lord the duke's?
    Hieronimo.
The next way from me.
    2 Portingale.
To his house, we mean.
    Hieronimo.
O, hard by, 'tis yon house that you see.
    2 Portingale.
You could not tell us if his son were there?
    Hieronimo.
Who, my lord *Lorenzo*?
    1 Portingale.
Ay, sir.
    [*He goes in at one door, and comes out at another.*
    Hieronimo.
O forbear, for other talk for us far fitter were;
But if you be importunate [2] to know
The way to him, and where to find him out,
Then list to me, and I'll resolve your doubt:
There is a path upon your left-hand side,

1 *next* omitt. 1618, 23, 33.   2 *importune* 1618, 23.
                                                   That

Well, heaven is heaven still!
And there is *Nemesis*, and furies,
And things call'd whips,
And they sometimes do meet with murderers:
They do not always 'scape, that's some comfort.
Ay, ay, ay, and then time steals on, and steals, and steals,
Till violence leaps forth, like thunder
Wrap'd in a ball of fire,
And so doth bring confusion to them all.
Good leave have you: I pray you go,
For I'll leave, if you can leave me so.

That leadeth from a guilty confcience
Unto a foreft of diftruft and fear,
A darkfome place, and dangerous to pafs;
There fhall you meet with melancholy thoughts,
Whofe baleful humours if you but uphold; [1]
It will conduct you to defpair and death;
Whofe rocky cliffs when you have once beheld,
Within a hugy dale of lafting night,
That, [2] kindled with the world's iniquities,
Doth caft up filthy and detefted fumes:
Not far from thence, where murderers have built
An habitation for their curfed fouls,
There in a brazen cauldron, fix'd by *Jove*
In his fell wrath, upon a fulphur flame,
Yourfelves fhall find *Lorenzo* bathing him
In boiling lead and blood of innocents.

     1 *Portingale.*
 Ha, ha, ha.
     Hieronimo.
Ha, ha, ha! Why, ha, ha, ha? Farewel, good ha, ha, ha.   [*Exit.*
     2 *Portingale.*
Doubtlefs this man is paffing lunatick,
Or imperfection of his age doth make him dote.
Come, let's away, to feek my lord the duke. [*Exeunt.*

Enter Hieronimo, *with a poniard in one hand, and a rope in the other.*

     Hieronimo.
Now, fir, perhaps I come and fee the king;
The king fees me, and fain would hear my fuit.
Why is not this a ftrange and feld feen thing,
That ftanders by, with toys fhould ftrike me mute?
Go to, I fee their fhifts, and fay no more.

 1 *Whofe palefull humours if you but behold* 1618, 23, 33.
 2 *That's* ditto.

           Hieronimo,

Hieronimo, 'tis time for thee to trudge:
Down by the dale that flows with purple gore,
Standeth a fiery tow'r; there sits a judge
Upon a seat of steel, and molten brass,
And 'twixt his teeth he holds a firebrand,
That leads unto the lake where hell doth stand:
Away, *Hieronimo*, to him be gone;
He'll do thee justice for *Horatio*'s death.
Turn down this path, thou shalt be with him straight;
Or this, and then thou need'st not take thy breath,
This way, or that way: soft and fair, not so;
For if I hang or kill myself, let's know,
Who will revenge *Horatio*'s murder then?
No, no, fie, no; pardon me, I'll none of that.
     [*He flings away the dagger and halter.*
This way I'll take, and this way comes the king.
     [*He takes them up again.*
And here I'll have a fling at him, that's flat;
And, *Balthazar*, I'll be with thee to bring,
And thee, *Lorenzo*: here's the king, nay, stay;
And here, ay here: there goes the hare away.

   Enter King, *Ambassador,* Castile, *and* Lorenzo.
      King.
Now show, ambassador, what our viceroy saith:
Hath he receiv'd the articles we sent?
      Hieronimo.
Justice! O, justice to *Hieronimo!*
      Lorenzo.
Back, seest thou not the king is busy?
      Hieronimo.
O, is he so?
      King.
Who is he that interrupts our business?
      Hieronimo.
Not I: *Hieronimo,* beware; go by, go by.

        Ambassador.

Ambassador.

Renowned king, he hath receiv'd and read
Thy kingly proffers, and thy promis'd league:
And as a man extremely overjoy'd,
To hear his son so princely entertain'd,
Whose death he had so solemnly bewail'd;
This for thy further satisfaction
And kingly love, he kindly lets thee know:
First, for the marriage of his princely son
With *Bel-imperia,* thy beloved niece,
The news are more delightful to his soul,
Than myrrh or incense to th' offended heavens:
In person therefore will he come himself,
To see the marriage rites solemnized:
And in the presence of the court of *Spain,*
To knit a sure inextricable [1] band
Of kingly love, and everlasting league,
Betwixt the crowns of *Spain* and *Portingale;*
There will he give his crown to *Balthazar,*
And make a queen of *Bel-imperia.*

King.

Brother, how like you this our viceroy's love?

Castile.

No doubt, my lord, it is an argument
Of honourable care to keep his friend,
And wondrous zeal to *Balthazar* his son;
Nor am I least indebted to his grace,
That bends his liking to my daughter thus.

Ambassador.

Now last, dread lord, here hath his highness sent,
(Although he send not that his son return)
His ransome due to *Don Horatio.*

Hieronimo.

Horatio! who calls *Horatio?*

King.

And well remember'd, thank his majesty:
Here, see it given to *Horatio.*

[1] *inexerable* second edit.
inexplicable 1618, 22, 33.

Hieronimo.

Hieronimo.
Juſtice! O juſtice! juſtice! gentle king.
King.
Who is that? *Hieronimo?*
Hieronimo.
Juſtice! O juſtice! O my ſon, my ſon,
My ſon, whom nought can ranſome or redeem.
Lorenzo.
Hieronimo, you are not well advis'd.
Hieronimo.
Away, *Lorenzo*, hinder me no more,
For thou haſt made me bankrupt of my bliſs;
Give me my ſon, you ſhall not ranſome him.
Away, I'll rip the bowels of the earth,
                  [*He diggeth with his dagger.*
And ferry over to the *Elyſian* plains,
And bring my ſon to ſhow his deadly wounds.
Stand from about me, I'll make a pickaxe of my poniard,
And here ſurrender up my marſhalſhip;
For I'll go marſhal up the [1] fiends in hell,
To be avenged on you all for this.
King.
What means this outrage?
Will none of you reſtrain his fury?
Hieronimo.
Nay, ſoft and fair, you ſhall not need to ſtrive:
Needs muſt he go that the devils drive.   [*Exit.*
King.
What accident hath hap'd, [2] *Hieronimo?*
I have not ſeen him to demean him ſo.
Lorenzo.
My gracious lord, he is, with extreme pride,
Conceiv'd of young *Horatio* his ſon,
And covetous of having to himſelf
The ranſome of the young prince *Balthazar*,
Diſtract, and in a manner lunatick.

[1] *my* 1618, 23, 33.   [2] *bapt to* ditto.
King.

King.
Believe me, nephew, we are sorry for't,
This is the love that fathers bear their sons: —
But, gentle brother, go give to him this gold,
The prince's ransome; let him have his due.
For what he hath, *Horatio* shall not want,
Happily *Hieronimo* hath need thereof.
Lorenzo.
But if he be thus helplesly [1] distract,
'Tis requisite his office be resign'd,
And given to one of more discretion.
King.
We shall increase his melancholy so;
'Tis best that [2] we see farther in it first:
Till when, ourself will exempt the place.
And, brother, now bring in the ambassador,
That he may be a witness of the match,
'Twixt *Balthazar* and *Bel-imperia*;
And that we may prefix a certain time,
Wherein the marriage shall be solemniz'd,
That we may have thy lord the viceroy here.
Ambassador.
Therein your highness highly shall content
His majesty, that longs to hear from hence.
King.
On then, and hear you, [3] lord ambassador. *** [*Exeunt.*

1 *haplesly* 1618, 23, 33. 2 *that* omitted ditto.
3 *your* ditto.   Enter

*** *See note, page* 40.
Enter Jaques, *and* Pedro.
Jaques.
I wonder, *Pedro*, why our master thus,
At midnight sends us with our torches light,
When man, and bird, and beast, are all at rest,
Save those that watch for rape and bloody murder.
Pedro.
O *Jaques*, know thou that our master's mind

THE SPANISH TRAGEDY.

Enter Hieronimo, *with a book in his hand.*
Hieronimo.
Vindicta mihi.
Ay, heaven will be reveng'd of every ill;
Nor will they suffer murder un-repay'd:
                                            Then

Is much distraught since his *Horatio* died:
And now his aged years should sleep in rest,
His heart in quiet, like a desperate man,
Grows lunatick and childish, for his son:
Sometimes as he doth at his table sit,
He speaks as if *Horatio* stood by him;
Then starting in a rage, falls on the earth,
Cries out *Horatio*, where is my *Horatio*?
So that with extreme grief, and cutting sorrow,
There is not left in him one inch of man:
See, here he comes.

Enter Hieronimo.
Hieronimo.
I pry through every crevise of each wall,
Look at each tree, and search through every brake,
Beat on the bushes, stamp our grand-dame earth,
Dive in the water, and stare up to heaven:
Yet cannot I behold my son *Horatio*.
How now, who's there, sprights, sprights?
Pedro.
We are your servants that attend you, sir.
Hieronimo.
What make you with your torches in the dark?
Pedro.
You bid us light them, and attend you here.
Hieronimo.
No, no, you are deceiv'd, not I, you are deceiv'd:
Was I so mad to bid you light your torches now?
Light me your torches at the mid of noon,
When as the sun-god rides in all his glory;
Light me your torches then.
Pedro.
Then we burn day-light.

Then stay, *Hieronimo*, attend their will;
For mortal men may not appoint their time, [1]
    Per scelus semper tutum est sceleribus iter.

    [1] *a time* 1618, 23, 33.

                                        Strike

               Hieronimo.
Let it be burnt, night is a murd'rous slut,
That would not have her treasons to be seen:
And yonder pale-fac'd *Hecate* there, the moon,
Doth give consent to that is done in darkness:
And all those stars that gaze upon her face,
Are aglets on her sleeve, pins on her train;
And those that should be powerful and divine,
Do sleep in darkness when they most should shine.
               Pedro.
Provoke them not, fair sir, with tempting words,
The heavens are gracious, and your miseries and sorrow
Make you speak you know not what.
               Hieronimo.
Villain, thou ly'st, and thou dost nought'
But tell me I am mad: thou ly'st, I am not mad:
I know thee to be *Pedro*, and he *Jaques*;
I'll prove it to thee; and, were I mad, how could I?
Where was she the same night, when my *Horatio* was murder'd?
She should have shone: search thou the book:
Had the moon shone in my boy's face, there was a kind of grace,
That I know, nay I do know had the murd'rer seen him,
His weapon would have fallen, and cut the earth;
Had he been fram'd of nought but blood and death:
Alack, when mischief doth it knows not what,
What shall we say to mischief?

              Enter Isabella.
               Isabella.
Dear *Hieronimo*, come in a-doors,
O seek not means so to increase thy sorrow.
               Hieronimo.
Indeed, *Isabella*, we do nothing here;
I do not cry, ask *Pedro* and *Jaques*:
Not I indeed, we are very merry, very merry.
               Isabella.
How? be merry here, be merry here?

Strike, and ſtrike home, where wrong is offer'd thee;
For evils unto ills conductors be,
And death's the worſt of reſolution;

For

Is not this the place, and this the very tree,
Where my *Horatio* died, where he was murder'd?
     Hieronimo.
Was, do not ſay what: let her weep it out;
This was the tree, I ſet it of a kernel:
And when our hot *Spain* could not let it grow,
But that the infant and the humane ſap
Began to wither, duly twice a morning,
Would I be ſprinkling it with fountain water:
At laſt it grew, and grew, and bore, and bore;
Till at the length it grew a gallows, and did bear our ſon:
It bore thy fruit and mine: O wicked, wicked plant!
       [*One knocks within at the door.*
See who knocks there?
     Pedro.
 It is a painter, ſir.
     Hieronimo.
Bid him come in, and paint ſome comfort,
For ſurely there's none lives but painted comfort:
Let him come in, one knows not what may chance:
God's will, that I ſhould ſet this tree.
But even ſo maſters, ungrateful ſervants, rear'd from nought,
And then they hate them that did bring them up.

    Enter the Painter.
     Painter.
God bleſs you, ſir.
     Hieronimo.
Wherefore? why, thou ſcornful villain?
How, where, or by what means ſhould I be bleſt?
     Iſabella.
What wouldſt thou have, good fellow?
     Painter.
 Juſtice, madam.
     Hieronimo.
O ambitious beggar, wouldſt thou have that,
That lives not in the world?
Why, all the undelved mines cannot buy
An ounce of juſtice. 'tis a jewel ſo ineſtimable.

I tell

For he that thinks with patience to contend,
To quiet life, his life shall easily end.

Fata si miseros juvant, habes salutem;
Fata si vitam negaut, habes sepulchrum.

If

I tell thee, God hath engrossed all justice in his hands,
And there is none but what comes from him.
Painter.
O then I see, that God must right me for my murder'd son.
Hieronimo.
How? was thy son murder'd?
Painter.
Ay, sir, no man did hold a son so dear.
Hieronimo.
What, not as thine? that's a lie,
As massy as the earth: I had a son,
Whose least unvalued hair did weigh
A thousand of thy sons, and he was murder'd.
Painter.
Alas, sir, I had no more but he.
Hieronimo.
Nor I, nor I: but this same one of mine,
Was worth a legion. But all is one.
Pedro, Jaques: go in a doors Isabella, go,
And this good fellow here, and I,
Will range this hideous orchard up and down,
Like to two lions reaved of their young.
Go in a doors, I say. [*Exeunt.*
[*The painter and he sits down.*
Come, let's talk wisely now.
Was thy son murder'd?
Painter.
Ay, sir.
Hieronimo.
So was mine.
How dost thou take it? art thou not sometime mad?
Is there no tricks that comes before thine eyes?
Painter.
O lord, yes, sir.
Hieronimo.
Art a painter? canst paint me a tear, or a wound?
A groan, or a sigh? canst paint me such a tree as this?

Painter.

If destiny thy miseries do ease,
Then hast thou health; and happy shalt thou be:
If destiny deny thee life, *Hieronimo*,
Yet shalt thou¹ be assured of a tomb:

¹ *thou shalt* 1623, 33.

Painter.
Sir, I am sure you have heard of my painting:
My name's *Bazardo*.
Hieronimo.
Bazardo! 'fore God an excellent fellow. Look you, sir,
Do you see? I'd have you paint me my gallery,
In your oil colours matted, and draw me five
Years younger than I am: do you see, sir? let five
Years go: let them go like the marshal of *Spain*,
My wife *Isabella* standing by me,
With a speaking look to my son *Horatio*,
Which should intend to this, or some such like purpose:
God bless thee, my sweet son; and my hand leaning upon his head thus,
sir; do you see? may it be done?
Painter.
Very well, sir.
Hieronimo.
Nay, I pray, mark me, sir:
Then, sir, would I have you paint me this tree, this very tree:
Canst paint a doleful cry?
Painter.
Seemingly, sir.
Hieronimo.
Nay, it should cry; but all is one.
Well, sir, paint me a youth run through and through with villains swords,
    hanging upon this tree.
Canst thou draw a murd'rer?
Painter.
I'll warrant you, sir;
I have the pattern of the most notorious villains,
That ever liv'd in all *Spain*.
Hieronimo.
O, let them be worse, worse: stretch thine art,
And let their beards be of *Judas* his own colour,
And let their eye-brows jutty over: in any case observe that;
Then, sir, after some violent noise,

If neither; yet let this thy comfort be,
Heaven covereth him that hath no burial.
And to conclude, I will revenge his death:
But how? not as the vulgar wits of men,
With open, but inevitable ills,
As by a secret, yet a certain mean,
              Which

Bring me forth in my shirt, and my gown under mine arm, With my torch in my hand, and my sword rear'd up thus: And with these words:
  What noise is this? who calls Hieronimo?
May it be done?
       Painter.
 Yes, sir.
       Hieronimo.
 Well, sir, then bring me forth, bring me through alley and alley, still with a distracted countenance going along, and let my hair heave up my night-cap.
 Let the clouds scowl, make the moon dark, the stars extinct, the winds blowing, the bells tolling, the owls shrieking, the toads croaking, the minutes jarring, and the clock striking twelve.
 And then at last, sir, starting, behold a man hanging, and tott'ring, and tott'ring, as you know the wind will wave a man, and I with a trice to cut him down.
 And looking upon him by the advantage of my torch, find it to be my son *Horatio.*
There you may a passion, there you may show a passion.
Draw me like old *Priam* of *Troy,*
Crying the house is o' fire, the house is o' fire,
As the torch over thy head; make me curse,
Make me rave, make me cry, make me mad,
Make me well again, make me curse hell,
Invocate, and in the end leave me
In a trance, and so forth.
       Painter.
 And is this the end?
       Hieronimo.
 O no, there is no end: the end is death and madness;
As I am never better than when I am mad;
Then methinks I am a brave fellow;
Then I do wonders, but reason abuseth me;
And there's the torment, there's the hell;
At the last, sir, bring me to one of the murderers;
Were he as strong as *Hector,* thus would I
Tear and drag him up and down.
  [*He beats the painter in, then comes out again, with a book in his hand.*

Which under kindſhip will be cloaked beſt.
Wiſe men will take their opportunity,
Cloſely, and ſafely, fitting things to time.
But in extremes advantage hath no time :
And therefore all times fit not for revenge.
Thus therefore will I reſt me in unreſt,
Diſſembling quiet in unquietneſs;
Not ſeeming that I know their villanies,
That my ſimplicity may make them think,
That ignorantly I will let all ¹ ſlip;
For ignorance I wot, and well they know,

Remedium malorum mors eſt.

Nor aught avails it me to menace them,
Who, as a wintry ſtorm upon a plain,
Will bear me down with their nobility.
No, no, *Hieronimo*, thou muſt enjoin
Thine eyes to obſervation, and thy tongue
To milder ſpeeches than thy ſpirit affords, ²
Thy heart to patience, and thy hands to reſt,
Thy cap to courteſy, and thy knee to bow,
Till to revenge thou know, when, where, and how.
[*A noiſe within.*
How now, what noiſe ? what coil is that you keep ?

Enter a Servant.

Servant.
Here are a ſort of poor petitioners,
That are importunate, and it ſhall pleaſe you, ſir,
That you ſhould plead their caſes ³ to the king.
Hieronimo.
That I ſhould plead their ſeveral actions ?
Why let them enter, and let me ſee them.

1 *it* 1618, 23, 33.   2 *ſpirits affoord* ditto.
3 *cauſes* 1623, 33.

Enter

Enter three Citizens, and an Old Man.

1 *Citizen.*
So, I tell you this, for learning, and for law,
There is not any advocate in *Spain*
That can prevail, or will take half the pain,
That he will, in pursuit of equity.

Hieronimo.
Come near, you men, that thus importune me;—
Now must I bear a face of gravity,
For thus¹ I us'd before my marshalship,
To plead in causes as corrigidor.—
Come on, sirs, what's the matter?

2 *Citizen.*
Sir, an action.

Hieronimo.
Of battery?

1 *Citizen.*
Mine of debt.

Hieronimo.
Give place.

2 *Citizen.*
No, sir, mine is an action of the case.

3 *Citizen.*
Mine an *Ejectione firma* by a lease.

Hieronimo.
Content you, sirs, are you determin'd
That I should plead your several actions?

1 *Citizen.*
Ay, sir, and here's my declaration.

2 *Citizen.*
And here's my band.

3 *Citizen.*
And here is my lease.

[*They give him papers.*

¹ *this* 1618, 23, 33.

Hieronimo.

THE SPANISH TRAGEDY.

Hieronimo.
But wherefore stands yon ¹ silly man so mute,
With mournful eyes and hands to heaven uprear'd?—
Come hither, father, let me know thy cause.
Senex.
O worthy sir, my cause but slightly known,
May move the hearts of warlike *Myrmidons*,
And melt the corsick rocks with ruthful ² tears.
Hieronimo.
Say, father, tell me what's thy suit?
Senex.
No, sir, could my woes
Give way unto my most distressful words,
Then should I not in paper (as you see)
With ink bewray, what blood began in me.
Hieronimo.
What's here? *The humble supplication of* Don Bazulto,
for his murdered son.
Senex.
Ay, sir.
Hieronimo.
No, sir, it was my murdered son: O my son,
O my son, o my son *Horatio!*
But mine, or thine, *Bazulto,* be content.
Here take my handkerchief, and wipe thine eyes,
Whiles wretched I, in thy mishaps may see
The lively portrait of my dying self.
[*He draweth out a bloody napkin.*
O no, not this, *Horatio*, this was thine;
And when I dy'd it in thy dearest blood,
This was a token 'twixt thy soul and me,
That of thy death revenged I should be.
But here, take this, and this—what, my purse?
Ay this, and that, and all of them are thine;
For all as one are our extremities.
1 *Citizen.*
O, see the kindness of *Hieronimo!*

1 *stand you* 1618, 23, 33.   3 *rueful* ditto.
                                2 *Citizen.*

2 Citizen.
This gentleness shows him a gentleman.
Hieronimo.
See, see, o fee thy shame, *Hieronimo*;
See here a loving father to his son;
Behold the sorrows and the sad laments,
That he delivereth [1] for his son's decease.
If love's [2] effects so strive in lesser things,
If love enforce such moods in meaner wits,
If love express [3] such power in poor estates:
Hieronimo, when as a raging sea,
Toss'd with the wind and tide, o'erturneth then
The upper billows, course of waves to keep,
Whilst lesser waters labour in the deep:
Then shamest thou not, *Hieronimo*, to neglect
The sweet [4] revenge of thy *Horatio?*
Though on this earth justice will not be found,
I'll down to hell, and in this passion,
Knock at the dismal gates of *Pluto's* court;
Getting by force (as once *Alcides* did) [5]
A troop of furies, and tormenting hags,
To torture *Don Lorenzo* and the rest.
Yet left the triple-headed porter should
Deny my passage to the slimy strond,
The *Thracian* poet thou shalt counterfeit: —
Come on, [6] old father, be my *Orpheus*;
And if thou canst † no notes upon the harp,
Then found the burden of thy sore heart's grief
Till we do gain, that *Proserpine* may grant
Revenge on them that murdered my son.
Then will I rent and tear them thus, and thus,
Shivering their limbs in pieces with my teeth.
[*Tears the papers.*

1 *delivered* 1618, 23, 33.   2 *love* 1618.
3 *enforce* 1611, 23, 33.   4 *swift* ditto.
5 *did* omitted 1618.
6 *on* omitted 1618, 23, 33.

† *canst no notes*, i. e. understandest not, hast no knowledge of, or power in. So *Spenser*, and others.   1 *Citizen.*

1 Citizen.
O sir, my declaration!
[*Exit* Hieronimo, *and they after.*
2 Citizen.
Save my bond.

Reenter Hieronimo.

2 Citizen.
Save my bond.
3 Citizen.
Alas! my lease, it cost me ten pound,
And you, my lord, have torn the same.
Hieronimo.
That cannot be, I gave it ¹ never a wound;
Show me one drop of blood fall from the same:
How is it possible I should slay it then?
Tush, no; run after, catch me if you can.
[*Exeunt all but the Old Man.*

Bazulto *remains till* Hieronimo *enters again, who staring him in the face speaks.*

Hieronimo.
And art thou come, *Horatio*, from the depth,
To ask for justice in this upper earth,
To tell thy father thou art unreveng'd,
To wring more tears from *Isabella's* eyes,
Whose lights are dim'd with overlong laments?
Go back, my son, complain to *Æacus*,
For here's no justice; gentle boy, be gone,
For justice is exiled from the earth:
Hieronimo will bear thee company.
Thy mother cries on righteous *Rhadamant*,
For just revenge against the murderers.
Senex.
Alas, my lord, whence springs this troubled speech?

¹ *them* 1618, 23, 33.

Hieronimo.

Hieronimo.
But let me look on my *Horatio.*
Sweet boy, how[1] art thou[2] chang'd in death's black
    shade!
Had *Proserpine* no pity on thy youth,
But suffer'd thy fair crimson-colour'd spring,
With withered winter to be blasted thus?
Horatio, thou art older[3] than thy father:
Ah ruthless father, that favour thus transforms!
Bazulto.
Ah, my good lord, I am not your young son.
Hieronimo.
What, not my son? thou then[4] a fury art,
Sent from the empty kingdom of black night,
To summon me to make appearance
Before grim *Minos* and just *Rhadamant,*
To plague *Hieronimo* that is remiss,
And seeks not vengeance for *Horatio's* death.
Bazulto.
I am a grieved man and not a ghost,
That came for justice for my murder'd son.
Hieronimo.
Ay, now I know thee, now thou nam'st thy son:
Thou art the lively image of my grief;
Within thy face, my sorrows I may see:
Thy eyes are gum'd[5] with tears; thy cheeks are wan,
Thy forehead troubled, and thy muttering lips
Murmur sad words abruptly broken off,
By force of windy sighs thy spirit breathes,
And all this sorrow riseth for thy son:
And selfsame sorrow feel I for my son.
Come in, old man, thou shalt to *Isabel:*
Lean on my arm: I thee, thou me shalt stay,
And thou and I and she will sing a song,

[1] *how* omitted 1618.   [2] *thou art* 1623, 33.
[3] *elder* 1618, 23, 33.   [4] *then thou* 1633.
[5] *dim'd* 1618, 23, 33.

Three

Three parts in one; but all of difcords fram'd:
Talk not of cords, but let us now be gone,
For with a cord *Horatio* was slain. [*Exeunt.*

Enter King of Spain, *the Duke, Viceroy, and* Lorenzo,
Balthazar, Don Pedro, *and* Bel-imperia.
 King.
Go, brother, 'tis the duke of *Caſtile's* cauſe,
Salute the viceroy in our name.
 Caſtile.
I go.
 Viceroy.
Go forth, *Don Pedro*, for thy nephew's ſake,
And greet the duke of *Caſtile.*
 Pedro.
It ſhall be ſo. 1
 King.
And now to meet theſe 2 *Portingales:*
For as we now are, ſo ſometimes were theſe,
Kings and commanders of the weſtern *Indies.* —
Welcome, brave viceroy, to the court of *Spain,*
And welcome all his honourable train.
'Tis not unknown to us, for why you come,
Or have ſo kingly croſs'd the raging ſeas:
Sufficeth 3 it in this, we note the troth,
And more than common love you lend to us.
So is it that mine honourable niece,
For it beſeems us now that it be known,
Already is betroth'd to *Balthazar:*
And by appointment and our condeſcent,
To morrow are they 4 to be married.
To this intent we entertain thyſelf,
Thy followers, their pleaſure, 5 and our peace.

1 *be ſir.* 1618. *be done ſir,* 1623.
2 *the* 1618, 23, 33.   3 *ſufficed* ditto.
4 *they are* 1633.   5 *pleaſures* 1623, 33.

Speak

THE SPANISH TRAGEDY.

Speak, men of *Portingale*, shall it be so?
If ay, say so: if not, say flatly no.
          Viceroy.
  Renowned king, I come not as thou think'st,
With doubtful followers, unresolved men,
But such as have upon thine articles,
Confirm'd thy motion, and contented me.
Know, sovereign, I come to solemnize
The marriage of thy beloved niece,
Fair *Bel-imperia*, with my *Balthazar*,
With thee, my son; whom sith I live so see,
Here take my crown, I give it her and thee:
And let me live a solitary life,
In ceaseless prayers,
To think how strangely heav'n hath thee preserv'd.
          King.
  See, brother, see, how nature strives in him!
Come, worthy viceroy, and accompany
Thy friend, with thine extremities:
A place more private fits this princely mood.
          Viceroy.
  Or here, or where your highness thinks it good.
          [*Exeunt all but* Cast. *and* Lorenzo.
          Castile.
  Nay, stay, *Lorenzo*, let me talk with you:
See'st thou this entertainment of these kings?
          Lorenzo.
  I do, my lord, and joy to see the same.
          Castile.
And knowest thou why this meeting is?
          Lorenzo.
  For her, my lord, whom *Balthazar* doth love,
And to confirm the promis'd marriage.
          Castile.
  She is thy sister.
          Lorenzo.
  Who, *Bel-imperia?* Ay, my gracious lord;
And this is the day that I have long'd so happily to see.
          Castile.

Castile.
Thou would'st be loath that any fault of thine,
Should intercept her in her happiness.
Lorenzo.
Heav'ns will not let *Lorenzo* err so much.
Castile.
Why then, *Lorenzo*, listen to my words:
It is suspected, and reported too,
That thou, *Lorenzo*, wrong'st *Hieronimo*;
And in his suits towards his majesty
Still keep'st him back, and seek'st to cross his suit.
Lorenzo.
That I, my lord?
Castile.
I tell thee, son, myself have heard it said,
When (to my sorrow) I have been asham'd
To answer for thee, though thou art [1] my son.
Lorenzo, know'st thou not the common love
And kindness that *Hieronimo* hath won
By his deserts, within the court of *Spain?*
Or seest thou not the king my brother's care
In his behalf, and to procure his health?
Lorenzo, shouldst thou thwart his passions,
And he exclaim against thee to the king,
What honour were't in this assembly,
Or what a scandal were't among the kings,
To hear *Hieronimo* exclaim on thee?
Tell me, and look thou tell me truly too, [2]
Whence grows the ground of this report in court?
Lorenzo.
My lord, it lies not in *Lorenzo*'s power
To stop the vulgar, liberal of their tongues:
A small advantage makes a water-breach,
And no man lives, that long contenteth all.
Castile.
Myself have seen thee busy to keep back

[1] *wert* 1618, 23, 33.   [2] *too* omitted ditto.

Him

Him and his supplications from the king.
Lorenzo.
 Yourself, my lord, have seen his passions,
That ill-beseem'd the presence of a king:
And for I pitied him in his distress,
I held him thence with kind and courteous words,
As free from malice to *Hieronimo*,
As to my soul, my lord.
Castile.
Hieronimo, my son, mistakes thee then.
Lorenzo.
 My gracious father, believe me, so he doth;
But what's a silly man distract in mind,
To think upon the murder of his son?
Alas! how easy is it for him to err?
But for his satisfaction, and the world's,
'Twere good, my lord, that¹ *Hieronimo* and I
Were reconcil'd, if he misconstrue me.
Castile.
Lorenzo, thou hast said, it shall be so:—
Go one of you, and call *Hieronimo*.

Enter Balthazar, *and* Bel-imperia.
Balthazar.
 Come *Bel-imperia*, *Balthazar's* content,
My sorrow's ease, and sovereign of my bliss,
Sith heaven hath ordain'd thee² to be mine:
Disperse those clouds and melancholy looks,
And clear³ them up with those thy sun-bright eyes,
Wherein my hope and heaven's fair beauty lies.
Bel-imperia.
 My looks, my lord, are fitting for my love;
Which new begun, can show no brighter yet.

1 *that* omitted 1623, 33.
2 *heav'n hath thee ordained* 1623, 33.
3 *cheare* 1618, 23, 33.

Balthaza-.

Balthazar.
New-kindled flames should burn as morning sun.
Bel-imperia.
But not too fast, left heat and all be done.
I see my lord, my father.
Balthazar.
Truce, my love, I will go salute him.
Castile.
Welcome, *Balthazar*, welcome, brave prince,
The pledge of *Castile's* peace;—
And welcome, *Bel-imperia*: how now, girl?
Why com'st thou sadly to salute us thus?
Content thyself, for I am satisfied;
It is not now as when *Andrea* liv'd,
We have forgotten, and forgiven that,
And thou art graced with a happier love:—
But, *Balthazar*, here comes *Hieronimo*;
I'll have a word with him.

Enter Hieronimo, *and a Servant.*
Hieronimo.
And where's the duke?
Servant.
Yonder.
Hieronimo.
Even so: what new device have they devised trow?
Pocas palabras, mild as the lamb;
Is't [1] I will be reveng'd? No, I am not the man.
Castile.
Welcome, *Hieronimo*.
Lorenzo.
Welcome, *Hieronimo*.
Balthazar.
Welcome, *Hieronimo*.

[1] *Hist, I will be reveng'd:* 1633.

Hieronimo.
My lords, I thank you for *Horatio.*
　　　　　Castile.
Hieronimo, the reason that I sent
To speak with you, is this.
　　　　　Hieronimo.
What, so short?
Then I'll be gone, I thank you for't.
　　　　　Castile.
Nay, stay, *Hieronimo:* — go call him, son.
　　　　　Lorenzo.
Hieronimo, my father craves a word with you.
　　　　　Hieronimo.
With me, sir? why, my lord, I thought you had done.
　　　　　Lorenzo.
No; 'would he had!
　　　　　Castile.
Hieronimo, I hear
You find yourself aggrieved at my son,
Because you have not access unto the king;
And say, 'tis he that intercepts your suits.
　　　　　Hieronimo.
Why, is not this a miserable thing, my lord?
　　　　　Castile.
Hieronimo, I hope you have no cause,
And would be loath that one of your deserts
Should once have reason to suspect my son,
Considering how I think of you myself.
　　　　　Hieronimo.
Your son *Lorenzo!* whom, my noble lord?
The hope of *Spain,* mine honourable friend?
Grant me the combat of them, if they dare:
　　　　　[*Draws out his sword.*
I'll meet him face to face to tell me so.
These be the scandalous reports of such,
As love not me, and hate my lord too much;
Should I suspect *Lorenzo* would prevent,
Or cross my suit, that lov'd my son so well?
My lord, I am asham'd it should be said. *Lorenzo.*

THE SPANISH TRAGEDY.

Lorenzo.
Hieronimo, I never gave you caufe.
Hieronimo.
My good lord, I know you did not.
Caftile.
There paufe;
And for the fatisfaction of the world,
Hieronimo, frequent my homely houfe,
The duke of *Caftile, Cyprian's* ancient feat;
And when thou wilt, ufe me, my fon, and it:
But here before prince *Balthazar* and me,
Embrace each other, and be perfect friends.
Hieronimo.
Ay, marry, my lord, and fhall;
Friends, quoth he? fee, I'll be friends with you all:
Efpecially with you, my lovely lord;
For divers caufes it is fit for us,
That we be friends, the world is fufpicious,
And men may think what we imagine not.
Balthazar.
Why this is friendly done, *Hieronimo.*
Lorenzo.
And that, I hope, old grudges are forgot,
Hieronimo.
What elfe? it were a fhame it fhould not be fo.
Caftile.
Come on, *Hieronimo,* at my requeft,
Let us entreat your company to day. [*Exeunt.*
Hieronimo.
Your lordfhip's to command.—*Pha!*—Keep your way.

† *Mi! chi mi fa piu carrezze che non fuole,*
  Tradito mi ha, o tradir mi vuole.

Enter Ghoft, and Revenge.
Ghoft.
Awake, *Erictho, Cerberus,* awake,

† *Me. Chi mi fa? Pui Correzza Che non fule*
  Tradito viha otrade vule. Quartos.   Solicit

Solicit *Pluto*, gentle *Proserpine*,
To combat *Acheron*, and *Erebus* in hell;
For ne'er by *Styx* and *Phlegethon*,
Nor ferried *Charon* to the fiery lakes,
Such fearful fights, as poor *Andrea* see.
Revenge, awake.
Revenge.
Awake, for why? 1
Ghost.
Awake, *Revenge*, for thou art ill advis'd
To sleep, awake: what, thou 2 art warn'd to watch.
Revenge.
Content thyself, and do not trouble me.
Ghost.
Awake, *Revenge*; if love, as love hath had,
Have yet the power or prevalence in hell:
Hieronimo with *Lorenzo* is join'd in league,
And intercepts our passage to revenge:
Awake, *Revenge*, or we are wobegone.
Revenge.
Thus wordlings ground what they have dream'd upon.
Content thyself, *Andrea*, though I sleep,
Yet is 3 my mood soliciting their souls:
Sufficeth thee that poor *Hieronimo*
Cannot forget his son *Horatio*;
Nor dies *Revenge*, although he sleep a while:
For in unquiet, quietness is feign'd, 4
And slumb'ring is a common worldly wile.
Behold, *Andrea*, for an instance, how
Revenge hath slept, and then imagine thou,
What 'tis to be subject to destiny.

1 *Rev. Awake, for why?* omitted 1618, 23, 33.
2 *thou* omitted ditto.   3 *in* ditto.
4 *found* ditto.

Enter

Enter a dumb show.

Ghost.
Awake, *Revenge,* reveal this myſtery.

Revenge.
The two firſt the nuptial torches bore
As brightly ¹ burning as the mid-day's ſun:
But after them doth *Hymen* hie as faſt,
Clothed in ſable, and a ſaffron robe,
And blows them out, and quencheth them with blood,
As diſcontent that things continue ſo.

Ghost.
Sufficeth me thy meaning's underſtood,
And thanks to ² thee, and thoſe infernal powers,
That will not tolerate a lover's wo:
Reſt thee, for I will ſit to ³ ſee the reſt.

Revenge.
Then ⁴ argue not, for thou haſt thy requeſt. [*Exeunt.*

ACT V.

Enter Bel-imperia, *and* Hieronimo.

Bel-imperia.

IS this the love thou bear'ſt *Horatio?*
Is this the kindneſs that thou counterfeit'ſt?
Are theſe the fruits of thine inceſſant tears?
Hieronimo, are theſe thy paſſions,
Thy proteſtations, and thy deep laments,
That thou wert wont to weary men withal?

1 *bright* 1618, 23, 33.   2 *unto* ditto.
3 *and* ditto,   4 *Thus* 1618.

O unkind

O unkind father! o deceitful world!
With what excuses canst thou show thyself?
With what dishonour, and the hate of men,
From this dishonour, and the hate of men;
Thus to neglect the loss and life [1] of him,
Whom both my letters, and thine own belief,
Assures thee to be causeless slaughtered?
Hieronimo, for shame, *Hieronimo*,
Be not a history to after times
Of such ingratitude unto thy son:
Unhappy mothers of such children then,
But monstrous fathers to forget so soon
The death of those, whom they with care and cost
Have tender'd so, thus careless should be lost.
Myself, a stranger in respect of thee,
So lov'd his life, as still I wish their deaths.
Nor shall his death be unreveng'd by me,
Although I bear it out for fashion's [2] sake:
For here I swear, in sight of heaven and earth,
Shouldst thou neglect the love thou shouldst retain,
And give it over, and devise no more,
Myself should send their hateful souls to hell,
That wrought his downfal, with extremest death.

Hieronimo.

   But may it be, that *Bel-imperia*
Vows such revenge as she hath deign'd to say?
Why then I see, that heav'n applies our drift,
And all the saints do sit soliciting
For vengeance on those cursed murderers.
Madam, 'tis true, and now I find it so:
I found a letter, written in your name,
And in that letter, how *Horatio* dy'd.
Pardon, o pardon, *Bel-imperia*,
My fear and care in not believing it;
Nor think, I thoughtless think upon a mean,
To let his death be unreveng'd at full:

[1] *life and loss* 1618, 23, 33.   [2] *fashion* 1623, 33.

And

THE SPANISH TRAGEDY.

And here I vow, fo you but give confent,
And will conceal my refolution,
I will ere long determine of their deaths,
That caufelefs thus have murdered my fon.
 Bel-imperia.
Hieronimo, I will confent, conceal,
And aught that ¹ may effect for thine avail,
Join with thee to revenge *Horatio's* death.
 Hieronimo.
On, ² then; whatfoever I devife,
Let me entreat you, grace my practifes:
For why, the plot's already in mine head.
Here they are.

   Enter Balthazar, *and* Lorenzo.
    Balthazar.
How now, *Hieronimo*? what, courting *Bel-imperia*?
 Hieronimo.
Ay, my lord, fuch courting as, I promife you,
She hath my heart; but you, my lord, have hers.
 Lorenzo.
But now, *Hieronimo*, or never, we are to entreat your
 help.
 Hieronimo.
My help? why, my good lords, affure yourfelves of me;
For you have given me caufe, ay, by my faith ³ have you.
 Balthazar.
It pleas'd you at th' entertainment of the ambaffador,
To grace the king fo much as with a fhow:
Now were your ftudy fo well furnifhed,
As for the paffing of the firft night's fport,
To entertain my father with the like,
Or any fuch like pleafing motion,
Affure yourfelf it would content them well.
 Hieronimo.
Is this all?

1 *what* 1633.   2 *O then* 1618, 23, 33.
3 *by mine honour* ditto.   *Lorenzo.*

Lorenzo.
Ay, this is all.
Hieronimo.
Why then, I'll fit you; say no more:
When I was young, I gave my mind,
And ply'd myself to fruitless poetry;
Which though it profit the professor nought,
Yet is it passing [1] pleasing to the world.
Lorenzo.
And how for that?
Hieronimo.
Marry, my good lord, thus:
And yet, methinks, you are too quick with us.
When in *Toledo*, there I studied,
It was my chance to write a tragedy,
See here, my lords, [*Shows them a book.*
Which, long forgot, I found this other day:
Now would your lordships favour me so much
As but to grace me with your acting it,
I mean, each one of you to play a part,
Assure you it will prove most passing strange,
And wondrous plausible to that assembly.
Balthazar.
What, would you have us play a tragedy?
Hieronimo.
Why, *Nero* thought it no disparagement,
And kings and emperors have ta'en delight,
To make experience of their wits in plays.
Lorenzo.
Nay, be not angry, good *Hieronimo*;
The prince but asked a question.
Balthazar.
In faith, *Hieronimo*, and you be in earnest,
I'll make one.
Lorenzo.
And I another.

[1] *it is* 1633.

Hieronimo.

Hieronimo.
Now, my good lord, could you entreat
Your fister *Bel-imperia* to make one,
For what's a play without a woman in't?
Bel-imperia.
Little entreaty shall serve me, *Hieronimo*;
For I must needs be employed in your play.
Hieronimo.
Why, this is well: I tell you, lordings,
It was determined to have been acted
By gentlemen and scholars too;
Such as could tell what to speak.
Balthazar.
And now it shall be play'd 1 by princes and courtiers,
Such as can tell how to speak;
If, as it is our country manner,
You will but let us know the argument.
Hieronimo.
That shall I roundly. The chronicles of *Spain*,
Record this written of a knight of 2 *Rhodes:*
He was betroth'd, and wedded at the length,
To one *Perseda* an *Italian* dame,
Whose beauty ravish'd all that her beheld;
Especially the soul of *Solyman*,
Who at the marriage was the chiefest guest.
By sundry means sought *Solyman* to win
Perseda's love, and could not gain the same:
Then 'gan he break his passions to a friend,
One of his bashaws, whom he held full dear;
Her had this bashaw long solicited,
And saw she was not otherwise to be won,
But by her husband's death, this knight of *Rhodes*;
Whom presently by treachery he slew:
She, stirr'd with an exceeding hate therefore,
As cause of this slew *Solyman:*
And, to escape the bashaw's tyranny,

1 *said* 1618, 23, 33.   2 *of the Rhodes:* 1618.

Did

Did stab herself: and this¹ the tragedy.
Lorenzo.
Ay, sir.
Bel-imperia.
But say, *Hieronimo*, what then became of him,
That was the bashaw?
Hieronimo.
Marry, thus; mov'd with remorse of his misdeeds,
Ran to a mountain top, and hung¹ himself.
Balthazar.
But which of us is to perform that part?
Hieronimo.
O, that will I, my lords, make no doubt of it:
I'll play the murderer, I warrant you;
For I already have conceited that.
Balthazar.
And what shall I?
Hieronimo.
Great *Solyman*, the 3 *Turkish* emperor.
Lorenzo.
And I?
Hieronimo.
Erastus, the knight of *Rhodes*.
Bel-imperia.
And I?
Hieronimo.
Perseda, chaste, and resolute. —
And here, my lords, are several abstracts drawn,
For each of you to note your parts,
And act it as occasion's offered you.
You must provide a *Turkish* cap,
A black mustachio, and a falchin.
[*Gives a paper to* Balthazar.
You with a cross, like to 4 a knight of *Rhodes*.
[*Gives another to* Lorenzo.
And, madam, you must attire yourself
[*Gives* Bel-imperia *another.*

1 *this is* 1618, 23, 33.   3 *hang'd* ditto.
3 *that* 1618.   4 *to* omitt. ditto.   Like

Like *Phœbe*, *Flora*, or the huntrefs, †
Which to your difcretion fhall feem beft.
And as for me, my lords, I'll look to one,
And with the ranfome that the viceroy fent,
So furnifh and perform this tragedy,
As ¹ all the world fhall fay, *Hieronimo*
Was liberal in gracing of it fo.
Balthazar.
Hieronimo, methinks a comedy were better.
Hieronimo.
A comedy! fie! comedies are fit for common wits:
But to prefent a kingly troop withal,
Give me a ftately written tragedy;
Tragœdia cothurnata, fitting kings,
Containing matter, and not common things.
My lords, all this muft be perform'd,
As fitting for the firft night's revelling.
The *Italian* tragedians were fo fharp of wit,
That in one hour's meditation,
They would perform any thing in action.
Lorenzo.
And well it may, for I have feen the like.
In *Paris* 'mongft the *French* tragedians.
Hieronimo.
In *Paris?* mafs, and well remember'd,
There's one thing more that refts for us to do.
Balthazar.
What's that, *Hieronimo*? forget not any thing.
Hieronimo.
Each one of us muft act his part
In unknown languages,
That it may breed the ² more variety:—
As you, my lord, in *Latin*,—I in *Greek*,—
You in *Italian*,—and for becaufe I know
That *Bel-imperia* hath practifed the *French*,

¹ *That* 1623, 33.   ² *the* omitted 1618, 23, 33.
† i.e. *Diana*.

In

In courtly *French* shall all her phrases be.
    Bel-imperia.
 You mean to try my cunning then, *Hieronimo?*
    Balthazar.
But this will be a mere confusion,
And hardly shall we all be understood.
    Hieronimo.
It must be so; for the conclusion
Shall prove the invention, and all was good:
And I myself in an oration,
And with a strange and wondrous show besides,
That I will have there behind a curtain,
Assure thyself shall make the matter known:
And all shall be concluded in one scene,
For there's no pleasure ta'en in tediousness.
    Balthazar.
 How like you this?
    Lorenzo.
 Why thus, my lord, we must resolve
To sooth his humours up.
    Balthazar.
 On [1] then, *Hieronimo*, farewel till soon.
    Hieronimo.
 You'll ply this gear?
    Lorenzo.
 I warrant you. [*Exeunt all but* Hieronimo.
    Hieronimo.
Why [2] so: now shall I see the fall of *Babylon*,
Wrought by the heav'ns in this confusion.
And if the world like not this tragedy,
Hard is the hap of old *Hieronimo*. [*Exit.*

   Enter Isabella, *with a weapon.*
    Isabella.
Tell me no more: O monstrous homicides!
Since neither piety, nor pity moves
The king to justice or compassion,

[1] *O then* 1633. [2] *I, why.* , I will

I will revenge myself upon this place,
Where thus they murder'd ¹ my beloved son.
  [*She cuts down the arbour.*
Down with these branches, and these loathsome boughs
Of this unfortunate and fatal pine:
Down with them, *Isabella,* rent them up,
And burn the roots from whence the rest is sprung.
I will not leave a root, a stalk, a tree,
A bough, a branch, a blossom, nor a leaf,
No, not an herb within this garden plot.
Accursed complot of my misery!
Fruitless for ever may this garden be,
Barren the earth, and blissless ² whosoever
Imagines not to keep it unmanur'd!
An eastern wind commix'd with noisome airs
Shall blast the plants, and the young saplings:
The earth with serpents shall be pestered,
And passengers for fear to be infect,
Shall stand aloof; and, looking at it, tell,
There, murder'd, died the son of *Isabell.*
Ay, here he died, and here I him embrace.
See where his ghost solicites with his wounds, ³
Revenge on her that should revenge his death.
Hieronimo, make haste to see thy son;
For sorrow and despair hath cited me,
To hear *Horatio* plead with *Rhadamant:*
Make haste, *Hieronimo*; to hold excus'd ⁴
Thy negligence in pursuit of their deaths,
Whose hateful wrath bereav'd him of his breath,—
Ah nay, ⁵ thou dost delay their deaths,
Forgiv'st the murd'rers of thy noble son,
And none but I bestir me to no end:

1 *Where they murdered* 1618, 23.
  Where they have murder'd 1633.
2 *blesless* 1618, 23, 33.
3 *solicited with his wounds,* ditto.
4 *to hold exclude* ditto.   5 *ha* ditto.

And

And as I curse this tree from further fruit,
So shall my womb be cursed for his sake;
And with this weapon will I wound the breast,
The hapless breast that gave *Horatio* suck.

[*She stabs herself.*

Enter Hieronimo, *he knocks up the curtain.*

Enter the duke of Castile.

Castile.
How now, *Hieronimo,* where's your 1 fellows,
That you take all this pain?
Hieronimo.
O, sir, it is for the author's credit,
To look that all things may go well:
But, good my lord, let me entreat your grace,
To give the king the copy of the play:
This is the argument of what we show.
Castile.
I will, *Hieronimo.*
Hieronimo.
One thing more, my good 2 lord.
Castile.
What's that?
Hieronimo,
Let me entreat your grace,
That, when the train are 3 pass'd into the gallery,
You would vouchsafe to throw me down the key.
Castile.
I will, *Hieronimo.* [*Exit Cast.*
Hieronimo.
What, are you ready *Balthazar?*
Bring a chair and a cushion for the king.

1 *thy* 1618, 23, 33.   2 *good my* 1633.
is 1618, 23, 33.

Enter

THE SPANISH TRAGEDY.

Enter Balthazar, *with a chair.*

Well done, *Balthazar*, hang up the title:
Our scene is *Rhodes:* what, is your beard on?
Balthazar.
Half on, the other is in my hand.
Hieronimo.
Despatch for shame, are you so long? [*Exit* Bal.
Bethink thyself, *Hieronimo*,
Recall thy wits, recount thy former wrongs,
Thou hast receiv'd by murder of thy son.
And lastly, not least, how *Isabell*,
Once his mother, and thy [1] dearest wife,
All wobegone for him, hath slain herself.
Behoves thee then, *Hieronimo*, to be reveng'd:
The plot is lay'd of dire revenge;
On,[2] then, *Hieronimo*, pursue revenge:
For nothing wants, but acting of revenge. [*Exit.*

Enter Spanish *King*, *Viceroy*, *Duke of* Castile, *and their train*

King.
Now, *Viceroy*, shall we see the tragedy
Of *Solyman* the *Turkish* emperor,
Perform'd of pleasure by your [3] son the prince,
My nephew, *Don Lorenzo*, and my niece?
Viceroy.
Who, *Bel-imperia?*
King.
Ay, and *Hieronimo* our marshal,
At whose request they deign [4] to do't themselves:
These be our pastimes in the court of *Spain.*
Here, brother, you shall be the book-keeper,
This is the argument of that they show.
[*Gives him a book.*

1 *my* 1623, 33.   2 *On them* 1618, 23, 33.
3 *our* ditto.   4 *denie* 1618.

Gentlemen,

Gentlemen, this play of Hieronimo, *in sundry Languages, was thought good to be set down in English, more largely, for the easier understanding to every publick reader.*

Enter Balthazar, Bel-imperia, *and* Hieronimo.

Balthazar.

BAshaw, that *Rhodes* is ours, yield heav'ns the honour,
And holy *Mahomet* our sacred prophet:
And be thou grac'd with every excellence,
That *Solyman* can give, or thou desire.
But thy desert in conquering *Rhodes* is less,
Than in reserving this fair christian [1] nymph
Perseda, blissful lamp of excellence,
Whose eyes compel like powerful adamant,
The warlike heart of *Solyman* to wait.

King.

See, *Viceroy*, that is *Balthazar* your son,
That represents the emperor *Solyman*:
How well he acts his amorous passion!

Viceroy.

Ay, *Bel-imperia* hath taught him that.

Castile.

That's because his mind runs all on *Bel-imperia*.

Hieronimo.

Whatever joy earth yields, betide [2] your majesty.

Balthazar.

Earth yields no joy without *Perseda's* love.

Hieronimo.

Let then [3] *Perseda* on your grace attend.

Balthazar.

She shall not wait on me, but I on her,
Drawn by the influence of her lights, I yield:
But let my friend the *Rhodian* knight come forth,
Erastus, dearer than my life to me,
That he may see *Perseda* my belov'd.

1 *christian* omitted 1633.   2 *betinde* 1618.
3 *Then let* 1618, 23, 33.

Enter

THE SPANISH TRAGEDY. 113

Enter Eraſtus.
King.
Here comes *Lorenzo:* — Look upon the plot,
And tell me, brother, what part plays he?
Bel-imperia.
Ah, my *Eraſtus*, welcome to *Perſeda.*
Lorenzo.
Thrice happy is *Eraſtus*, that thou liv'ſt:
Rhodes' loſs is nothing to *Eraſtus*' joy,
Sith his *Perſeda* lives, his life ſurvives.
Balthazar.
Ah, baſhaw, here is love between *Eraſtus*
And fair *Perſeda*, ſovereign of my ſoul.
Hieronimo.
Remove *Eraſtus*, mighty *Solyman*,
And then *Perſeda* will be quickly won.
Balthazar.
Eraſtus is my friend; and, while he lives,
Perſeda never will remove her love.
Hieronimo.
Let not *Eraſtus* live to grieve great *Solyman*.
Balthazar.
Dear is *Eraſtus* in our princely eye.
Hieronimo.
But if he be your rival, let him die.
Balthazar.
Why, let him die; ſo love commandeth me:
Yet grieve I, that *Eraſtus* ſhould ſo die.
Hieronimo.
Eraſtus, *Solyman* ſaluteth thee,
And lets thee wit by me his highneſs' will,
Which is, thou ſhouldſt be thus employed.
[*Stabs him.*
Bel-imperia.
Ay me, *Eraſtus!* — See, *Solyman*, *Eraſtus* ſlain.

Vol. II.   H   *Balthazar.*

Balthazar.
Yet liveth *Solyman* to comfort thee:
Fair queen of beauty, let not favour die,
But with a gracious eye behold his grief,
That with *Perseda's* beauty is increas'd,
If by *Perseda's* grief be not releas'd.
Bel-imperia.
Tyrant, defist foliciting vain fuits;
Relentlefs are mine ears to thy laments,
As thy butcher is pitilefs and bafe,
Which feiz'd on my *Eraftus,* harmlefs knight:
Yet by thy pow'r thou thinkeft to command;
And to thy power *Perseda* doth obey:
But, were fhe able, thus fhe would revenge
Thy treacheries on thee, ignoble prince: [*Stabs him.*
And on herfelf fhe would be thus reveng'd.
[*Stabs herfelf.*
King.
Well faid, old marfhal, this was bravely done.
Hieronimo.
But *Bel-imperia* plays *Perseda* well.
Viceroy.
Were this in earneft, *Bel-imperia,*
You would be better to my fon than fo.
King.
But now what follows for [1] *Hieronimo?*
Hieronimo.
Marry, this follows for *Hieronimo:*
Here break we off our fundry languages,
And thus conclude I in our vulgar tongue.
Happily you think (but bootlefs are [2] your thoughts)
That this is fabuloufly counterfeit;
And that we do as all tragedians do,
To die to-day (for fafhioning our fcene,
The death of *Ajax,* or fome *Roman* peer)
And in a minute ftarting up again,

[1] *for* omitted 1618, 23, 33.   [2] *be* ditto.

Revive

Revive to pleafe to-morrow's audience:
No, princes; know, I am *Hieronimo,*
The hopelefs father of a haplefs fon,
Whofe tongue is tun'd ² to tell his lateft tale,
Not to excufe grofs errours in the play.
I fee, your looks urge inftance of thefe words;
Behold the reafon urging me to this:
                                                                [*He fhows his dead fon.*
See here my fhow, look on this fpectacle;
Here lay my hope, and here my hope hath end:
Here lay my heart, and here my heart was flain:
Here lay my treafure, here my treafure loft:
Here lay my blifs, and here my blifs bereft:
But hope, heart, treafure, joy, and blifs,
All fled, fail'd, died; yea, all decay'd with this.
From forth thefe wounds came breath that gave me life;
They murder'd me, that made thefe fatal marks:
The caufe was love, whence grew this mortal hate;
The hate, *Lorenzo* and young *Balthazar,*
The love, my fon to *Bel-imperia:*
But night, the coverer of accurfed crimes,
With pitchy filence hufh'd thefe traytors ² harms,
And lent them leave, for they had forted leifure,
To take advantage in my garden plot,
Upon my fon, my dear *Horatio:*
There mercilefs they butcher'd up my boy,
In black dark night, to pale dim cruel death.
He fhrieks, I heard; and yet, methinks, I hear
His difmal outcry echo in the air:
With fooneft fpeed I hafted to the noife;
Where hanging on a tree I found my fon,
Through girt with wounds, and flaughter'd as you fee:
And griev'd I, think you, at this fpectacle?
Speak, *Portingale,* whofe lofs refembles ³ mine,
If thou can'ft weep upon thy *Balthazar,*

1 *turn'd* 1618.   2 *the trait'rous* 1623, 23. 33.
3 *refemble* 1618, 23.

'Tis

'Tis like, I wail'd [1] for my *Horatio*.—
And you, my lord, whose reconciled son
March'd in a net, and thought himself unseen,
And rated me for brainsick lunacy,
With, [2] — God, amend that mad *Hieronimo*;
How can you brook our play's catastrophe?
And here behold this bloody handkerchief,
Which at *Horatio's* death I, weeping, dip'd
Within the river of his bleeding wounds:
It as propitious, see, I have reserv'd, [3]
And never hath it left my [4] bloody heart,
Soliciting rememb'rance of my vow,
With these, o these accursed murderers;
Which now perform'd, my heart is satisfy'd.
And to this end the bashaw I became,
That might revenge me on *Lorenzo's* life;
Who therefore was appointed to the part,
And was to represent the knight of *Rhodes*,
That I might kill him more conveniently:—
So, *Viceroy*, was this *Balthazar* thy son,
That *Solyman*, which *Bel-imperia*,
In person of *Perseda*, murdered,
Solely appointed to that tragick part,
That she might slay him that offended her.
Poor *Bel-imperia* miss'd her part in this;
For though the story saith, she should have died,
Yet I of kindness, and of care to her,
Did otherwise determine of her end;
But love of him, whom they did hate too [5] much,
Did urge her resolution to be such.—
And, princes, now behold *Hieronimo*,
Author and actor in this tragedy,
Bearing his latest fortune in his fist;

1 *waile* 1633.   2 *Which* 1618, 23, 33.
3 *preserv'd* ditto. 4 *bleeding* 1623, 33.
5 *so* 1623, 33.

THE SPANISH TRAGEDY. 117

And will as refolute conclude his part,
As any of the actors gone before.—
And, gentles,¹ thus I end my play:
Urge no more words, I have no more to fay.
                           [*He runs to hang himfelf.*
            King.
  O hearken, *Viceroy,* — hold *Hieronimo,* —
Brother, my nephew and thy fon are flain.
            Viceroy.
  We are betray'd, my *Balthazar* is flain:
Break ope the doors; run, fave *Hieronimo.*
                      [*They run in and hold* Hieronimo.
Hieronimo, do but inform the king of thefe events,
Upon mine honour, thou fhalt have no harm.
            Hieronimo.
Viceroy, I will not truft thee with my life,
Which I this day have offer'd to my fon.—
Accurfed wretch, why ftay'ft² thou him that was refolv'd
  to die?
            King.
  Speak, traitor! damned bloody murderer, fpeak!
For now I have thee, I will make thee fpeak:
Why haft thou done this undeferving deed?
            Viceroy.
  Why haft thou murdered my *Balthazar?*
           Caftile.
  Why haft thou butcher'd both my children thus? *⁎⁎*

1 *gentlies* 1623, 33.   2 *ftaidft* 1tto.
                                     Hieronimo.

⁎⁎ *See note, pge 40.*
            Hieronimo.
But are you fure, that they are dead?
            Caftile.
Ay, flain too fure.
            Hieronimo.
  What, and yours too?
                                                               Viceroy.

118   THE SPANISH TRAGEDY.

Hieronimo.
O, good words: as dear to me was my *Horatio*,
As yours, or yours, or yours, my lord, to you.
My guiltless son was by *Lorenzo* slain,
And by *Lorenzo* and that *Balthazar*
Am I at last revenged thoroughly;
Upon whose souls may heav'ns be yet aveng'd ¹
With greater far than these afflictions. *⁎*

¹ *revenged* 1618, 23, 33.

Castile.

Viceroy.
Ay, all are dead; not one of them survive.
Hieronimo.
Nay, then I care not: come, and we shall be friends:
Let us lay our heads together.
See, here's a goodly noose will hold them all.
Viceroy.
O damned devil, how secure he is!
Hieronimo.
Secure? why dost thou wonder at it?
All thee, *Viceroy*, this day I have seen reveng'd,
That in that fight am gown a prouder monarch,
Had I e'er sat under the crown of *Spain*.
As many lives as there be stars,
I'd give the heavens to go to as those lives,
But I would all, ay, and my soul to boot,
See thee ride in this red pool.
Castile.
Speak, who were thy confederates in this?
Viceroy.
That was thy daughter *Bel-imperia*;
For by her hand my *Balthazar* was slain:
I saw her stab him.

⁎ *see note, page* 40.

Methinks, since I grew inward with revenge,
I cannot look with scorn enough on death.
King.
What, dost thou ¹ mock us, slave? — Bring tortures forth.

¹ *thou* omitted 1613, 33.

Hieronimo.

Castile.
But who were thy confederates in this?
Viceroy.
That was thy daughter, *Bel-imperia*;
For by her hand my *Balthazar* was slain:
I saw her stab him.
King.
Why speak'st thou not?
Hieronimo.
What lesser liberty can kings afford
Than harmless silence? then, afford it me:
Sufficeth, I may not, nor I will not tell thee.
King.
Fetch forth the tortures. —
Traitor as thou art, I'll make thee tell. *Hieronimo.*

Hieronimo.
Do, do, do; and mean time I'll torture you:
You had a son, as I take it; and your son
Should have been married to your daughter: ha, was't not so?
You had a son too, he was my liege's nephew:
He was proud and politick: had he liv'd,
He might ha' come to wear the crown of *Spain*:
I think 'twas so; 'twas I that kill'd him,
Look you, this same hand was it that stab'd
His heart, do you see this hand,
For one *Horatio*, if you ever knew him?
A youth, one that they hang'd up in his father's garden,
One that did force your valiant son to yield,
While your valiant son did take him prisoner.
Viceroy.
Be deaf, my senses, I can hear no more.
King.
Fall, heaven, and cover us with thy sad ruins.
Castile.
Roll all the world within thy pitchy cloud.
Hieronimo.
Now do I applaud what I have acted.
Nunc mors; cæde, manus. 1
Now to express the rupture of my part,
First take my tongue, and afterward my heart.

1 *Nunc mers* † *cadæ manus,* 1618,
† *mens* 1623, 33.

Hieronimo.
Indeed, thou may'st torment me as his wretched son
Hath done in mur'dring my *Horatio;*
But never shalt thou force me, to reveal
The thing which I have vow'd inviolate:
And therefore, in despite of all thy threats,
Pleas'd with their deaths, and eas'd with their revenge,
First take my tongue, and afterwards my heart.
[*He bites out his tongue.*
King.
O monstrous resolution of a wretch!—
See, viceroy, he hath bitten forth his tongue,
Rather than to reveal what we requir'd.
Castile.
Yet can he write.
King.
And if in this he satisfy us not,
We will devise th' extremest kind of death
That ever was invented for a wretch.
[*He makes signs for a knife to mend his pen.*
Castile.
O, he would have a knife to mend his pen.
Viceroy.
Here; and advise thee, that thou write the troth.—
Look to my brother, save *Hieronimo.*
[*He with the knife stabs the duke and himself.*
King.
What age hath ever heard such monstrous deeds?
My brother, and the whole succeeding hope
That ɪ *Spain* expected after my decease!
Go bear his body hence, that we may mourn
The loss of our beloved brother's death,
That he may be intomb'd whate'er befall:
I am the next, the nearest, last of all.
Viceroy.
And thou, *Don Pedro,* do the like for us:

ɪ *Of* 1618, 23, 33.

Take

Take up our haplefs fon, untimely flain;
Set me with him, and he with woful me,
Upon the main maft of a fhip unman'd,
And let the wind and tide hale me along
To *Sylla's* barking and untamed gulph;
Or to the loathfome pool of *Acheron*,
To weep my want for ¹ my fweet *Balthazar*:
Spain hath no refuge for a *Portingale*.. *[Exeunt.*

The trumpets found a dead march: the King of Spain
mourning after his brother's body; and the King of
Portingale *bearing the body of his fon.*

Enter Ghoſt, and Revenge.

Ghoſt.
Ay, now my hopes have end in their effects,
When blood and forrow finifh my defires:
Horatio murder'd in his father's bower;
Vilde *Serberine* by *Pedringano* flain;
Falfe *Pedringano* hang'd by quaint device;
Fair *Ifabella* by herfelf mifdone;
Prince *Balthazar* by *Bel-imperia* ftab'd;
The duke of *Caſtile*, and his wicked fon,
Both done to death by old *Hieronimo*.
My *Bel-imperia* fall'n, as *Dido* fell;
And good *Hieronimo* flain by himfelf.
Ay, thefe were fpectacles to pleafe my foul,
Now will I beg at lovely *Proſerpine*,
That, by the virtue of her princely doom,
I may confort my friends in pleafing fort,
And on my foes work juft and fharp revenge.
I'll lead my friend *Horatio* through thofe fields,
Where never-dying wars are ftill inur'd:

I'll lead fair *Isabella* to that train
Where pity weeps, but never feeleth pain:
I'll lead my *Bel-imperia* to those joys
That vestal virgins and fair queens possess:
I'll lead *Hieronimo* where *Orpheus* plays,
Adding sweet pleasure to eternal days.
But say, *Revenge*, (for thou must help, or none)
Against the rest how shall my hate be shown?

     Revenge.
 This hand shall hale them down to deepest hell,
Where none [1] but furies, bugs, and tortures dwell.

    Ghost.
 Then, sweet *Revenge*, do this at my request:
Let me be judge, and doom them to unrest.
Let loose poor *Titius* from the vulture's gripe,
And let *Don Cyprian* supply his room;
Place *Don Lorenzo* on *Ixion*'s wheel,
And let the lover's endless pains surcease;
Juno forgets old wrath, and grants him ease;
Hang *Balthazar* about *Chimera*'s neck,
And let him there bewail his bloody love,
Ripining at our joys that are above:
Let *Serberine* go roll the fatal stone,
And take from *Sisiphus* his endless moan:
False *Pedringano*, for his treachery,
Let him be drag'd through boiling *Acheron*,
And there live, dying still in endless flames,
Blaspheming Gods and all their holy names.

    Revenge.
 Then haste we down to meet thy friends and foes;
To place thy friends in ease, the rest in woes:
For here, though death hath [2] end their misery,
I'll there begin their endless tragedy.   [*Exeunt.*

  1 *nought* 1618, 23, 33. 2 *doth* 1623, 33.

THE LOVE OF

KING DAVID

AND

FAIR BETHSABE

WITH THE

TRAGEDY OF ABSALON

THE LOVE OF KING DAVID AND FAIR BETHSABE: &c.

—*was written by the ingenious* George Peele, *formerly
ſtudent of* Chriſt-Church, Oxford, *and maſter of arts in the
year* 1579. *He was city poet, and had the ordering of the
pageants; lived on the bank ſide over againſt* Black Friers;
*left a wife and daughter behind him, and died before or in the
year* 1598. *He was almoſt as famous for his tricks and merry
pranks as* Scoggan *or* Tarleton: *and as there are books of
others in print, ſo there are of his; eſpecially one, entitled
'* Merrie conceited jeſts of Geo. Peele, gentleman, ſometime
'ſtudent in Oxford: wherein is ſhewed the courſe of his life
'how he lived. A man very well known in the city of* London
'*and elſewhere.* London, *printed for* Hen. Bell. 4to.
'1627." *pages* 21. black letter. *Though they are not ſo
properly jeſts as tales or tricks of a ſharper.* Geo. Peele's
*chriſtian pen (as it is called) is ſaid to have put an end to
the famous Tragedy of* Mahomet and Irene the fair Greek
in the pamphlet above of Peele's *jeſts.* p. 14. *A tragedy that
Langbaine ſeems never to have heard of. See* Cha. Goring's
Irene the fair Greek, 4to. 1798. [Oldys' MS. *notes on*
Langbaine.

Naſh *in his epiſtle to the gentlemen ſtudents of both univer-
ſities, prefixed to* Greene's Arcadia, 4to. black letter, *re-
ommends his friend,* Peele, "*as the chief ſupporter of plea-
'ſance now living, the* Atlas *of poetrie, and primus ver-
'borum artifex : whoſe firſt increaſe,* 'The Arraignment of
'Paris, *might plead to their opinions his pregnant dexteritie
'of wit, and manifold varietie of invention.*" *He wrote,
beſides the plays already mentioned,* "The character of Ed-
'ward the firſt, ſirnamed Edward Longſhanks, with his
'return from the Holy Land : alſo the Life of Llewellin rebel
'in* Wales: *Laſtly, the ſinking of Queen* Elinor *at* Charing-
roſs, *and riſing again at* Potters Hithe, *now named* Queen
Hithe. 1593." Peele *wrote likewiſe* The Honour of the
Garter, *a Poem Gratulatorie ; and dedicated it to the Earl of
Northumberland, calling it the* Firſtling *conſecrated to his
noble name.*

The

The play here presented to the reader,
Scriptural *History, abounds with the most m*
fine genius; and a genuine spirit of poetry
whole. It is printed from the edition of 15(
acts, with all its peculiarities of stage direc
ther account of this excellent poet, see Ath(
p. 300. *and the ingenious Mr.* Farmer's *Ess(*
of Shakespeare.

D R A

DRAMATIS PERSONÆ.

KING DAVID.
King HANON.
King MACHAAS.
ABSALON,
AMMON,
ANONIA, } DAVID's *Sons.*
SALOMON,
CHILEAB,
JOAB, *Captain of the hoſt to* DAVID.
AMASA, *Captain of the hoſt to* ABSALON.
URIAS, *Huſband to* BETHSABE.
NATHAN, *a Prophet.*
ABIATHAR, *High-prieſt.*
JONATHAN, *his Son.*
SADOC, *a Prieſt.*
AHIMEAS, *his Son.*
CUSAY,
ITHAY, } *Friends to* DAVID.
ACHITOPHEL, *Friend to* ABSALON.
JONADAB, *Friend to* AMMON.
ABISAI, *Nephew to* DAVID.
SEMEI, DAVID's *enemy.*
JETHRAY, *Servant to* AMMON.

BETHSABE, *Wife to* URIAS.
THAMAR, DAVID's *daughter.*
Widow of THECOA.
Handmaid to BETHSABE.
DAVID's *Concubines.*

Meſſenger, Soldiers, Train, Shepherds, Servants, &c.

PROLOGUE.

OF Israel's sweetest singer now I sing,
    His holy style and happy victories;
Whose muse was dip'd in that inspiring dew,
Arch-angels stilled from the breath of Jove,
Decking her temples with the glorious flowers,
Heav'ns rain'd on tops of Sion and mount Sinai.
Upon the bosom of his ivory lute
The cherubins and angels lay'd their breasts;
And, when his consecrated fingers struck
The golden wires of his ravishing harp,
He gave alarum to the host of heaven,
That, wing'd with light'ning, brake the clouds, and cast
Their crystal armour at his conquering feet.
Of this sweet poet Jove's musician,
And of his beauteous son, I prease to sing. —
Then help, divine Adonai, to conduct
Upon the wings of my well temper'd verse
The hearers minds above the towers of heaven,
And guide them so in this thrice haughty flight,
Their mounting feathers scorch not with the fire,
That none can temper but thy holy hand:
To thee for succour flies my feeble muse,
And at thy feet her iron pen doth use.

DAVID AND BETHSABE.

He draws a curtain and discovers Bethsabe *with her maid bathing over a spring: she sings, and* David *sits above viewing her.*

THE SONG.

HOT sun, cool fire, temper'd with sweet air,
Black shade, fair nurse, shadow my white hair:
Shine, sun; burn, fire; breathe, air, and ease me;
Black shade, fair nurse, shroud me, and please me:
Shadow, my sweet nurse, keep me from burning,
Make not my glad cause cause of mourning.

    Let not my beauty's fire
    Inflame unstay'd desire,
    Nor pierce any bright eye
    That wand'reth lightly.

        Bethsabe.
Come, gentle *Zephyr*, trick'd with those perfumes
That erst in *Eden* sweeten'd *Adam's* love,
And stroke my bosom with the silken fan:
This shade, sun-proof, is yet no proof for thee;
Thy body, smoother than this waveless spring,
And purer than the substance of the same,
Can creep through that his lances cannot pierce:
Thou, and thy sister, soft and sacred air,
Goddess of life, and governess of health,
Keeps ev'ry fountain fresh and arbour sweet;

No brazen gate her paſſage can repulſe,
Nor buſhy [1] thicket bar thy ſubtle breath:
Then deck thee with thy looſe delightſome robes,
And on thy wings bring delicate perfumes,
To play the wantons with us through the leaves.

David.
What tunes, what words, what looks, what wonders, pierce
My ſoul, incenſed with a ſudden fire?
What tree, what ſhade, what ſpring, what paradiſe,
Enjoys the beauty of ſo fair a dame?
Fair *Eva*, plac'd in perfect happineſs,
Lending her praiſe-notes to the liberal heavens,
Struck with the accents of arch-angels tunes,
Wrought not more pleaſure to her huſband's thoughts,
Than this fair woman's words and notes to mine.
May that ſweet plain that bears her pleaſant weight,
Be ſtill enamel'd with diſcolour'd flowers;
That precious fount, bear ſand of pureſt gold;
And, for the pebble, let the ſilver ſtreams
That pierce earth's bowels to maintain the ſource,
Play upon rubies, ſapphires, chryſolites;
The brims let be embrac'd with golden curls
Of moſs that ſleeps with ſound the waters make,
For joy to feed the fount with their recourſe;
Let all the graſs that beautifies her bower
Bear manna ev'ry morn inſtead of dew,
Or let the dew be ſweeter far than that
That hangs, like chains of pearl, on *Hermon* hill,
Or balm which trickled from old *Aaron's* beard. —
Cuſay, come up, and ſerve thy lord the king.

Enter Cuſay.

Cuſay.
What ſervice doth my lord the king command?

[1] *buſhly*

David.

David.
See, *Cufay*, fee, the flower of *Ifrael*,
The faireft daughter that obeys the king,
In all the land the lord fubdu'd to me;
Fairer than *Ifaac's* lover at the well,
Brighter than infide bark of new-hew'n cedar,
Sweeter than flames of fine perfumed myrrh,
And comelier than the filver clouds that dance
On *Zephyr's* wings before the king of heaven.
Cufay.
Is it not *Bethfabe* the *Hethite's* wife,
Urias, now at *Rabath'* fiege with *Joab*?
David.
Go know, and bring her quickly to the king;
Tell her, her graces have found grace with him.
Cufay.
I will, my lord. [*Exit* Cufay *to* Bethfabe.
David.
Bright *Bethfabe* fhall wafh in *David's* bower
In water mix'd with pureft almond flower,
And bathe her beauty in the milk of kids;
Bright *Bethfabe* gives earth to my defires;
Verdure to earth; and to that verdure flowers;
To flowers fweet odours; and to odours wings,
That carry pleafures to the hearts of kings.
[Cufay *to* Bethfabe, *fhe ftarting as fomething affright*.
Cufay.
Fair *Bethfabe*, the king of *Ifrael*
From forth his princely tower hath feen thee bathe;
And thy fweet graces have found grace with him:
Come then, and kneel unto him where he ftands;
The king is gracious, and hath liberal hands.
Bethfabe.
Ah! what is *Bethfabe* to pleafe the king?
Or what is *David*, that he fhould defire
For fickle beauty's fake his fervant's wife?

Cufay.

Cusay.
David, thou know'st, fair dame, is wise and just,
Elected to the heart of *Israel's* God;
Then do not thou expostulate with him
For any action that contents his soul.
Bethsabe.
My lord the king, elect to God's own heart,
Should not his gracious jealousy incense,
Whose thoughts are chaste; I hate incontinence.
Cusay.
Woman, thou wrong'st the king, and doubt'st his honour,
Whose truth maintains the crown of *Israel,*
Making him stay that bad me bring thee straight.
Bethsabe.
The king's poor handmaid will obey my lord.
Cusay.
Then come, and do thy duty to his grace;
And do what seemeth favour in his sight. [*Exeunt.*
David.
Now comes my lover tripping like the roe,
And brings my longings tangled in her hair:
To joy her love I'll build a kingly bower,
Seated in hearing of a hundred streams,
That, for their homage to her sovereign joys,
Shall, as the serpents fold into their nests
In oblique turnings, wind the nimble waves
About the circles of her curious walks;
And with their murmur summon easeful sleep,
To lay his golden sceptre on her brows. —
Open the doors, and entertain my love;
Open, I say; and, as you open, sing,
Welcome, fair *Bethsabe,* king *David's* darling.

Enter Cusay, *with* Bethsabe.

David.
Welcome, fair *Bethsabe,* king *David's* darling;

Thy

Thy bones fair covering, erft difcover'd fair,
And all mine eyes with all thy beauties pierc'd:
As heav'n's bright eye burns moft, when moft he climbs
The crooked *Zodiack* with his fiery fphere,
And fhineth fartheft from this earthly globe;
So, fince thy beauty fcorch'd my conquer'd foul,
I call'd thee nearer for my nearer cure.
      Bethfabe.
Too near, my lord, was your unarmed heart,
When fartheft off my haplefs beauty pierc'd;
And, 'would this dreary day had turn'd to night,
Or that fome pitchy cloud had cloak'd the fun,
Before their lights had caus'd my lord to fee
His name difparag'd, and my chaftity!
      David.
My love, if want of love have left thy foul
A fharper fenfe of honour than thy king,
(For love leads princes fometimes from their feats,)
As erft my heart was hurt, difpleafing thee,
So come and tafte thy eafe with eafing me.
      Bethfabe.
One med'cine cannot heal our diff'rent harms;
But, rather, make both rankle at the bone:
Then, let the king be cunning in his cure,
Left, flatt'ring both, both perifh in his hand.
      David.
Leave it to me, my deareft *Bethfabe,*
Whofe fkill is converfant in deeper cures:—
And, *Cufay,* hafte thou to my fervant *Joab,*
Commanding him to fend *Urias* home
With all the fpeed can poffibly be us'd.
      Cufay.
Cufay will fly about the king's defire. [*Exeunt.*

Enter Joab, Abisai, Urias, *and others,
with drum and ensign.*

Joab.
Courage, ye mighty men of *Israel*,
And charge your fatal instruments of war
Upon the bosom of proud *Ammon's* sons,
That have disguis'd your king's ambassadors,
Cut half their beards, and half their garments off,
In spite of *Israel*, and his daughters sons;
Ye fight the holy battles of *Jehovah*,
King *David's* God, and ours, and *Jacob's* God,
That guides your weapons to their conquering strokes,
Orders your footsteps, and directs your thoughts
To stratagems that harbour victory:
He casts his sacred eyesight from on high,
And sees your foes run seeking for their deaths,
Laughing their labours, and their hopes, to scorn;
Whilst 'twixt your bodies, and their blunted swords,
He puts on armour of his honour's proof,
And makes their weapons wound the senseless winds.

Abisai.
Before this city *Rabath* we will lie,
And shoot forth shafts as thick and dangerous
As was the hail that *Moses* mix'd with fire,
And threw with fury round about the fields,
Devouring *Pharaoh's* friends, and *Egypt's* fruits.

Urias.
First, mighty captains, *Joab*, and *Abisai*,
Let us assault, and scale this kingly tower,
Where all their conduits, and their fountains are;
Then we may easily take the city too.

Joab.
Well hath *Urias* counsell'd our attempts;
And as he spake us, so assault the tower:
And *Hanon* now, the king of *Ammon's* son,
Repulse our conquering passage if he dare.

Hanon *with king* Machaas, *and others,
upon the walls.*

Hanon.
What would the shepherd's dogs of *Israel*
Snatch from the mighty issue of king *Ammon,*
The valiant *Ammonites,* and haughty *Syrians?*
'Tis not your late succeffive victories
Can make us yield, or quail our courages;
But if ye dare assay to scale this tower,
Our angry swords shall smite ye to the ground,
And venge our losses on your hateful lives.

Joab.
Hanon, thy father *Nahas* gave relief
To holy *David* in his haplels exile,
Lived his fixed date, and died in peace;
But thou, instead of reaping his reward,
Hast trod it under foot, and scorn'd our king:
Therefore thy days shall end with violence,
And to our swords thy vital bloud shall cleave.

Machaas.
Hence, thou that bear'st poor *Israel's* shepherd's hook,
The proud lieutenant of that base-born king,
And keep within the compass of his fold;
For, if ye seek to feed on *Ammon's* fruits,
And stray into the *Syrians* fruitful *Medes,*
The mastiffs of our land shall worry you,
And pull the wezands [1] from your greedy throats.

Abisai.
Who can endure these *Pagans* blasphemies?

Urias.
My foul repines at this disparagement.

Joab.
Assault, ye valiant men of *David's* host,
And beat these railing dastards from their doors.

[1] *weesels*

Assault,

*Assault, and they win the tower,
and* Joab *speaks above.*
Thus have we won the tower, which we will keep,
Maugre the sons of *Ammon* and of *Syria.*

Enter Cusay, *beneath.*
Cusay.
Where is lord *Joab,* leader of the host?
Joab.
Here is lord *Joab,* leader of the host.—
Cusay, come up, for we have won the hold. [*He comes.*
Cusay.
In happy hour then is Cusay come.
Joab.
What news then brings lord *Cusay* from the king?
Cusay.
His majesty commands thee out of hand
To send him home *Urias* from the wars,
For matter of some service he shall do.
Urias.
'Tis for no choler hath surpris'd the king,
I hope, lord *Cusay,* 'gainst his servant's truth?
Cusay.
No; rather, to prefer *Urias*' truth.
Joab.
Here, take him with thee then, and go in peace;
And tell my lord the king that I have fought
Against the city *Rabath* with success,
And scaled where the royal palace is,
The conduit heads, and all their sweetest springs:
Then let him come in person to these walls,
With all the soldiers he can bring besides,
And take the city as his own exploit:
Lest I surprize it, and the people give
The glory of the conquest to my name.
Cusay.
We will, lord *Joab*; and, great *Israel's* God

Bless

Bless in thy hands the battles of our king!
            Joab.
Farewel, *Urias*; haste away the king.
            Urias.
As sure as *Joab* breathes a victor here,
Urias will haste him, and his own return.   [*Exeunt.*
            Abisai.
Let us descend, and ope the palace' gate,
Taking our soldiers in to keep the hold.
            Joab.
Let us, *Abisai*: — and, ye sons of *Judah*,
Be valiant, and maintain your victory.   [*Exeunt.*

  Ammon, Jonadab, Jethray *and* Ammon's *Page.*
            Jonadab.
What means my lord, the king's beloved son,
That wears upon his right triumphant arm,
The power of *Israel* for a royal favour,
That holds upon the tables of his hands
Banquets of honour, and all thought's content,
To suffer pale and grisly abstinence
To sit and feed upon his fainting cheeks,
And suck away the blood that cheers his looks?
            Ammon.
Ah, *Jonadab*, it is my sister's looks,
On whose sweet beauty I bestow my blood;
That makes me look so amourously lean;
Her beauty having seiz'd upon my heart,
So merrily consecrate to her content,
Sets now such guard about his vital blood,
And views the passage with such piercing eyes,
That none can scape to cheer my pining cheeks,
But all is thought too little for her love.
            Jonadab.
Then from her heart thy looks shall be releaved,
And thou shalt joy her as thy soul desires.
            Ammon.

Ammon.
How can it be, my sweet friend *Jonadab*,
Since *Thamar* is a virgin and my sister?
Jonadab.
Thus it shall be: lie down upon thy bed,
Feigning thee fever-sick, and ill at ease;
And, when the king shall come to visit thee,
Desire thy sister *Thamar* may be sent
To dress some dainties for thy malady:
Then when thou hast her solely with thyself,
Enforce some favour to thy manly love.—
See, where she comes; entreat her in with thee.

Enter Thamar.

Thamar.
What aileth *Ammon* with such sickly looks,
To daunt the favour of his lovely face?
Ammon.
Sweet *Thamar*, sick, and wish some wholesome cates,
Dress'd with the cunning of thy dainty hands.
Thamar.
That hath the king commanded at my hands;
Then, come, and rest thee, while I make thee ready
Some dainties, easeful to thy crased soul.
Ammon.
I go, sweet sister, eased with thy sight.

Exeunt. Restat Jonadab.
Jonadab.
Why should a prince, whose power may command,
Obey the rebel passions of his love,
When they contend but 'gainst his conscience,
And may be govern'd, or suppress'd, by will?
Now, *Ammon*, loose those loving knots of blood,
That soak'd the courage from thy kingly heart,
And give it' passage to thy wither'd cheeks.
Now, *Thamar*, ripen'd are the holy fruits
That grew on plants of thy virginity;

And

And rotten is thy name in *Israel*:
Poor *Thamar*, little did thy lovely hands
Foretel an action of such violence,
As to contend with *Ammon's* lusty arms,
Sinew'd with vigour of his kindless love:
Fair *Thamar*, now dishonour hunts thy foot,
And follows thee through ev'ry covert shade,
Discovering thy shame and nakedness,
Even from the valleys of *Jehosaphat*
Up to the lofty mounts of *Lebanon*;
Where cedars, stir'd with anger of the winds,
Sounding in storms the tale of thy disgrace,
Tremble with fury, and with murmur shake
Earth with their feet, and with their heads the heavens,
Beating the clouds into their swiftest rack,
To bear this wonder round about the world. [*Exit.*

Ammon *thrusting out* Thamar.

Ammon.
Hence from my bed, whose sight offends my soul,
As doth the parbreak of disgorged bears.

Thamar.
Unkind, unprincely, and unmanly *Ammon*,
To force, and then refuse thy sister's love;
Adding unto the fright of thy offence
The baneful torment of my publish'd shame!
O, do not this dishonour to thy love,
Nor clog thy soul with such increasing sin;
This second evil far exceeds the first.

Ammon.
Jethray, come, thrust this woman from my sight,
And bolt the door upon her if she strive.

Jethray.
Go, madam, go, away, you must be gone;
My lord hath done with you: I pray, depart.
[*He shuts her out.*

Thamar.

Thamar.
Whither, alas! ah, whither shall I fly
With folded arms, and all-amazed soul,
Cast as was *Eva* from that glorious soil,
(Where all delights sat bating wing'd with thoughts,
Ready to nestle in her naked breasts)
To bare and barren vales with floods made waste,
To desert woods, and hills with light'ning scorch'd,
With death, with shame, with hell, with horrour fit;
There will I wander from my father's face,
There *Absalon*, my brother *Absalon*,
Sweet *Absalon* shall hear his sister mourn,
There will I live with my windy sighs,
Night ravens and owls to rend my bloody side,
Which with a rusty weapon I will wound,
And make them passage to my panting heart.
Why talk'st thou, wretch, and leav'st the deed undone?

Enter Absalon.

Rend hair, and garments, as thy heart is rent
With inward fury of a thousand griefs,
And scatter them by these unhallow'd doors,
To figure *Ammon's* resting cruelty,
And tragick spoil of *Thamar's* chastity.
Absalon.
What causeth *Thamar* to exclaim so much?
Thamar.
The cause that *Thamar* shameth to disclose.
Absalon.
Say, I thy brother will revenge that cause.
Thamar.
Ammon, our father's son, hath forced me,
And thrust me from him as the scorn of *Israel*.
Absalon.
Hath *Ammon* forced thee? by *David's* hand,
And by the covenant God hath made with him,
Ammon shall bear his violence to hell;

Traitor

Traitor to heav'n, traitor to *David's* throne,
Traitor to *Abfalon* and *Ifrael*.
This fact hath *Jacob's* ruler feen from heaven,
And through a cloud of fmoke, and tower of fire,
(As he rides vaunting him upon the greens)
Shall tear his chariot wheels with violent winds,
And throw his body in the bloody fea;
At him the thunder fhall difcharge his bolt;
And his fair fpoufe, with bright and fiery wings,
Sit ever burning on his hateful bones:
Myfelf, as fwift as thunder, or his fpoufe,
Will hunt occafion with a fecret hate,
To work falfe *Ammon* an ungracious end.—
Go in, my fifter; reft thee in my houfe;
And God, in time, fhall take this fhame from thee.
     Thamar.
Nor God, nor time, will do that good for me.
   [*Exit* Thamar. *Reftat* Abfalon.

   Enter David, *with his train.*
     David.
My *Abfalon*, what mak'ft thou here alone,
And bear'ft fuch difcontentment in thy brows?
     Abfalon.
Great caufe hath *Abfalon* to be difpleas'd,
And in his heart to fhroud the wounds of wrath.
     David.
'Gainft whom fhould *Abfalon* be thus difpleas'd?
     Abfalon.
'Gainft wicked *Ammon* thy ungracious fon,
My brother, and fair *Thamar's* by the king,
My ftep-brother, by mother, and by kind;
He hath difhonour'd *David's* holinefs,
And fix'd a blot of lightnefs on his throne,
Forcing my fifter *Thamar* when he feign'd
A ficknefs, fprung from root of heinous luft,

         David

David.

Hath *Ammon* brought this evil on my houſe,
And ſuffer'd ſin to ſmite his father's bones?
Smite, *David*, deadlier than the voice of heaven,
And let hate's fire be kindled in thy heart;
Frame in the arches of thy angry brows,
Making thy forehead, like a comet, ſhine,
To force falſe *Ammon* tremble at thy looks.
Sin with his ſev'nfold crown, and purple robe,
Begins his triumphs in my guilty throne;
There ſits he watching with his hundred eyes
Our idle minutes, and our wanton thoughts;
And with his baits, made of our frail deſires,
Gives us the hook that hales our ſouls to hell:
But with the ſpirit of my kingdom's God
I'll thruſt the flattering tyrant from his throne,
And ſcourge his bondſlaves from my hallow'd court
With rods of iron, and thorns of ſharpen'd ſteel. —
Then, *Abſalon*, revenge not thou this ſin;
Leave it to me, and I will chaſten him.

Abſalon.

I am content; then, grant, my lord the king,
Himſelf with all his other lords would come
Up to my ſheep-feaſt on the plain of *Hazor*.

David.

Nay, my fair ſon, myſelf, with all my lords,
Will bring thee too much charge; yet ſome ſhall go.

Abſalon.

But let my lord the king himſelf take pains;
The time of year is pleaſant for your grace,
And gladſome ſummer in her ſhady robes,
Crowned with roſes and with planted flowers,
With all her nymphs ſhall entertain my lord,
That from the thicket of my verdant groves,
Will ſprinkle honey dews about his breaſt,
And caſt ſweet balm upon his kingly head:
Then grant thy ſervant's boon, and go, my lord.

David.

DAVID AND BETHSABE.

David.
Let it content my sweet son *Absalon*,
That I may stay, and take my other lords.
Absalon.
But shall thy best beloved *Ammon* go?
David.
What needeth it, that *Ammon* go with thee?
Absalon.
Yet do thy son and servant so much grace.
David.
Ammon shall go, and all my other lords,
Because I will give grace to *Absalon*.

Enter Cusay, *and* Urias, *with others.*
Cusay.
Pleaseth my lord the king, his servant *Joab*
Hath sent *Urias* from the *Syrian* wars.
David.
Welcome, *Urias*, from the *Syrian* wars,
Welcome to *David* as his dearest lord.
Urias
Thanks be to *Israel's* God, and *David's* grace,
Urias finds such greeting with the king.
David.
No other greeting shall *Urias* find
As long as *David* sways th' elected seat,
And consecrated throne of *Israel*.
Tell me, *Urias*, of my servant *Joab*;
Fights he with truth the battles of our God,
And for the honour of the Lord's anointed?
Urias.
Thy servant *Joab* fights the chosen wars
With truth, with honour, and with high success;
And 'gainst the wicked king of *Ammon's* sons,
Hath by the finger of our sovereign's God,
Besieg'd the city *Rabath*, and atchiev'd
The court of waters, where the conduits run,

And

And all the *Ammonites* delightsome springs:
Therefore he wisheth *David's* mightiness
Should number out the host of *Israel*,
And come in person to the city *Rabath*,
That so her conquests may be made the king's,
And *Joab* fight as his inferiour.
     David.
 This hath not God, and *Joab's* prowess done,
Without *Urias'* valour, I am sure,
Who, since his true conversion from a *Hethite*,
To an adopted son of *Israel*,
Hath fought like one whose arms were lift by heaven,
And whose bright sword was edg'd with *Israel's* wrath:
Go therefore home, *Urias*, take thy rest;
Visit thy wife, and houshold, with the joys
A victor and a favourite of the king's
Should exercise with honour after arms.
     Urias.
 Thy servant's bones are yet not half so craz'd,
Nor constitute on such a sickly mould,
That for so little service he should faint,
And seek, as cowards, refuge of his home:
Nor are his thoughts so sensually stir'd,
To stay the arms with which the lord would smite
And fill their circle with his conquer'd foes,
For wanton bosom of a flattering wife.
     David.
 Urias hath a beauteous sober wife,
Yet young, and fram'd of tempting flesh and blood;
Then, when the king hath summon'd thee from arms,
If thou unkindly shouldst refrain her bed,
Sin might be lay'd upon *Urias'* soul,
If *Bethsabe* by frailty hurt her fame:
Then go, *Urias*, solace in her love;
Whom God hath knit to thee, tremble to lose.
     Urias.
 The king is much too tender of my ease;
The ark, and *Israel*, and *Judah*, dwell

DAVID AND BETHSABE.

In palaces, and rich pavilions,
But *Joab*, and his brother in the fields,
Suffering the wrath of winter and the sun:
And shall *Urias* (of more shame than they)
Banquet and loiter in the work of heaven?
As sure as thy soul doth live, my lord,
Mine ears shall never lean to such delight,
When holy labour calls me forth to fight.
    David.
Then, be it with *Urias'* manly heart
As best his fame may shine in *Israel.*
    Urias.
Thus shall *Urias'* heart be best content,
Till thou dismiss me back to *Joab's* bands;
This ground before the king my master's doors,
         [*He lies down.*
Shall be my couch, and this unwearied arm,
The proper pillar of a soldier's head;
For never will I lodge within my house,
Till *Joab* triumph in my secret vows.
    David.
Then fetch some flagons of our purest wine,
That we may welcome home our hardy friend
With full carouses to his fortunes past,
And to the honours of his future arms;
Then will I send him back to *Rabath'* siege,
And follow with the strength of *Israel.*

Enter one with the flagons of wine.

Arise, *Urias*; come, and pledge the king.
    Urias.
If *David* think me worthy such a grace, [*He riseth.*
I will be bold, and pledge my lord the king.
    David.
Absalon, and *Cusay*, both shall drink
To good *Urias*, and his happiness.

Vol. II.   K   *Absalon.*

Absalon.
We will, my lord, to pleafe *Urias*' foul.
David.
I will begin, *Urias*, to thyfelf,
And all the treafure of the *Ammonites*,
Which here I promife to impart to thee,
And bind that promife with a full caroufe.
Urias.
What feemeth pleafant in my fov'reign's eyes,
That fhall *Urias* do till he be dead.
David.
Fill him the cup; follow, ye lords, that love
Your fovereign's health, and do as he hath done.
Abfalon.
Ill may he thrive, or live in *Ifrael*,
That loves not *David*, or denies his charge.—
Urias, here is to *Abifai's* health,
Lord *Joab's* brother, and thy loving friend.
Urias.
I pledge lord *Abfalon*, and *Abifai's* health. [*He drinks.*
Cufay.
Here now, *Urias*, to the health of *Joab*,
And to the pleafant journey we fhall have,
When we return to mighty *Rabath*' fiege.
Urias.
Cufay, I pledge thee all with all my heart.—
Give me fome drink, ye fervants of the king;
Give me my drink. [*He drinks.*
David.
Well done, my good *Urias*; drink thy fill,
That in thy fulnefs *David* may rejoice.
Urias.
I will, my lord.
Abfalon.
Now, lord *Urias*, one caroufe to me.
Urias.
No, fir, I'll drink to the king;
Your father is a better man than you.
David.

DAVID AND BETHSABE.

David.
Do so, *Urias*; I will pledge thee straight.
Urias.
I will, indeed, my lord, and sovereign;
I'll once in my days be so bold.
David.
Fill him his glass.
Urias.
Fill me my glass. [*He gives him the glass.*
David.
Quickly, I say, *Urias*; quickly, I say.
Urias.
Here, my lord, by your favour now I drink to you.
David.
I pledge thee, good *Urias*, presently. [*He drinks.*
Absalon.
Here then, *Urias*, once again for me,
And to the health of *David's* children.
Urias.
David's children?
Absalon.
Ay, *David's* children; wilt thou pledge me, man?
Urias.
Pledge me, man!
Absalon.
Pledge me, I say, or else thou lov'st us not.
Urias.
What, do you talk? do you talk?
I'll no more, I'll lie down here.
David.
Rather, *Urias*, go thou home and sleep.
Urias.
O, ho, sir; would you make me break my sentence?
[*He lies down.*
Home, sir! no, indeed, sir: I'll sleep upon mine arm,
Like a soldier, sleep like a man as long as I live in *Israel.*

K 2 *David.*

David.
If nought will serve to save his wife's renown,
I'll send him with a letter unto *Joab*
To put him in the forefront of the wars,
That so my purposes may take effect.—
Help him in, sirs.   [*Exit* Dav. *and* Abs.
Cusay.
Come, rise, *Urias*; get thee in and sleep.
Urias.
I will not go home, sir; that's flat.
Cusay.
Then come, and rest thee upon *David's* bed.
Urias.
On, afore, my lords; on, afore.   [*Exeunt.*

CHORUS.

O proud revolt of a presumptuous man,
Laying his bridle in the neck of sin,
Ready to bear him past his grave to hell.
Like as the fatal raven, that in his voice
Carries the dreadful summons of our deaths,
Flies by the fair *Arabian* spiceries,
Her pleasant gardens, and delightsome parks,
Seeming to curse them with his hoarse exclaims,
And yet doth stoop with hungry violence
Upon a piece of hateful carrion:
So wretched man, displeas'd with those delights
Would yield a quick'ning favour to his soul,
Pursues with eager and unstanched thirst
The greedy longings of his loathsome flesh.
If holy *David* so shook hands with sin,
What shall our baser spirits glory in?
This kingly giving lust her rein
Pursues the sequel with a greater ill.
Urias in the forefront of the wars
Is murder'd by the hateful heathens sword,

And

And *David* joys his too dear *Bethsabe*.
Suppose this past, and that the child is born,
Whose death the prophet solemnly doth mourn.

Enter Bethsabe, *with her handmaid.*

Bethsabe.
Mourn, *Bethsabe*, bewail thy foolishness,
Thy sin, thy shame, the sorrow of thy soul :
Sin, shame, and sorrow swarm about thy soul;
And in the gates, and entrance of thy heart,
Sadness, with wreathed arms, hangs her complaint.
No comfort from the ten-string'd instrument,
The tinckling cymbal, or the ivory lute ;
Nor doth the sound of *David's* kingly harp,
Make glad the broken heart of *Bethsabe :*
Jerusalem is fill'd with thy complaint,
And in the streets of *Sion* sits thy grief.
The babe is sick, sick to the death, I fear,
The fruit that sprung from thee to *David's* house :
Nor may the pot of honey and of oil,
Glad *David*, or his handmaid's countenance.
Urias, — wo is me to think hereon !
For who is it among the sons of men,
That saith not to my soul, the king hath sin'd ;
David hath done amiss, and *Bethsabe*
Lay'd snares of death unto *Urias'* life ? —
My sweet *Urias*, fall'n into the pit
Art thou, and gone ev'n to the gates of hell
For *Bethsabe*, that wouldst not shroud her shame.
O, what is it to serve the lust of kings !
How lion-like thy rage, when we resist !
But, *Bethsabe*, in humbleness attend
The grace that God will to his handmaid send. [*Exit.*

David *in his gown walking sadly.*
To him Nathan.
David.
The babe is sick, and sad is *David's* heart,
To see the guiltless bear the guilty's pain.
David, hang up thy harp; hang down thy head;
And dash thy ivory lute against the stones.
The dew, that on the hill of *Hermon* falls,
Rains not on *Sion's* tops, and lofty towers;
And *David's* thoughts are spent in pensiveness:
The plains of *Gath* and *Ascalon* rejoice.
The babe is sick, sweet babe, that *Bethsabe*
With woman's pain brought forth to *Israel.*

Enter Nathan.
But what saith *Nathan* to his lord the king?
Nathan.
Thus *Nathan* saith unto his lord the king:
There were two men both dwellers in one town,
The one was mighty, and exceeding rich
In oxen, sheep, and cattle of the field;
The other poor, having nor ox, nor calf,
Nor other cattle, save one little lamb,
Which he had bought and nourish'd by the hand;
And it grew up, and fed with him and his,
And eat and drank, as he and his were wont,
And in his bosom slept, and was to live
As was his daughter or his dearest child.
There came a stranger to this wealthy man;
And he refus'd, and spar'd to take his own,
Or of his store to dress or make him meat,
But took the poor man's sheep, partly, poor man's store,
And dress'd it for this stranger in his house.
What, tell me, shall be done to him for this?

David.

DAVID AND BETHSABE.

David.
Now as the lord doth live, this wicked man
Is judg'd, and shall become the child of death;
Fourfold to the poor man shall he restore,
That without mercy took his lamb away.
Nathan.
Thou art the man; and thou hast judg'd thyself.
David, thus faith the Lord thy God by me:
I thee anointed king in *Israel,*
And sav'd thee from the tyranny of *Saul;*
Thy master's house I gave thee to possess;
His wives into thy bosom did I give,
And *Judah,* and *Jerusalem* withal;
And might, thou know'st, if this had been too small,
Have given thee more:
Wherefore then hast thou gone so far astray,
And hast done evil, and sinned in my sight?
Urias thou hast killed with the sword;
Yea, with the sword of the uncircumcised
Thou hast him slain: wherefore, from this day forth,
The sword shall never go from thee and thine;
For thou hast ta'en this *Hethite's* wife to thee:
Wherefore behold, I will, faith *Jacob's* God,
In thine own house stir evil up to thee;
Yea, I before thy face, will take thy wives,
And give them to thy neighbour to possess:
This shall be done to *David* in the day,
That *Israel* openly may see thy shame.
David.
Nathan, I have against the Lord, I have
Sinned; o, sinned grievously: and, lo!
From heaven's throne doth *David* throw himself,
And groan and grovel to the gates of hell.
[*He falls down.*
Nathan.
David, stand up; thus faith the Lord by me:
David the king shall live, for he hath seen
The true repentant sorrow of thy heart;

But,

But, for thou haft in this mifdeed of thine
Stir'd up the enemies of *Ifrael*
To triumph, and blafpheme the God of hofts,
And fay, He fet a wicked man to reign
Over his loved people and his tribes;
The child fhall furely die, that erft was born,
His mother's fin, his kingly father's fcorn.
          [*Exit* Nathan.
     David.
 How juft is *Jacob's* God in all his works!
But muft it die, that *David* loveth fo?
O, that the mighty one of *Ifrael*,
Nill change his doom, and fays the babe muft die.
Mourn, *Ifrael*, and weep in *Sion* gates;
Wither, ye cedar trees of *Lebanon*;
Ye fprouting almonds with your flow'ring tops,
Droop, drown, and drench in *Hebron's* fearful ftreams:
The babe muft die that was to *David* born,
His mother's fin, his kingly father's fcorn.
          [David *fits fadly.*

   Enter Cufay *to* David *and his train.*

     Servus.
What tidings bringeth *Cufay* to the king?
     Cufay.
To thee, the fervant of king *David's* court,
This bringeth *Cufay*, as the prophet fpake:
The Lord hath furely ftricken to the death
The child new born by that *Urias'* wife,
That by the fons of *Ammon* erft was flain.
     Servus.
Cufay, be ftill; the king is vexed fore:
How fhall he fpeed that brings thefe tidings firft,
When, while the child was yet alive, we fpake,
And *David's* heart would not be comforted?
     David.
 Yea, *David's* heart will not be comforted?
              What

What murmur ye, the servants of the king?
What tidings telleth *Cusay* to the king? —
Say, *Cusay*, lives the child, or is he dead?
Cusay.
The child is dead, that of *Urias*' wife
David begat.
David.
Urias' wife, say'st thou?
The child is dead, then ceaseth *David's* shame:
Fetch me to eat, and give me wine to drink;
Water to wash, and oil to clear my looks;
Bring down your shalms, your cymbals, and your pipes;
Let *David's* harp and lute, his hand and voice,
Give laud to him that loveth *Israel*,
And sing his praise, that shendeth *David's* fame,
That put away his sin from out his sight,
And sent his shame into the streets of *Gath*. —
Bring ye to me the mother of the babe,
That I may wipe the tears from off her face,
And give her comfort with this hand of mine,
And deck fair *Bethsabe* with ornaments,
That she may bear to me another son,
That may be loved of the Lord of host;
For where he is, of force must *David* go,
But never may he come where *David* is.

*They bring in water, wine, and oil,
musick, and a banquet.*

Fair *Bethsabe*, sit thou, and sigh no more;
And sing and play, you servants of the king:
Now sleepeth *David's* sorrow with the dead,
And *Bethsabe* liveth to *Israel*.

They use all solemnities together and sing, &c.
David.
Now arms, and warlike engins for assault,
Prepare at once, ye men of *Israel*,

Ye

Ye men of *Judah* and *Jerusalem*,
That *Rabba* may be taken by the king,
Lest it be called after *Joab's* name,
Nor *David's* glory shine in *Sion's* streets;
To *Rabba* marcheth *David,* and his men,
To chastise *Ammon* and the wicked ones. [*Exeunt omnes.*

    Enter Absalon, *with two or three.*

        Absalon.
Set up your mules, and give them well to eat,
And let us meet our brothers at the feast;
Accursed is the master of this feast,
Dishonour of the house of *Israel,*
His sister's slander, and his mother's shame.
Shame be his share that could such ill contrive,
To ravish *Thamar*; and, without a pause,
To drive her shamefully from out his house:
But, may his wickedness find just reward!
Therefore doth *Absalon* conspire with you,
That *Ammon* die what time he sits to eat;
For in the holy temple have I sworn
Wreak of his villany in *Thamar's* rape.
And here he comes; bespeak him gently, all,
Whose death is deeply graved in my heart.

    Enter Ammon, *with* Adonia *and* Jonadab,
      to Absalon *and his company.*

        Ammon.
Our shearers are not far from hence, I wot;
And *Ammon* to you all his brethren
Giveth such welcome as our fathers erst
Were wont in *Judah* and *Jerusalem*:—
But, specially, lord *Absalon*, to thee,
The honour of thy house and progeny;

                               Sit

DAVID AND BETHSABE.

Sit down, and dine with me, king *David's* son,
Thou fair young man, whose hairs shine in mine eye,
Like golden wires of *David's* ivory lute.
                Absalon.
Ammon, where be thy shearers, and thy men,
That we may pour in plenty of thy wines,
And eat thy goats milk, and rejoice with thee?
                Ammon.
Here cometh *Ammon's* shearers, and his men;—
Absalon, sit and rejoice with me.

*Here enter a company of shepherds,
and dance and sing.*

                Ammon.
Drink, *Absalon*, in praise of *Israel*;
Welcome to *Ammon's* fields from *David's* court.
                Absalon.
Die with thy draught; perish, and die accurs'd;
Dishonour to the honour of us all;
Die for the villany to *Thamar* done,
Unworthy thou to be king *David's* son.   [*Exit* Abs.
                Jonadab.
O, what hath *Absalon* for *Thamar* done,
Murder'd his brother, great king's *David's* son!
                Adonia.
Run, *Jonadab*, away, and make it known,
What cruelty this *Absalon* hath shown.—
Ammon, thy brother *Adonia* shall
Bury thy body among the dead men's bones;
And we will make complaint to *Israel*
Of *Ammon's* death, and pride of *Absalon*.
                            [*Exeunt omnes.*

Enter

Enter David *with* Joab, Abisai, Cusay, *with drum and ensign against* Rabba.

David.
This is the town of the uncircumcised,
The city of the kingdom, this is it,
Rabba, where wicked *Hannon* sitteth king:
Despoil this king, this *Hannon* of his crown;
Unpeople *Rabba*, and the streets thereof;
For in their blood, and slaughter of the slain,
Lieth the honour of king *David's* line. —
Joab, — *Abisai*, — and the rest of you,
Fight ye this day for great *Jerusalem*.

Joab.
And see, where *Hannon* shows him on the walls;
Why then do we forbear to give assault,
That *Israel* may, as it is promised,
Subdue the daughters of the *Gentiles* tribes;
All this must be perform'd by *David's* hand.

David.
Hark to me, *Hannon*, and remember well:
As sure as he doth live that kept my host,
What time our young men by the pool of *Gibeon*,
Went forth against the strength of *Isbofeth*,
And twelve to twelve did with their weapons play,
So sure art thou, and thy men of war,
To feel the sword of *Israel* this day;
Because thou hast defied *Jacob's* God,
And suffer'd *Rabba* with the *Philistine*,
To rail upon the tribe of *Benjamin*.

Hannon.
Hark, man: as sure as *Saul* thy master fell,
And gor'd his sides upon the mountain tops
And *Jonathan*, *Abinadab*, and *Melchisua*,
Water'd the dales and deeps of *Ascalon*
With bloody streams, that from *Gilboa* ran
In channels through the wilderness of *Ziph*,
What time the sword of the uncircumcised

Was

Was drunken with the blood of *Ifrael*;
So fure fhall David perifh with his men,
Under the walls of *Rabba*, *Hannon's* town.
                    Joab.
Hannon, the God of *Ifrael* hath faid,
David the king fhall wear that crown of thine,
That weighs a talent of the fineft gold,
And triumph in the fpoil of *Hannon's* town,
When *Ifrael* fhall hale thy people hence,
And turn them to the tile-kiln, man and child,
And put them under harrows made of iron,
And hew their bones with axes, and their limbs
With iron fwords divide and tear in twain.
Hannon, this fhall be done to thee and thine,
Becaufe thou haft defied *Ifrael.*—
To arms, to arms, that *Rabba* feel revenge,
And *Hannon's* town become king *David's* fpoil.
            [*Alarum, excurfions, affault, exeunt omnes.*

Then the trumpets, and David *with* Hannon's *crown.*
                    David.
Now clattering arms, and wrathful ftorms of war,
Have thunder'd over *Rabba's* rafed towers;
The wreakful ire of great *Johova's* arm,
That for his people made the gates to rend,
And cloth'd the *Cherubins* in fiery coats,
To fight againft the wicked *Hannon's* town,
Pay thanks, ye men of *Juda*, to the king,
The God of *Sion* and *Jerufalem*,
That hath exalted *Ifrael* to this;
And crowned *David* with this diadem.
                    Joab.
Beauteous and bright is he among the tribes;
As when the fun attir'd in glift'ring robe,
Comes dancing from his oriental gate,
And bridegroom-like hurls through the gloomy air
His radiant beams, fuch doth king *David* fhow,
                                    Crown'd

Crown'd with the honour of his enemies town,
Shining in riches like the firmament,
The ftarry vault that overhangs the earth:
So looketh *David* king of *Ifrael*.
Abifai.
Joab, why doth not *David* mount his throne,
Whom heav'n hath beautified with *Hannon's* crown?
Sound trumpets, fhalms, and inftruments of praife,
To *Jacob's* God for *David's* victory.

Enter Jonadab.
Jonadab.
Why doth the king of *Ifrael* rejoice?
Why fitteth *David* crown'd with *Rabba's* rule?
Behold, there hath great heavinefs befall'n
In *Ammon's* fields by *Abfalon's* mifdeed!
And *Ammon's* fhearers, and their feaft of mirth
Abfalon hath overturn'ed with his fword;
Nor liveth any of king *David's* fons
To bring this bitter tidings to the king.
David.
Ay me, how foon are *David's* triumphs dafh'd!
How fuddenly declineth *David's* pride!
As doth the daylight fettle in the weft,
So dim is *David's* glory, and his gite.
Die, *David*; for to thee is left no feed
That may revive thy name in *Ifrael*.
Jonadab.
In *Ifrael* is left of *David's* feed.

Enter Adonia, *with other fons.*
Comfort your lord, you fervants of the king.—
Behold, thy fons return in mourning weeds,
And only *Ammon Abfalon* hath flain.
David.
Welcome, my fons; dearer to me you are

Than

Than is this golden crown, or *Hannon's* spoil:
O tell me then, tell me my sons, I say,
How cometh it to pass, that *Absalon*
Hath slain his brother *Ammon* with the sword?
    Adonia.
 Thy sons, o king, went up to *Ammon's* fields
To feast with him, and eat his bread and oil;
And *Absalon* upon his mule doth come,
And to his men he saith, when *Ammon's* heart
Is merry and secure, then strike him dead,
Because he forced *Thamar* shamefully,
And hated her, and threw her forth his doors:
And this did he; and they with him conspire,
And kill thy son in wreak of *Thamar's* wrong.
    David.
 How long shall *Judah* and *Jerusalem*
Complain, and water *Sion* with their tears?
How long shall *Israel* lament in vain,
And not a man among the mighty ones
Will hear the sorrows of king *David's* heart? —
Ammon, thy life was pleasing to thy lord,
As to mine ears the musick of my lute,
Or songs that *David* tuneth to his harp;
And *Absalon* hath ta'en from me away
The gladness of my sad distressed soul.
    [*Ex. omnes. Manet* David.

   Enter widow of Thecoa.
    Widow.
 God save king *David*, king of *Israel*,
And bless the gates of *Sion* for his sake!
    David.
 Woman, why mournest thou? rise from the earth;
Tell me what sorrow hath befall'n thy soul.
    Widow.
 Thy servant's soul, o king, is troubled sore,
And grievous is the anguish of her heart;
And from *Thecoa* doth thy handmaid come.
    David.

David.
Tell me, and say, thou woman of *Thecoa*,
What aileth thee, or what is come to pass.
Widow.
Thy servant is a widow in *Thecoa*:
Two sons thy handmaid had; and they, my lord,
Fought in the field, where no man went betwixt,
And so the one did smite, and slay the other.
And lo, behold, the kindred doth arise,
And cry on him that smote his brother,
That he therefore may be the child of death;
For we will follow and destroy the heir.
So will they quench that sparkle that is left,
And leave nor name, nor issue on the earth
To me or to thy handmaid's husband dead.
David.
Woman, return; go home unto thy house:
I will take order that thy son be safe.
If any man say otherwise than well,
Bring him to me, and I shall chastise him:
For, as the lord doth live, shall not a hair
Shed from thy son, or fall upon the earth.
Woman, to God alone belongs revenge;
Shall then the kindred slay him for his sin?
Widow.
Well hath king *David* to his handmaid spoke;
But wherefore then hast thou determined
So hard a part against the righteous tribes,
To follow and pursue the banished;
When as to God alone belongs revenge?
Assuredly thou say'st against thyself;
Therefore, call home again the banished;
Call home the banished that he may live,
And raise to thee some fruit in *Israel*.
David.
Thou woman of *Thecoa*, answer me,
Answer me one thing I shall ask of thee:
Is not the hand of *Joab* in this work?

DAVID AND BETHSABE.

Tell me, is not his finger in this fact?
Widow.
It is, my lord; his hand is in this work:
Assure thee, *Joab*, captain of thy host,
Hath put these words into thy handmaid's mouth;
And thou art as an angel from on high,
To understand the meaning of my heart:
Lo, where he cometh to his lord the king.

Enter Joab.
David.
Say, *Joab*, didst thou send this woman in
To put this parable for *Absalon?*
Joab.
Joab, my lord, did bid this woman speak,
And she hath said; and thou hast understood.
David.
I have, and am content to do the thing;
Go, fetch my son, that he may live with me.
[Joab *kneels.*
Joab.
Now God be blessed for king *David's* life;
Thy servant *Joab* hath found grace with thee,
In that thou sparest *Absalon* thy child:
A beautiful and fair young man is he,
In all his body is no blemish seen;
His hair is like the wire of *David's* harp,
That twines about his bright and ivory neck:
In *Israel* is not such a goodly man;
And here I bring him to entreat for grace.

Enter Absalon, *with* Joab.
David.
Hast thou slain in the fields of *Hazor*—

Ah, *Absalon*, my son! ah, my son *Absalon!*
But wherefore do I vex thy spirit so?
Live, and return from *Gesur* to thy house;
Return from *Gesur* to *Jerusalem:*
What boots it to be bitter to thy soul?
Ammon is dead, and *Absalon* survives.

              Absalon.

Father, I have offended *Israel*;
I have offended *David*, and his house;
For *Thamar's* wrong hath *Absalon* misdone:
But *David's* heart is free from sharp revenge,
And *Joab* hath got grace for *Absalon*.

              David.

Depart with me, you men of *Israel*,
You that have follow'd *Rabba* with the sword;
And ransack *Ammon's* richest treasuries.—
Live, *Absalon*, my son, live once in peace:
Peace be with thee, and with *Jerusalem*.

           [*Exeunt omnes.* Manet Abs.

              Absalon.

David is gone, and *Absalon* remains,
Flow'ring in pleasant spring-time of his youth:
Why liveth *Absalon*, and is not honoured
Of tribes and elders, and the mightiest ones,
That round about his temples he may wear
Garlands and wreaths set on with reverence;
That every one that hath a cause to plead
Might come to *Absalon*, and call for right?
Then in the gates of *Sion* would I sit,
And publish laws in great *Jerusalem*;
And not a man should live in all the land,
But *Absalon* would do him reason's due;
Therefore, I shall address me as I may,
To love the men, and tribes of *Israel*. [*Exit.*

              Enter

DAVID AND BETHSABE. 163

Enter David, Ithay, Sadoc, Ahimaas, Jonathan, *with others*, David *barefoot, with some loose covering over his head, and all mourning.*

David.
Proud lust, the bloodiest traitor to our souls,
Whose greedy throat, nor earth, air, sea, or heaven,
Can glut or satisfy with any store,
Thou art the cause these torments suck my blood,
Piercing with venom of thy poison'd eyes
The strength and marrow of my tainted bones:
To punish *Pharaoh*, and his cursed host,
The waters shrunk at great *Adonai's* voice,
And sandy bottom of the sea appear'd,
Off'ring his service at his servant's feet;
And, to inflict a plague on *David's* sin,
He makes his bowels traitors to his breast,
Winding about his heart with mortal gripes.
Ah, *Absalon*, the wrath of heav'n inflames
Thy scorched bosom with ambitious heat,
And *Satan* sets thee on a lusty tower,
Showing thy thoughts the pride of *Israel*,
Of choice to cast thee on her ruthless stones,—
Weep with me then, ye sons of *Israel*,
  [*He lies down, and all the rest after him.*
Lie down with *David*, and with *David* mourn
Before the holy one that sees our hearts;
Season this heavy soil with showers of tears,
And fill the face of ev'ry flower with dew;
Weep, *Israel*, for *David's* soul dissolves,
Lading the fountains of his drowned eyes,
And pours her substance on the senseless earth.
Sadoc.
Weep, *Israel*; o, weep for *David's* soul,
Strewing the ground with hair and garments torn,
For tragick witness of your hearty woes.
Ahimaas.
O, 'would our eyes were conduits to our hearts,

L 2   And

DAVID AND BETHSABE.

And that our hearts were seas of liquid blood,
To pour in streams upon this holy mount,
For witness we would die for *David's* woes.

Jonadab.
Then should this mount of olives seem a plain,
Drown'd with a sea, that with our sighs should roar,
And in the murmur of his mounting waves,
Report our bleeding sorrows to the heavens,
For witness we would die for *David's* woes.

Ithay.
Earth cannot weep enough for *David's* woes;
Then weep, you heavens, and all you clouds, dissolve,
That piteous stars may see our miseries;
And drop their golden tears upon the ground,
For witness how they weep for *David's* woes.

Sadoc.
Now let my soveregin raise his prostrate bones,
And mourn not as a faithless man would do;
But be assur'd, that *Jacob's* righteous God,
That promis'd never to forsake your throne,
Will still be just, and pure in his vows.

David.
Sadoc, high-priest, preserver of the ark,
Whose sacred virtue keeps the chosen crown,
I know, my God is spotless in his vows,
And that these hairs shall greet my grave in peace;
But that my son should wrong his tender'd soul,
And fight against his father's happiness,
Turns all my hopes into despair of him,
And that despair feeds all my veins with grief.

Ithay.
Think of it, *David,* as a fatal plague
Which grief preserveth, but preventeth not;
And turn thy drooping eyes upon the troops,
That, of affection to thy worthiness,
Do swarm about the person of the king:
Cherish their valours, and their zealous loves,
With pleasant looks, and sweet encouragements.

David.
Methinks, the voice of *Ithay* fills mine ears.
Ithay.
Let not the voice of *Ithay* loath thine ears,
Whose heart would balm thy bosom with his tears.
David.
But wherefore goest thou to the wars with us?
Thou art a stranger here in *Israel*,
And son to *Achis*, mighty king of *Gath*;
Therefore return, and with thy father stay:
Thou cam'st but yesterday; and should I now
Let thee partake these troubles here with us?
Keep both thyself, and all thy soldiers safe;
Let me abide the hazards of these arms,
And God requite the friendship thou hast show'd.
Ithay.
As sure as *Israel's* God gives *David* life,
What place or peril shall contain the king,
The same will *Ithay* share in life and death.
David.
Then, gentle *Ithay*, be thou still with us,
A joy to *David*, and a grace to *Israel*.—
Go, *Sadoc*, now, and bear the ark of God
Into the great *Jerusalem* again:
If I find favour in his gracious eyes,
Then will he lay his hand upon my heart
Yet once again before I visit death;
Giving it strength, and virtue to mine eyes
To taste the comforts, and behold the form
Of his fair ark, and holy tabernacle:
But, if he say, my wonted love is worn,
And I have no delight in *David* now,
Here lie I armed with an humble heart
T' embrace the pains that anger shall impose,
And kiss the sword my lord shall kill me with.
Then, *Sadoc*, take *Ahimaas* thy son,
With *Jonathan* son to *Abiathar*;

And in thefe fields will I repofe myfelf,
Till they return from you fome certain news.
    Sadoc.
Thy fervants will with joy obey the king,
And hope to cheer his heart with happy news.
    [*Ex.* Sadoc, Ahim. *and* Jonathan.
    Ithay.
Now that it be no grief unto the king,
Let me for good inform his majefty,
That with unkind and gracelefs *Abfalon*,
Achitophel your ancient counfellor
Directs the ftate of this rebellion.
    David.
Then doth it aim with danger at my crown.—
O thou, that hold'ft his raging bloody bound
Within the circle of the filver moon,
That girds earth's centre with his watry fcarf,
Limit the counfel of *Achitophel*,
No bounds extending to my foul's diftrefs,
But turn his wifdom into foolifhnefs.

   Enter Cufay, *with his coat turned,*
    and head covered.
    Cufay.
Happinefs and honour to my lord the king.
    David.
What happinefs or honour may betide
His ftate that toils in my extremities?
    Cufay.
O, let my gracious fov'reign ceafe thefe griefs,
Unlefs he wifh his fervant *Cufay's* death;
Whofe life depends upon my lord's relief:
Then, let my prefence with my fighs, perfume
The pleafant clofet of my fov'reign's foul.
    David.
No, *Cufay*, no; thy prefence unto me
Will be a burden, fince I tender thee,

       And

And cannot brook ¹ thy sighs for *David's* sake:
But if thou turn to fair *Jerusalem*,
And say to *Absalon*, as thou hast been
A trusty friend unto his father's seat,
So thou wilt be to him, and call him king,
Achitophel's counsel may be brought to nought.
Then having *Sadoc* and *Abiathar*,
All three may learn the secrets of my son,
Sending the message by *Abimaas*,
And friendly *Jonathan*, who both are there.
    Cusay.
 Then rise, referring the success to heaven.
    David.
Cusay, I rise; though with unwieldy bones
I carry arms against my *Absalon*.   [*Exeunt.*

 Absalon, Amasa, Achitophel, *with the concubines* ¹
  David, *and others in great state*; Absalon *crowned.*
    Absalon.
Now you that were my father's concubines,
Liquor to his inchaste and lustful fire,
Have seen his honour shaken in his house,
Which I possess in sight of all the world:
I bring you forth for foils to my renown,
And to eclipse the glory of your king,
Whose life is with his honour fast inclos'd
Within the entrails of a jetty cloud,
Whose dissolution shall pour down in showers
The substance of his life and swelling pride;
Then shall the stars light earth with rich aspects,
And heav'n shall burn in love with *Absalon*,
Whose beauty will suffice to chase all mists,
And clothe the sun's sphere with a triple fire,
Sooner than his clear eyes should suffer stain,
Or be offended with a low'ring day.

   ¹ *breake*

       ¹ *Concubines.*

1 Concubine.
Thy father's honour, graceless *Absalon*,
And ours thus beaten with thy violent arms,
Will cry for vengeance to the host of heaven,
Whose power is ever arm'd against the proud,
And will dart plagues at thy aspiring head,
For doing this disgrace to *David's* throne.

2 Concubine.
To *David's* throne, to *David's* holy throne,
Whose sceptre angels guard with swords of fire,
And sit as eagles on his conquering fist,
Ready to prey upon his enemies:
Then think not thou, the captain of his foes,
Wert thou much swifter than *Azahell* was,
That could outpace the nimple-footed roe,
To scape the fury of their thumping beaks,
Or dreadful scope of their commanding wings.

Achitophel.
Let not my lord the king of *Israel*
Be angry with a silly woman's threats;
But with the pleasure he hath erst enjoy'd,
Turn them into their cabinets again,
Till *David's* conquest be their overthrow.

Absalon.
Into your bowers, ye daughters of disdain,
Gotten by fury of unbridled lust,
And wash your couches with your mourning tears,
For grief that *David's* kingdom is decay'd.

1 Concubine.
No, *Absalon*, his kingdom is enchain'd
Fast to the finger of great *Jacob's* God,
Which will not lose it for a rebel's love. [*Exeunt.*

Amasa.
If I might give advice unto the king,
These concubines should buy their taunts with blood.

Absalon.
Amasa, no; but let thy martial sword

Empty

Empty the veins ¹ of *David's* armed men,
And let thefe foolifh women fcape our hands
To recompenfe the fhame they have fuftain'd.
Firft, *Abfalon* was by the trumpet's found
Proclaim'd through *Hebron* king of *Ifrael*;
And now is fet in fair *Jerufalem*
With complete ftate, and glory of a crown.
Fifty fair footmen by my chariot run,
And to the air whofe rupture rings my fame,
Where'er I ride they offer reverence.
Why fhould not *Abfalon*, that in his face
Carries the final purpofe of his God,
That is, to work him grace in *Ifrael*,
Endeavour to atchieve with all his ftrength,
The ftate that moft may fatisfy his joy,
Keeping his ftatutes and his covenants pure?
His thunder is entangled in my hair,
And with my beauty is his lightning quench'd;
I am the man he made to glory in,
When by the errours of my father's fin
He loft the path that led him into the land
Wherewith our chofen anceftors were blefs'd.

Enter Cufay.
  Cufay.
Long may the beauteous king of *Ifrael* live!
To whom the people do by thoufands fwarm.
  Abfalon.
What meaneth, *Cufay*, fo to greet his foe?
Is this the love thou fhowd'ft to *David's* foul,
To whofe affiftance thou haft vow'd thy life?
Why leav'ft thou him in this extremity?
  Cufay.
Becaufe the Lord, and *Ifrael* choofeth thee;
And as before I ferv'd thy father's turn,
With counfel acceptable in his fight,
So likewife will I now obey his fon.

1 *pains*   *Abfalon.*

Abſalon.

Then welcome, *Cuſay*, to king *Abſalon.* —
And now, my lords, and loving counſellors,
I think it time to exerciſe our arms
Againſt forſaken *David* and his hoſt. —
Give counſel firſt, my good *Achitophel*,
What times and orders we may beſt obſerve,
For proſp'rous manage of theſe high exploits.

Achitophel.

Let me chooſe out twelve thouſand valiant men;
And, while the night hides with her ſable miſts
The cloſe endeavours cunning ſoldiers uſe,
I will aſſault thy diſcontented ſire;
And, while with weakneſs of their weary arms,
Surcharg'd with toil to ſhun thy ſudden power,
The people fly in huge diſorder'd troops
To ſave their lives, and leave the king alone,
Then will I ſmite him with his lateſt wound,
And bring the people to thy feet in peace.

Abſalon.

Well hath *Achitophel* given his advice. —
Yet let us hear what *Cuſay* counſels us,
Whoſe great experience is well worth the ear.

Cuſay.

Though wife *Achitophel* be much more meet
To purchaſe hearing with my lord the king,
For all his former counſels, than myſelf,
Yet, not offending *Abſalon* or him,
This time it is not good, nor worth purſuit;
For, well thou know'ſt, thy father's men are ſtrong,
Chafing as ſhe-bears robbed of their whelps.
Beſides the king himſelf a valiant man,
Train'd up in feats and ſtratagems of war;
And will not, for prevention of the worſt,
Lodge with the common ſoldiers in the field:
But now, I know, his wonted policies
Have taught him lurk within ſome ſecret cave,
Guarded with all his ſtouteſt ſoldiers;
Which, —if the forefront of his battle faint,

Will

Will yet give out that *Abſalon* doth fly,
And ſo thy ſoldiers be diſcouraged:
David himſelf withal, whoſe angry heart
Is as a lion's, letted of his walk,
Will fight himſelf, and all his men to one,
Before a few ſhall vanquiſh him by fear.
My counſel therefore is, with trumpet's ſound
To gather men from *Dan* to *Berſabe*,
That they may march in number like ſea ſands,
That neſtle cloſe in one [1] another's neck:
So ſhall we come upon him in our ſtrength,
Like to the dew that falls in ſhowers from heaven,
And leave him not a man to march withal.
Beſides, if any city ſuccour him,
The numbers of our men ſhall fetch us ropes,
And we will pull it down the river's ſtream,
That not a ſtone be left to keep us out.
     Abſalon.
 What ſays my lord to *Cuſay's* counſel now?
     Amaſa.
 I fancy *Cuſay's* counſel better far
Than that is given us from *Achitophel*;
And ſo, I think, doth ev'ry ſoldier here.
     All.
 Cuſay's counſel is better than *Achitophel's.*
     Abſalon.
 Then march we after *Cuſay's* counſel all;
Sound trumpets through the bounds of *Iſrael*,
And muſter all the men will ſerve the king,
That *Abſalon* may glut his longing ſoul
With ſole fruition of his father's crown. [*Exeunt.*
     Achitophel.
 Ill ſhall they fare that follow thy attempts,
That ſcorn'ſt the counſel of *Achitophel.* *Reſtat* Cuſay.

    1 *one* omitted.

           Cuſay.

DAVID AND BETHSABE.

Cusay.
Thus hath the power of *Jacob's* jealous God
Fulfill'd his servant *David's* drifts by me,
And brought *Achitophel's* advice to scorn.

Enter Sadoc, Abiathar, Ahimaas, *and* Jonathan.

Sadoc.
God save lord *Cusay*, and direct his zeal
To purchase *David's* conquest 'gainst his son.
Abiathar.
What secrets hast thou glean'd from *Absalon*?
Cusay.
These, sacred priests, that bear the ark of God:
Achitophel advis'd him in the night
To let him choose twelve thousand fighting men,
And he would come on *David* at unwares,
While he was weary with his violent toil:
But I advis'd to get a greater host,
And gather men from *Dan* to *Bersabe*,
To come upon him strongly in the fields.
Then send *Ahimaas* and *Jonathan*
To signify these secrets to the king,
And will him not to stay this night abroad;
But get him over *Jordan* presently,
Lest he and all his people kiss the sword.
Sadoc.
Then go, *Ahimaas*, and *Jonathan*,
And straight convey this message to the king.
Ahimaas.
Father, we will, if *Absalon's* chief spies
Prevent not this device, and stay us here. [*Exeunt.*

Semei solus.

The man of *Israel*, that hath rul'd as king,
Or, rather, as the tyrant of the land,
Bolstering his hateful head upon the throne,

That

That God unworthily hath bless'd him with,
Shall now, I hope, lay it as low as hell,
And be depos'd from his detested chair.
O, that my bosom could by nature bear
A sea of poison, to be pour'd upon
His cursed head that sacred balm hath grac'd,
And confecrated king of *Ifrael!*
Or, 'would my breath were made the smoke of hell,
Infected with the sighs of damned souls,
Or with the reeking of that serpent's gorge,
That feeds on adders, toads, and venomous roots,
That, as I open'd my revenging lips
To curse the shepherd for his tyranny,
My words might cast rank poison to his pores,
And make his swoln and rankling sinews crack,
Like to the combat blows that break the clouds,
When *Jove's* stout champions fight with fire:
See, where he cometh that my soul abhors.
I have prepar'd my pocket full of stones
To cast at him, mingled with earth and dust,
Which, bursting with disdain, I greet him with.

David, Joab, Abysai, Ithay,
with others.

Come forth, thou murderer, and wicked man:
The lord hath brought upon thy cursed head
The guiltless blood of *Saul* and all his sons,
Whose royal throne thy baseness hath usurp'd;
And, to revenge it deeply on thy soul,
The Lord hath giv'n the kingdom to thy son,
And he shall wreak the trait'rous wrongs of *Saul:*
Even as thy sin hath still importun'd heaven,
So shall thy murders and adultery
Be punish'd in the sight of *Ifrael,*
As thou deserv'st with blood, with death, and hell.
Hence, murd'rer, hence. [*throws at him.*

Abisai.

Abisai.
Why doth this dead dog curse my lord the king?
Let me alone to take away his head.
David.
Why medleth thus the son of *Zeruia*
To interrupt the action of our God?
Semei useth me with this reproach,
Because the lord hath sent him to reprove
The sins of *David*, printed in his brows
With blood, that blusheth for his conscience guilt;
Who dares then ask him, why he curseth me?
Semei.
If then thy conscience tell thee thou hast sin'd,
And that thy life is odious to the world,
Command thy followers to shun thy face;
And by thyself here make away thy soul,
That I may stand and glory in thy shame.
David.
I am not desp'rate, *Semei*, like thyself,
But trust unto the covenant of my God,
Founded on mercy with repentance built,
And finish'd with the glory of my soul.
Semei.
A murd'rer, and hope for mercy in thy end!
Hate and destruction sit upon thy brows,
To watch the issue of thy damned ghost;
Which with thy latest gasp they'll take and tear,
Hurling in ev'ry pain of hell a piece.
Hence, murderer, thou shame to *Israel*,
Foul lecher, drunkard, plague to heav'n and earth.
[*He throws at him.*
Joab.
What, is it piety in *David's* thoughts,
So to abhor from laws of policy
In this extremity of his distress,
To give his subjects cause of carelesness!
Send hence the dog with sorrow to his grave.

David.

David.
Why should the sons of *Zeruia* seek to check
His spirit, which the Lord hath thus inspir'd?
Behold, my son which issued from my flesh,
With equal fury seeks to take my life;
How much more then the son of *Jemini*,
Chiefly, since he doth nought but God's command?
It may be, he will look on me this day
With gracious eyes, and for his cursing bless
The heart of *David* in his bitterness.
Semei.
What, dost thou fret my soul with sufferance?
O, that the souls of *Ishoseth* and *Abner*,
Which thou sent'st swimming to their graves in blood,
With wounds fresh bleeding, gasping for revenge,
Were here to execute my burning hate!
But I will hunt thy foot with curses still;
Hence, monster, murderer, mirror of contempt.
[*He throws dust again.*

Enter Ahimaas *and* Jonathan.
Abimaas.
Long life to *David*, to his enemies death.
David.
Welcome, *Abimaas*, and *Jonathan*:
What news sends *Cusay* to thy lord the king?
Abimaas.
Cusay would wish my lord the king,
To pass the river *Jordan* presently,
Lest he and all his people perish here;
For wife *Athitophel* hath counsell'd *Absalon*
To take advantage of your weary arms,
And come this night upon you in the fields.
But yet the Lord hath made his counsel scorn,
And *Cusay's* policy with praise preferr'd;
Which was to number every *Israelite*,
And so assault you in their pride of strength.
Jonathan.

Jonathan.
Abiathar besides entreats the king
To send his men of war against his son,
And hazard not his person in the field.
David.
Thanks to *Abiathar*, and to you both,
And to my *Cusay*, whom the Lord requite;
But ten times treble thanks to his soft hand,
Whose pleasant touch hath made my heart to dance,
And play him praises in my zealous breast,
That turn'd the counsel of *Achitophel*
After the prayers of his servant's lips.
Now will we pass the river all this night,
And in the morning sound the voice of war,
The voice of bloody and unkindly war.
Joab.
Then tell us how thou wilt divide thy men,
And who shall have the special charge herein.
David.
Joab, thyself shall for thy charge conduct
The first third part of all my valiant men;
The second shall *Abisai's* valour lead;
The third fair *Ithay*, which I most should grace,
For comfort he hath done to *David's* woes;
And I myself will follow in the midst.
Ithay.
That let not *David*; for, though we should fly,
Ten thousand of us were not half so much
Esteem'd with *David's* enemies, as himself;
Thy people, loving thee, deny thee this.
David.
What seems them best, then that will *David* do:—
But now, my lords, and captains, hear his voice,
That never yet pierc'd piteous heav'n in vain;
Then let it not slip lightly through your ears;
For my sake spare the young man *Absalon*.—
Joab, thyself didst once use friendly words
To reconcile my heart incens'd to him;

If then thy love be to thy kinſman found,
And thou wilt prove a perfect *Iſraelite*,
Friend him with deeds, and touch no hair of him,
Not that fair hair with which the wanton winds
Delight to play, and loves to make it curl,
Wherein the nightingales would build their neſts;
And make ſweet bow'rs in ev'ry golden treſs,
To ſing their lover every night aſleep.
O, ſpoil not, *Joab*, *Jove's* fair ornaments,
Which he hath ſent to ſolace *David's* ſoul. —
The beſt, ye ſee, my lords, are ſwift to ſin;
To ſin our feet are waſh'd with milk of roes,
And dried again with coals of lightening. —
O Lord, thou ſee'ſt, the proudeſt ſins, poor ſlave,
And with his bridle pull'ſt him to the grave;
For my ſake then, ſpare lovely *Abſalon*.
     Ithay.
 We will, my lord, for thy ſake favour him. [*Exeunt*.

   Achitophel *ſolus, with a halter*.
     Achitophel.
 Now hath *Achitophel* order'd his houſe,
And taken leave of every pleaſure there;
Hereon depends *Achitophel's* delights,
And in this circle muſt his life be clos'd.
The wiſe *Achitophel*, whoſe counſel prov'd
Ever as found for fortunate ſucceſs,
As if men aſk'd the oracle of God,
Is now us'd like the fool of *Iſrael*:
Then ſet thy angry ſoul upon her wings,
And let her fly into the ſhade of death;
And for my death let heaven for ever weep,
Making huge floods upon the land I leave,
To raviſh them, and all their faireſt fruits.
Let all the ſighs I breath'd for this diſgrace,
Hang on my hedges like eternal miſts,

As mourning garments for their master's death.
Ope, earth, and take thy miserable son
Into the bowels of thy cursed womb;
Once in a surfeit thou didst spew him forth,
Now for fell hunger suck him in again;
And be his body poison to thy veins:
And now thou hellish instrument of heaven,
Once execute th' arrest of *Jove's* just doom,
And stop his breast that curseth *Israel*. [*l*

Enter Absalon, Amasa, *with all his train.*

Absalon.
Now for the crown and throne of *Israel*,
To be confirm'd with virtue of my sword,
And writ with *David's* blood upon the blade;
Now, *Jove*, let forth the golden firmament,
And look on him with all thy fiery eyes,
Which thou hast made to give their glories light;
To show thou lov'st the virtue of thy hand,
Let fall a wreath of stars upon my head,
Whose influence may govern *Israel*,
With state exceeding all her other kings. —
Fight, lords, and captains, that your sov'reign's face
May shine in honour brighter than the sun;
And with the virtue of my beauteous rays
Make this fair land as fruitful as the fields,
That with sweet milk and honey overflow'd.
God, in the whizzing of a pleasant wind,
Shall march upon the tops of mulberry trees,
To cool all breasts that burn with any griefs,
As whilom he was good to *Moyses'* men.
By day the lord shall sit within a cloud,
To guide your footsteps to the fields of joy;
And in the night a pillar, bright as fire,
Shall go before you, like a second sun,
Wherein the essence of his godhead is;
That, day and night, you may be brought to peace,

And never swerve from that delightsome path,
That leads your souls to perfect happiness:
This shall he do for joy when I am king. —
Then fight, brave captains, that these joys may fly
Into your bosoms with sweet victory. [*Exeunt.*

The battle, and Absalon *hangs by the hair.*
Absalon.
What angry angel, sitting in these shades,
Hath lay'd his cruel hands upon my hair,
And holds my body thus 'twixt heaven and earth?
Hath *Absalon* no soldier near his hand
That may untwine me this unpleasant curl,
Or wound this tree that ravisheth his lord?
O God, behold the glory of thy hand,
And choicest fruit of nature's workmanship,
Hang, like a rotten branch, upon this tree,
Fit for the axe, and ready for the fire.
Since thou withhold'st all ordinary help,
To loose my body from this bond of death,
O, let my beauty fill these senseless plants
With sense and pow'r to loose me from this plague,
And work some wonder to prevent his death,
Whose life thou mad'st a special miracle.

Enter Joab, *with another Soldier.*
Soldier.
My lord, I saw the young prince *Absalon*
Hang by the hair upon a shady oak,
And could by no means get himself unloos'd.
Joab.
Why slew'st thou not the wicked *Absalon*,
That rebel to his father and to heaven,
That so I might have giv'n thee for thy pains,
Ten silver shekles and a golden waist.

DAVID AND BETHSABE.

Soldier.
Not for a thousand shekles would I slay
The son of *David*, whom, his father charg'd,
Nor thou, *Abisai*, nor the son of *Gath*,
Should touch with stroke of deadly violence.
The charge was giv'n in hearing of us all;
And, had I done it, then, I know, thyself,
Before thou wouldst abide the king's rebuke,
Wouldst have accus'd me as a man of death.

Joab.
I must not now stand trifling here with thee.

Absalon.
Help, *Joab*, help; o, help thy *Absalon*;
Let not thy angry thoughts be lay'd in blood,
In blood of him, that sometimes nourish'd thee,
And soften'd thy sweet heart with friendly love:
O, give me once again my father's sight,
My dearest father, and my princely sovereign;
That, shedding tears of blood before his face,
The ground may witness, and the heavens record,
My last submission found and full of ruth.

Joab.
Rebel to nature, hate to heav'n and earth,
Shall I give help to him that thirsts the soul
Of his dear father, and my sov'reign lord!
Now see, the Lord hath tangled in a tree
The health and glory of thy stubborn heart,
And made thy pride curb'd with a senseless plant:
Now, *Absalon*, how doth the Lord regard
The beauty, whereupon thy hope was built,
And which thou thought'st his grace did glory in?
Find'st thou not now, with fear of instant death,
That God affects not any painted shape,
Or goodly personage, when the virtuous soul
Is stuff'd with nought but pride and stubborness?
But, preach I to thee, while I should revenge
Thy cursed sin that staineth *Israel*,
And makes her fields blush with her children's blood?

Take that as part of thy deserved plague,
Which worthily no torment can inflict.
    Absalon.
O *Joab, Joab,* cruel, ruthless *Joab!*
Herewith thou wound'st thy kingly sov'reign's heart,
Whose heav'nly temper hates his children's blood,
And will be sick, I know, for *Absalon.*—
O my dear father, that thy melting eyes
Might pierce this thicket to behold thy son,
Thy dearest son, gor'd with a mortal dart!—
Yet, *Joab*, pity me; pity my father, *Joab*;
Pity his soul's distress that mourns my life,
And will be dead, I know, to hear my death.
    Joab.
If he were so remorseful of thy state,
Why sent he me against thee with the sword?
All *Joab* means to pleasure thee withal
Is, to despatch thee quickly of thy pain:
Hold, *Absalon, Joab's* pity is in this;
In this, proud *Absalon,* is *Joab's* love. [*He goes out.*
    Absalon.
Such love, such pity *Israel's* God send thee,
And for his love to *David* pity me.
Ah, my fear father! see, thy bowels bleed;
See death assault thy dearest *Absalon*;
See, pity, pardon, pray for *Absalon.*

   Enter five or six Soldiers.
    Soldier.
See, where the rebel in his glory hangs:—
Where is the virtue of thy beauty, *Absalon?*
Will any of us here now fear thy looks?
Or be in love with that thy golden hair,
Wherein was wrap'd rebellion 'gainst thy sire,
And cords prepar'd to stop thy father's breath?
Our captain *Joab* hath begun to us;
And here's an end to thee and all thy sins.—
             Come,

Come, let us take the beauteous rebel down,
And in some ditch amidst this darksome wood,
Bury his bulk beneath a heap of stones,
Whose stony heart did hunt his father's death.

Enter in triumph with drum and ensign,
Joab, Abisai, *and Soldiers to* Absalon.

Joab.
Well done, tall soldiers; take the traitor down,
And in this miry ditch inter his bones,
Covering his hateful breast with heaps of stones.
This shady thicket of dark *Ephraim*
Shall ever lower on his cursed grave;
Night ravens and owls shall ring his fatal knell,
And sit exclaiming on his damned soul;
There shall they heap their preys of carrion,
Till all his grave be clad with stinking bones,
That it may loath the sense of every man:
So shall his end breed horrour to his name,
And to his trait'rous fact eternal shame.   [*Exeunt.*

CHORUS.

O dreadful precedent of his just doom,
Whose holy heart is never touch'd with ruth
Of fickle beauty, or of glorious shapes,
But with the virtue of an upright soul,
Humble and zealous in his inward thoughts,
Though in his person loathsome and deformed.
Now, since this story lends us other store,
To make a third discourse of *David's* life,
Adding thereto his most renowned death,
And all their deaths, that at his death he judged,
Here end we this, and what here wants to please,
We will supply with treble willingness.

Trumpets

Trumpets sound: *Enter* Joab, Ahimaas, Cusay, Amasa, *with all the rest.*

Joab.
Soldiers of *Israel*, and ye sons of *Juda*,
That have contended in these irksome broils,
And rip'd old *Israel's* bowels with your swords;
The godless general of your stubborn arms
Is brought by *Israel's* helper to the grave,
A grave of shame, and scorn of all the tribes:
Now then, to save your honours from the dust,
And keep your bloods in temper by your bones,
Let *Joab's* ensign shrowd your manly heads,
Direct your eyes, your weapons, and your hearts,
To guard the life of *David* from his foes.
Errour hath mask'd your much too forward minds,
And you have sin'd against the chosen state,
Against his life, for whom your lives are bless'd,
And follow'd an usurper to the field;
In whose just death your deaths are threatened,
But *Joab* pities your disorder'd souls,
And therefore offers pardon, peace, and love,
To all that will be friendly reconcil'd
To *Israel's* weal, to *David*, and to heaven.—
Amasa, thou art leader of the host,
That under *Absalon* have rais'd their arms;
Then be a captain wise and politick,
Careful and loving for thy soldiers lives,
And lead them to this honourable league.

Amasa.
I will; at least, I'll do my best:
And for the gracious offer thou hast made
I give thee thanks, as much as for my head.—
Then, you deceiv'd poor souls of *Israel*,
Since now ye see the errours you incur'd,
With thanks and due submission be appeased;

And

And as ye see your captain's precedent,
Here cast we then our swords at *Joab's* feet,
Submitting with all zeal and reverence
Our goods and bodies to his gracious hands.
[*All stand up.*
          Joab.
Stand up, and take ye all your swords again;
David, and *Joab*, shall be blest herein.
          Abimaas.
Now let me go inform my lord the king
How God hath freed him from his enemies.
          Joab.
Another time, *Abimaas*, not now:—
But, *Cusay*, go thyself, and tell the king
The happy message of our good success.
          Cusay.
I will, my lord, and thank thee for thy grace.
[*Ex.* Cus.
          Abimaas.
What if thy servant should go too, my lord?
          Joab.
What news hast thou to bring since he is gone?
          Abimaas.
Yet do *Abimaas* so much content,
That he may run about so sweet a charge.
          Joab.
Run, if thou wilt; and peace be with thy steps:—
[*Ex.* Ahim.
Now follow, that you may salute the king
With humble hearts, and reconciled souls.
          Amasa.
We follow, *Joab*, to our gracious king;
And him our swords shall honour to our deaths.
[*Exeunt.*

David, Bethsabe, Salomon, Nathan, Adonia,
Chileab, *with their train.*

Bethsabe.
What means my lord, the lamp of *Israel*,
From whose bright eyes all eyes receive their light,
To dim the glory of his sweet aspects,
And paint his countenance with his heart's distress?
Why should his thoughts retain a sad conceit,
When every pleasure kneels before his throne,
And sues for sweet acceptance with his grace?
Take but your lute, and make the mountains dance,
Retrieve the sun's sphere, and restrain the clouds,
Give ears to trees, make savage lions tame,
Impose still silence to the loudest winds,
And fill the fairest day with foulest storms;
Then why should passions of much meaner power,
Bear head against the heart of *Israel?*
David.
Fair *Bethsabe*, thou mightst increase the strength
Of these thy arguments, drawn from my skill,
By urging thy sweet sight to my conceits,
Whose virtue ever serv'd for sacred balm
To cheer my pinings past all earthly joys:
But, *Bethsabe*, the daughter of the highest,
Whose beauty builds the towers of *Israel*,
She, that in chains of pearl and unicorn,
Leads at her train the ancient golden world,
The world that *Adam* held in paradise,
Whose breath refineth all infectious airs,
And makes the meadows smile at her repair;
She, she, my dearest *Bethsabe*,
Fair peace, the goddess of our graces here,
Is fled the streets of fair *Jerusalem*,
The fields of *Israel*, and the heart of *David*,
Leading my comforts in her golden chains,
Link'd to the life, and soul of *Absalon.*

Bethsabe.

Bethsabe.
Then is the pleasure of my sov'reign's heart
So wrap'd within the bosom of that son,
That *Salomon*, whom *Israel's* God affects,
And gave the name unto him for his love,
Should be no salve to comfort *David's* soul?
David.
Salomon, my love, is *David's* lord;
Our God hath nam'd him lord of *Israel:*
In him (for that, and since he is thy son,)
Must *David* needs be pleased at the heart;
And he shall surely sit upon my throne:
But *Absalon*, the beauty of my bones,
Fair *Absalon*, the counterfeit of love,
Sweet *Absalon*, the image of content,
Must claim a portion in his father's care,
And be in life and death king *David's* son.
Nathan.
Yet as my lord hath said, let *Salomon* reign,
Whom God in naming hath anointed king.
Now is he apt to learn th' eternal laws,
Whose knowledge being rooted in his youth
Will beautify his age with glorious fruits;
While *Absalon*, incens'd with graceless pride,
Usurps and stains the kingdom with his sin:
Let *Salomon* be made thy staff of age,
Fair *Israel's* rest, and honour of thy race.
David.
Tell me, my *Salomon*, wilt thou embrace
Thy father's precepts graved in thy heart,
And satisfy my zeal to thy renown,
With practice of such sacred principles
As shall concern the state of *Israel?*
Salomon.
My royal father, if the heav'nly zeal,
Which for my welfare feeds upon your soul,
Were not sustain'd with virtue of mine own,
If the sweet accents of your cheerful voice

Should

Should not each hour beat upon mine ears
As fweetly as the breath of heaven to him
That gafpeth fcorched with the fummer's fun;
I fhould be guilty of unpardoned fin,
Fearing the plague of heav'n, and fhame of earth:
But fince I vow myfelf to learn the fkill
And holy fecrets of his mighty hand
Whofe cunning tunes the mufick of my foul,
It would content me, father, firft to learn
How the eternal fram'd the firmament;
Which bodies lead their influence by fire;
And which are fill'd with hoary winter's ufe;
What fign is rainy; and what ftar is fair;
Why by the rules of true proportion
The year is ftill divided into months,
The months to days, the days to certain hours;
What fruitful race fhall fill the future world;
Or for what time fhall this round building ftand;
What magiftrates, what kings fhall keep in awe
Men's minds with bridles of th' eternal law.
     David.
 Wade not too far, my boy, in waves too deep:
The feeble eyes of our afpiring thoughts
Behold things prefent, and record things paft;
But things to come exceed our human reach,
And are not painted yet in angels eyes:
For thofe, fubmit thy fenfe, and fay — Thou power,
That now art framing of the future world,
Know'ft all to come, not by the courfe of heaven,
By frail conjectures of inferiour figns,
By monftrous floods, by flights and flocks of birds,
By bowels of a facrificed beaft,
Or by the figures of fome hidden art;
But by a true and natural prefage,
Laying the ground and perfect architect
Of all our actions now before thine eyes,
From *Adam* to the end of *Adam's* feed. —
O heav'n, protect my weaknefs with thy ftrength;
            So

So look on me that I may view thy face,
And see thefe fecrets written in thy brows. —
O *fun*, come dart thy rays upon my moon,
That now mine eyes, eclipfed to the earth,
May brightly be refin'd and fhine to heaven:
Transform me from this flefh, that I may live
Before my death, regenerate with thee. —
O thou great God, ravifh my earthly fprite,
That for the time a more than human fkill
May feed the organons of all my fenfe;
That, when I think, thy thoughts may be my guide,
And, when I fpeak, I may be made by choice
The perfect echo of thy heav'nly voice.
Thus fay, my fon, and thou fhalt learn them all.

Salomon.

A fecret fury ravifheth my foul,
Lifting my mind above her human bounds;
And, as the eagle, roufed from her ftand
With violent hunger tow'ring in the air,
Seizeth her feather'd prey, and thinks to feed,
But feeing then a cloud beneath her feet,
Lets fall the fowl, and is emboldened
With eyes intentive to bedare the fun,
And flyeth clofe unto his ftately fphere;
So *Salomon* mounted on the burning wings
Of zeal divine, lets fall his mortal food,
And cheers his fenfes with celeftial air,
Treads in the golden ftarry labyrinth,
And holds his eyes fix'd on *Jehova's* brows.
Good father, teach me further what to do.

Nathan.

See, *David*, how his haughty fpirit mounts,
Even now of height to wield a diadem;
Then make him promife, that he may fucceed,
And reft old *Ifrael's* bones from broils of war.

David.

Nathan, thou prophet, fprung from *Jeffe's* root,
I promife thee, and lovely *Bethfabe*,
My *Salomon* fhall govern after me.

Bethfabe.

Bethsabe.
He that hath touch'd thee with this righteous thought
Preserve the harbour of thy thoughts in peace.

Enter Messenger.

Messenger.
My lord, thy servants of the watch have seen
One running hitherward from forth the wars.
David.
If he be come alone, he bringeth news.
Messenger.
Another hath thy servant seen, my lord,
Whose running much resembles *Sadoc's* son.
David.
He is a good man, and good tidings brings.

Enter Ahimaas.

Ahimaas.
Peace and content be with my lord the king,
Whom *Israel's* God hath bless'd with victory.
David.
Tell me, *Ahimaas*, lives my *Absalon*?
Ahimaas.
I saw a troop of soldiers gathered,
But know not what the tumult might import.
David.
Stand by, until some other may inform
The heart of *David* with a happy truth.

Enter Cusay.

Cusay.
Happiness and honour live with *David's* soul,
Whom God hath bless'd with conquest of his foes.
David.
But, *Cusay*, lives the young man *Absalon*?
Cusay.

DAVID AND BETHSABE.

Cusay.
The stubborn enemies to *David's* peace,
And all that cast their darts against his crown,
Fare ever, like the young man *Absalon!*
For as he rid the woods of *Ephraim,*
Which fought for thee as much as all thy men,
His hair was tangled in a shady oak;
And hanging there, by *Joab* and his men,
Sustain'd the stroke of well deserved death.

David.
Hath *Absalon* sustain'd the stroke of death?
Die, *David,* for the death of *Absalon,*
And make these cursed news the bloody darts,
That through his bowels rip thy wretched breast.
Hence, *David,* walk the solitary woods,
And in some cedar's shade, the thunder flew,
And fire from heav'n hath made his branches black,
Sit mourning the decease of *Absalon;*
Against the body of that blasted plant
In thousand shivers break thy ivory lute,
Hanging thy stringless harp upon his boughs,
And through the hollow sapless sounding trunk
Bellow the torments that perplex thy soul.
There let the winds sit sighing till they burst;
Let tempest, muffled with a cloud of pitch,
Threaten the forests with her hellish face,
And, mounted fiercely on her iron wings,
Rend up the wretched engine by the roots
That held my dearest *Absalon* to death.
Then let them toss my broken lute to heaven,
Even to his hands that beats me with the strings,
To show how sadly his poor shepherd sings.
[*He goes to his pavilion and sits close awhile.*
Bethsabe.
Die, *Bethsabe,* to see thy *David* mourn,
To hear his tunes of anguish and of hell;
O, help my *David,* help thy *Bethsabe,*
[*She kneels down.*
Whose

Whose heart is pierced with thy breathy swords,
And bursts with burden of ten thousand griefs.
Now sit thy sorrows sucking of my blood;
O, that it might be poison to their powers,
And that their lips might draw my bosom dry,
So *David's* love might ease him, though she die.
     Nathan.
 These violent passions come not from above;
David and *Bethsabe* offend the Highest,
To mourn in this immeasurable sort.
     David.
 O *Absalon, Absalon,* o my son, my son!
'Would God that I had died for *Absalon!*
But he is dead; ah, dead; *Absalon* is dead:
And *David* lives to die for *Absalon.*
 [*He looks forth, and at the end sits close again.*

  Enter Joab, Abisai, Ithay, *with their train.*
     Joab.
Why lies the queen so prostrate on the ground?
Why is this company so tragick hued?
Why is the king now absent from his men,
And marcheth not in triumph through the gates?—
    [*He unfolds the pavilion.*
David, awake; if sleep have shut thine eyes,
Sleep of affection, that thou canst not see
The honour offer'd to the victor's head:
Joab brings conquest, pierced on his spear,
And joy from all the tribes of *Israel.*
     David.
 Thou man of blood, thou sepulchre of death,
Whose marble breast intombs my bowels quick,
Did I not charge thee, nay entreat thy hand
Even for my sake to spare my *Absalon?*
And hast thou now in spite of *David's* health,
And scorn to do my heart some happiness,
Giv'n him the sword, and spilt his purple soul?
     Joab.

DAVID AND BETHSABE.

Joab.
What, irks it *David*, that he victor breathes,
That *Juda*, and the fields of *Israel*,
Should cleanse their faces from their children's blood?
What, art thou weary of thy royal rule?
Is *Israel's* throne a serpent in thine eyes,
And he that set thee there, so far from thanks,
That thou must curse his servant for his sake?
Hast thou not said, that, as the morning light,
The cloudless morning, so should be thine house,
And not as flowers by the brightest rain,
Which grow up quickly, and as quickly fade?
Hast thou not said, the wicked are as thorns,
That cannot be preserved with the hand,
And that the man shall touch them, must be arm'd
With coats of iron, and garments made of steel,
Or with the shaft of a defenced spear?
And art thou angry he is now cut off,
That led the guiltless swarming to their deaths,
And was more wicked than an host of men?
Advance thee from thy melancholy den,
And deck thy body with thy blissful robes,
Or, by the Lord that sways the heav'n I swear,
I'll lead thine armies to another king,
Shall cheer them for their princely chivalry;
And not sit daunted, frowning in the dark,
When his fair looks, with oil and wine refresh'd,
Should dart into their bosoms gladsome beams,
And fill their stomachs with triumphant feasts,
That when elsewhere stern war shall sound his trump,
And call another battle to the field,
Fame still may bring thy valiant soldiers home,
And for their service happily confess
She wanted worthy trumps to sound their prowess:
Take thou this course and live, refuse and die.
Abisai.
Come, brother, let him sit there till he sink;
Some other shall advance the name of *Joab*.
[*Offers to go out.*
Bethsabe.

Bethsabe.
O, stay, my lords, stay; *David* mourns no more,
But riseth to give honour to your acts. [*Stay.*
[*He riseth up.*
David.
Then happy art thou, *David's* fairest son,
That, freed from the yoke of earthly toils,
And sequester'd from sense of human sins,
Thy soul shall joy the sacred cabinet
Of those divine ideas, that present
Thy changed spirit with a heav'n of bliss.
Then thou art gone; ay, thou art gone, my son;
To heaven, I hope, my *Absalon* is gone:
Thy soul there plac'd in honour of the saints,
Or angels clad with immortality,
Shall reap a sevenfold grace for all thy griefs;
Thy eyes, now no more eyes, but shining stars,
Shall deck the flaming heav'ns with novel lamps;
There shalt thou taste the drink of *Seraphins*,
And cheer thy feelings with archangels food;
Thy day of rest, thy holy sabbath day
Shall be eternal; and, the curtain drawn,
Thou shalt behold thy sov'reign face to face,
With wonder knit in triple unity,
Unity infinite and innumerable.—
Courage, brave captains; *Joab's* tale hath stir'd,
And made the suit of *Israel* prefer'd.
Joab.
Bravely resolv'd, and spoken like a king:
Now may old *Israel*, and his daughters sing. [*Exeunt.*

THE
TRAGEDY
OF
SOLIMAN AND PERSEDA:

WHEREIN IS LAY'D OPEN,

LOVE'S CONSTANCY,

FORTUNE'S INCONSTANCY,

AND

DEATH'S TRIUMPH.

THE TRAGEDY OF SOLIMAN AND PERSEDA,

— *is given from Mr.* Garrick's *copy, printed by* Edward Allde, 1599. *The author having concealed his name, we cannot pronounce by whom it was written. Though, might the editor be allowed to indulge a conjecture, he would ascribe it to* Kyd, *as it carries with it many internal marks of that author's manner of composition: the plan is similar to that of* The Spanish Tragedy, *and the same phrases frequently occur in both. It is farther observable, that in* The Spanish Tragedy *the story of* Eraftus *and* Perseda *is introduced by* Hieronimo; *in order, it should seem, to bespeak the attention of the audience to a more regular, and a more perfect representation of their tragical catastrophe.* Shakespeare *has frequently quoted passages out of this play, as the reader will occasionally observe. It is not divided into acts; at least, they are not particularly marked: but there is no doubt, that the author intended, each act should close with the* chorus; *and it is therefore divided accordingly.*

DRAMATIS

DRAMATIS PERSONÆ.

SOLIMAN, Emperor of the Turks.
HALEB, } his brothers.
AMURATH,
BRUSOR, his general.
Janisaries.
Lord Marshall.
PHILIPPO, Governour of Rhodes.
Prince of CYPRUS.[1]
ERASTUS, in love with PERSEDA.
GUELPIO, } his friends.
JULIO,
PISTON, his servant.
FERDINANDO, in love with LUCINA.
BASILISCO, a vainglorious knight.
A captain.
Knights.
Witnesses.
A Messenger.

PERSEDA, beloved of ERASTUS.
LUCINA, beloved of FERDINANDO.
Ladies.

CHORUS: Love, Fortune, Death.

[1] *Cipris*, passim.

THE
TRAGEDY
OF
SOLIMAN AND PERSEDA.

ACT I.

Enter Love, Fortune, Death.

Love.

WHAT, *Death*, and *Fortune* crofs the way of *Love?*
  Fortune.
Why, what is *Love,* but *Fortune's* tennis-ball?
  Death.
Nay, what are you both, but fubjects unto *Death?*
And I command you to forbear this place;
For here the mouth of fad *Melpomene*
Is wholly bent to tragedy's difcourfe:
And what are tragedies, but acts of death?
Here means the wrathful mufe, in feas of tears,
And loud laments, to tell a difmal tale;
A tale, wherein fhe lately hath beftow'd
The hufky humour of her bloody quill,
And now for tables takes her to her tongue.

Love.

THE TRAGEDY OF

Love.

Why thinks *Death*, *Love* knows not the hiſtory
Of brave *Eraſtus*, and his *Rhodian* dame?
'Twas I that made their hearts conſent to love;
And therefore come I now as fitteſt perſon
To ſerve for chorus to this tragedy:
Had I not been, they had not dy'd ſo ſoon.

Death.

Had I not been, they had not dy'd ſo ſoon.

Fortune.

Nay then, it ſeems, you both do miſs the mark:
Did not I change long love to ſudden hate;
And then rechange their hatred into love;
And then from love deliver them to death?
Fortune is chorus; *Love*, and *Death*, be gone.

Death.

I tell thee, *Fortune*, and thee, wanton *Love*,
I will not down to everlaſting night,
Till I have moraliz'd this tragedy,
Whoſe chiefeſt actor was my ſable dart.

Love.

Nor will I up unto the brightſome ſphere
From whence I ſprung, till in the chorus' place
I make it known to you and to the world,
What intereſt *Love* hath in tragedies.

Fortune.

Nay then, though *Fortune* have delight in change,
I'll ſtay my flight, and ceaſe to turn my wheel,
Till I have ſhown by demonſtration,
What int'reſt I have in a tragedy:
Tuſh! *Fortune* can do more than *Love*, or *Death*.

Love.

Why ſtay we then? let's give the actors leave;
And, as occaſion ſerves, make our return.   [*Exeunt.*

Enter

Enter Eraftus, *and* Perfeda.

Eraftus.
Why when, *Perfeda?* wilt thou not aſſure me,
But ſhall I, like a maftleſs ſhip at ſea,
Go ev'ry way, and not the way I would?
My love hath lafted from mine infancy,
And ftill increaſed, as I grew myſelf.
When did *Perfeda* paftime in the ftreets,
But her *Eraftus* over-ey'd her ſport?
When didſt thou, with thy ſampler in the ſun,
Sit ſewing with thy feres, but I was by,
Marking thy lily hand's dexterity;
Comparing it to twenty gracious things?
When didſt thou ſing a note that I could hear,
But I have fram'd a ditty to the tune,
Figuring *Perfeda* twenty kind of ways?
When didſt thou go to church on holydays,
But I have waited on thee to and fro,
Marking my times, as falcons watch their flight?
When I have miſs'd thee, how I have lamented,
As if my thoughts had been aſſured true.
Thus in my youth: now ſince I grew a man,
I have perfevered to let thee know
The meaning of my true heart's conftancy.
Then be not nice, *Perfeda*, as women wont
To hafty lovers whoſe fancy ſoon is fled;
My love is of a long continuance,
And merits not a ftranger's recompence.
Perfeda.
Enough, *Eraftus*, thy *Perfeda* knows:
She whom thou wouldſt have thine, *Eraftus*, knows.
Eraftus.
Nay, my *Perfeda* knows, and then 'tis well.
Perfeda.
Ay, watch you vantages? thine be it then,
I have forgot the reft, but that's the eſſect;
Which to effect, accept this carcanet:

My

My grandam on her death-bed gave it me,
And there, ev'n there I vow'd unto myself,
To keep the same, until my wand'ring eye
Should find a harbour for my heart to dwell.
Ev'n in thy breast do I elect my rest;
Let in my heart to keep thine company.
                Erastus.
  And, sweet *Perseda*, accept this ring
To equal it, receive my heart to boot;
It is no boot, for that was thine before:
And far more welcome is this change to me,
Than sunny days to naked savages,
Or news of pardon to a wretch condemn'd,
That waiteth for the fearful stroke of death:
As careful will I be to keep this chain,
As doth the mother keep her children
From water-pits, or falling in the fire.
Over mine armour will I hang this chain;
And, when long combat makes my body faint,
The sight of this shall show *Perseda's* name,
And add fresh courage to my fainting limbs.
This day the eager *Turk* of *Tripolis*,
The knight of *Malta*, honour'd for his worth,
And he that's titled by the golden spur,
The *Moor* upon his hot *Barbarian* horse,
The fiery *Spaniard*, bearing in his face
The impress of a noble warriour,
The sudden *Frenchman*, and the big-bon'd *Dane*,
And *English* archers, hardy men at arms,
'Yclepped lions of the western world;
Each one of these approved combatants,
Assembled from sev'ral corners of the world,
Are hither come to try their force in arms,
In honour of the prince of *Cyprus*' nuptials.
Amongst these worthies will *Erastus* troop,
Though like a gnat amongst a hive of bees:
Know me by this thy precious carcanet;

And,

And, if I thrive in valour as the glafs,
That takes the funbeams burning with his force,
I'll be the glafs, and thou that heav'nly fun,
From whence I'll borrow what I do atchieve:
And, fweet *Perfeda*, unnoted though I be,
Thy beauty yet fhall make me known ere night.
Perfeda.
Young flips are never graff'd in windy days;
Young fcholars never enter'd with the rod.
Ah, my *Eraftus*, there are *Europe's* knights,
That carry honour graven in their helms,
And they muft win it dear that win it thence:
Let not my beauty prick thee to thy bane,
Better fit ftill than rife and overta'en.
Eraftus.
Counfel me not, for my intent is fworn,
And be my fortune as my love deferves.
Perfeda.
So be thy fortune as thy features ferve,
And then *Eraftus* lives without compare.

Enter a Meffenger.

Here comes a *Meffenger* to hafte me hence.—
I know your meffage, hath the princefs fent for me?
Meffenger.
She hath, and defires you to confort her to the triumphs.

Enter Pifton.
Pifton.
Who faw my mafter?—O, fir, are you here?
The prince, and all the outlandifh gentlemen,
Are ready to go to the triumphs; they ftay for you.
Eraftus.
Go, firrah, bid my men bring my horfe, and a dozen ftaves.

Pifton.

Piston.
You shall have your horses, and two dozen of staves.
[*Exit* Piston.
Erastus.
Wish me good hap, *Perseda*, and I'll win
Such glory, as no time shall ere rase out,
Or end the period of my youth in blood.
Perseda.
Such fortune as the good *Andromache*
Wish'd valiant *Hector* wounded [1] with the *Greeks*,
I wish *Erastus* in his maiden wars:
O'ercome with valour these high-minded knights,
As with thy virtue thou hast conquer'd me.
Heav'ns hear my hearty prayer, and it effect. [*Exeunt*

Enter Philippo, *the Prince of* Cyprus, Basilisco,
and all the Knights.
Philippo.
Brave knights of *Christendom*, and *Turkish* both,
Assembled here in thirsty honour's cause,
To be enrolled in the brass-leav'd book
Of never wasting perpetuity,
Put lamb-like mildness to your lions strength,
And be our tilting like two brothers sports,
That exercise their war with friendly blows.—
Brave prince of *Cyprus*, and our son-in-law,
Welcome these worthies by their sev'ral countries;
For in thy honour hither are they come,
To grace thy nuptials with their deeds at arms.
Ciprus.
First, welcome, thrice renowned *Englishmen*,
Graced by thy country, but ten times more
By thy approved valour in the field;
Upon the onset of the enemy,
What is thy motto, when thou spur'st thy horse?

---

1 *wounded* perhaps for *wound*, the preterite of *wind*
i. e. encircled. In the margin of Q°. is written, "*rounded*
L. T."
Englishman

SOLIMAN AND PERSEDA.

Englishman.
In *Scotland* was I made a knight at arms,
Where for my country's caufe I charg'd my lance:
In *France* I took the ftandard from the king,
And give the flower of *Gallia* in my creſt:
Againſt the lightfoot *Iriſh* have I ferv'd,
And in my ſkin bear tokens of their kerns. 1
Our word of courage all the world hath heard,
Saint GEORGE *for* ENGLAND, *and faint* GEORGE *for me!*

Ciprus.
Like welcome unto thee, fair knight of *France,*
Well fam'd thou art for difcipline in war:
Upon th' encounter of thine enemy,
What is thy mot, renowned knight of *France?*

Frenchman.
In *Italy* I put my knighthood on,
Where in my ſhirt but with a ſingle rapier,
I combated a *Roman* much renown'd,
His weapon's point empoiſon'd for my bane,
And yet my ſtars did bode my victory.
Saint DENNIS *is for* FRANCE, *and that for me.*

Ciprus.
Welcome, *Caſtilian,* too amongſt the reſt;
For fame doth found thy valour with the reſt:
Upon the firſt encounter of thy foe,
What is thy word of courage, brave man of *Spain?*

Spaniard.
At fourteen years of age was I made knight,
When twenty thouſand *Spaniards* were in field,
What time a daring *Rutter* made a challenge,
To change a bullet with our fwift-flight ſhot;
And I with ſingle heed and level hit
The haughty challenger, and ſtruck him dead:
The golden fleece is that we cry upon,
And JAQUES, JAQUES, *is the* SPANIARD'S *choice.*

1 *ſkenes.*

Cyprus.

THE TRAGEDY OF

Ciprus.
Next, welcome unto thee, renowned *Turk*,
Not for thy lay, but for thy worth in arms:
Upon the first brave of thine enemy,
What is thy noted word of charge, brave *Turk?*
Brusor.
Against the *Sophy* in three pitched fields,
Under the conduct of great *Soliman*,
Have I been chief commander of an host,
And put the flint-heart *Persians* to the sword;
The desert plains of *Africk* have I stain'd
With blood of *Moors*, and there in three set battles fought,
March'd conqueror through *Asia*,
Along the coasts held by the *Pontinguize*;
Ev'n to the verge of gold, aboarding [1] *Spain*,
Hath *Brusor* led a valiant troop of *Turks*,
And made some *Christians* kneel to *Mahomet:*
Him we adore, and in his name I cry,
MAHOMET *for me and* SOLIMAN!
Ciprus.
Now, signior *Basilisco*, you we know,
And therefore give not you a stranger's welcome;
You are a *Rutter* born in *Germany:*
Upon the first encounter of your foe,
What is your brave upon the enemy?
Basilisco.
I fight not with my tongue; this is my oratrix.
            [*Laying his hand upon his sword.*
Ciprus.
Why, signior *Basilisco*, is it a she sword?
Basilisco.
Ay, and so are all blades with me: behold my instance;
Perdie, each female is the weaker vessel,
And the vigour of this arm infringeth
The temper of any blade, quoth my assertion,
And thereby gather, that this blade,

---

[1] *golde, aboording — aboarding*, coming to the coast. Fr. *Aboarder.*   Being

Being approved weaker than this limb,
May very well bear a feminine epitheton.
     Ciprus.
'Tis well prov'd; but what's the word that glories your country?
     Basilisco.
Sooth to say, the earth is my country,
As the air to the fowl, or the marine moisture
To the red-gill'd fish: I repute myself no coward;
For humility shall mount: I keep no table
To character my fore-passed conflicts.
As I remember, there happened a sore drought
In some part of *Belgia*, that the juicy grass
Was fear'd with the Sun-God's element:
I held it policy to put the men-children
Of that climate to the sword,
That the mothers tears might relieve the parched earth.
The men dy'd, the women wept, and the grass grew;
Else had my *Friesland* horse perished,
Whose loss would have more grieved me,
Than the ruin of that whole country.
Upon a time in *Ireland* I fought
On horseback with an hundred kerns,
From *Titan's* eastern uprise to his western downfal;
Insomuch that my steed began to faint:
I, conjecturing the cause to be want of water, dismounted,
In which place there was no such element;
Enraged therefore, with this scimitar,
All on foot, like an *Herculean* offspring,
Endured some three or four hours combat,
In which process, my body distill'd such dewy showers of sweat,
That from the warlike wrinckles of my front
My palfrey cool'd his thirst.
My mercy in conquest is equal with my manhood in fight,
The tear of an infant hath been the ransome of a conquer'd city;
         Whereby

Whereby I purchafed the furname of *Pitiez a domant.*
Rough words blow my choler,
As the wind doth *Mulciber's* workhoufe:
I have no word, becaufe no country,
Each place is my habitation;
Therefore each country's word mine to pronounce. —
Princes, what would you? I have feen much, heard more,
But done moft: to be brief, he that will try me,
Let him waft me with his arm; I am his for fome five
  lances:
Although it go againft my ftars to jeft,
Yet to gratulate this benign prince,
I will fupprefs my condition.
     Philippo.
 He is beholding to you greatly, fir: —
Mount, ye brave lordings, forwards to the tilt;
Myfelf will cenfure of your chivalry,
And with impartial eyes behold your deeds: —
Forward, brave ladies, place you to behold
The fair demeanor of thefe warlike knights. [*Exeunt.*

    Manet Bafilifco.

     Bafilifco.
 I am melancholy: an humour of *Venus* beleaguereth me.
I have rejected with contemptible frowns
The fweet glances of many amorous girls; or, rather,
  ladies:
But, certes, I am now captivated with the reflecting eye
Of that admirable comet *Perfeda.*
I will place her to behold my triumphs,
And do wonders in her fight:
O heav'ns! fhe comes, accompanied with a child,
Whofe chin bears no impreffion of manhood,
Not an hair, not an excrement.

            Enter

SOLIMAN AND PERSEDA.

Enter Eraſtus, Perſeda, *and* Piſton.
Eraſtus.
My ſweet *Perſeda!*   [*Exeunt* Eraſt. *and* Perſ.
Baſiliſco.
Peace, infant; thou blaſphemeſt.
Piſton.
You are deceived, ſir; he ſwore not.
Baſiliſco.
I tell thee, jeſter, he did worſe; he call'd that lady, his.
Piſton.
Jeſter! O *extempore, o flores.*
Baſiliſco.
O harſh, uneducate, illiterate peaſant!
Thou abuſeſt the phraſe of the *Latin.*
Piſton.
By gods fiſh, friend, take you the *Latins* part, I'll abuſe you too.
Baſiliſco.
What, *ſaunce* dread of our indignation?
Piſton.
Saunce? what language is that?
I think, thou art a word-maker by thine occupation.
Baſiliſco.
Ay? termeſt thou me of an occupation?
Nay then, this fiery humour of choler is ſuppreſs'd
By the thought of love. — Fair lady, —
Piſton.
Now, by my troth, ſhe is gone.
Baſiliſco.
Ay? hath the infant tranſported her hence?
He ſaw my anger figured in my brow,
And at his beſt advantage ſtole away;
But I will follow for revenge.
Piſton.
Nay, but hear you, ſir;
I muſt talk with you before you go.
          [Piſton *gets on his back, and pulls him down.*
Vol. II.   O   *Baſiliſco.*

Basilisco.
O, if thou be'st magnanimous, come before me.
Piston.
Nay, if thou be'st a right warriour, get from under me.
Basilisco.
What, wouldst thou have me a *Typhon*,
To bear up *Pelion*, or *Ossa?*
Piston.
Typhon me no *Typhons*,
But swear upon my dudgeon dagger,*
Not to go till I give thee leave;
But stay with me, and look upon the tilters.
Basilisco.
O, thou seekest thereby to dim my glory.
Piston.
I care not for that; wilt thou not swear?
Basilisco.
O, I swear, I swear.
[*He sweareth him on his dagger.*
Piston.
By the contents of this blade,—
Basilisco.
By the contents of this blade,—
Piston.
I the aforesaid *Basilisco*,—
Basilisco.
I the aforesaid *Basilisco*,—
Knight, good fellow; knight, knight.
Piston.
Knave, good fellow, knave, knave:
Will not offer to go from the side of *Piston*,—
Basilisco.
Will not offer to go from the side of *Piston*,—
Piston.
Without the leave of the said *Piston* obtained.
Basilisco.
Without the leave of the said *Piston* licensed,
Obtain'd, and granted.

* *See note, page* 29.

Piston.

SOLIMAN AND PERSEDA.

Piston.
Enjoy thy life, and live; I give it thee.
Basilisco.
I enjoy my life at thy hands, I confess it:
I am up; but that I am religious in mine oath,—
Piston.
What would you do, sir? what would you do?
Will you up the ladder, sir, and see the tilting?
  [*Then they go up the ladders, and they sound within to the first course.*
Basilisco.
Better a dog fawn on me than bark.
Piston.
Now, sir, how lik'st thou this course?
Basilisco.
Their lances were couch'd too high,
And their steeds ill-born.
Piston.
It may be so, it may be so:
    [*Sound to the second course.*
Now, sir, how like you this course?
Basilisco.
Pretty, pretty, but not famous;
Well for a learner, but not for a warriour.
Piston.
By my faith, methought it was excellent.
Basilisco.
Ay, in the eye of an infant a peacock's tail is glorious.
    [*Sound to the third course.*
Piston.
O, well ran; the bay horse with the blue tail
And the silver knight are both down:
By cock and pie, and mouse foot,
The *Englishman* is a fine knight.
Basilisco.
Now, by the marble face of the welkin,
He is a brave warriour.

THE TRAGEDY OF

Piston.
What an oath is there! fie upon thee, extortioner.
Basilisco.
Now comes in the infant that courts my mistress.
                           [*Sound to the fourth course.*
O that my lance were in my rest,
And my beaver clos'd for this encounter.
Piston.
O, well ran; my master hath overthrown the *Turk*.
Basilisco.
Now fie upon the *Turk*;
To be dismounted by a child, it vexeth me.
                           [*Sound to the fifth course.*
Piston.
O, well ran master; he hath overthrown the *Frenchman*.
Basilisco.
It is the fury of his horse, not the strength of his arm.
I would thou wouldst remit my oath,
That I might assail thy master.
Piston.
I give thee leave, go to thy destruction:
But, sirra, where's thy horse?
Basilisco.
Why my page stands holding him by the bridle.
Piston.
Well, go mount thee, go.
Basilisco.
I go, and fortune guide my lance.   [*Exit* Basilisco.
Piston.
Take the braggin'st knave in *Christendom* with thee.—
Truly, I am sorry for him:
He just like a knight! he'll just like a jade.
It is a world to hear the fool prate and brag;
He will jet as if it were a goose on a green:
He goes many times supperless to bed,
And yet he takes physick to make him lean.
Last night he was bidden to a gentlewoman's to supper,
And, because he would not be put to carve,

He

He wore his hand in a scarf, and said,— he was wounded:
He wears a colour'd lath in his scabbard,
And, when 'twas found upon him, he said, — he was
  wrathful,
He might not wear iron: he wears civet,
And, when it was ask'd him where he had that musk,
He said, — all his kindred smelt so.
Is not this a counterfeit fool?
Well; I'll up, and see how he speeds.
                              [*Sound the sixth course.*
Now, by the faith of a 'squire, he is a very faint knight;
Why, my master hath overthrown him
And his curtal both to the ground:
I shall have old laughing,
It will be better than the fox in the hole for me.

Sound. *Enter* Philippo, *Prince of* Ciprus, Erastus,
    Ferdinando, Lucina, *and all the Knights.*
                Ciprus.
Brave gentlemen, by all your free consents,
This knight unknown hath best demean'd himself:
According to the proclamation made,
The prize, and honour of the day is his; —
But now unmask thyself, that we may see,
What warlike wrinkles time hath character'd,
With age's print upon thy warlike face.
                Englishman.
Accord to his request, brave man at arms,
And let me see the face that vanquish'd me.
                Frenchman.
Unmask thyself, thou well approved knight.
                Turk.
I long to see thy face, brave warriour.
                Lucina.
Nay, valiant sir, we may not be deny'd;
Fair ladies should be coy to show their faces,
Lest that the sun should tan them with his beams:
I'll be your page this once for to disarm you.   *Pistis.*

THE TRAGEDY OF

Piston.
That's the reason, that he shall help
Your husband to arm his head.
O, the policy of this age is wonderful.
Philippo.
What, young *Erastus!* is it possible?
Ciprus.
Erastus, be thou honour'd for this deed.
Englishman.
So young, and of such good accomplishment!
Thrive, fair beginner, as this time doth promise,
In virtue, valour, and all worthiness:
Give me thy hand, I vow myself thy friend.
Erastus.
Thanks, worthy sir, whose favourable hand
Hath enter'd such a youngling in the war;—
And thanks unto you all, brave worthy sirs;
Impose me task, how I may do you good;
Erastus will be dutiful in all.
Philippo.
Leave protestations now, and let us hie
To tread *lavolta,* that is womens walk;
There spend we the remainder of the day.
[*Exeunt.* Manet *Ferd,*
Ferdinando.
Though over-born, and foiled in my course,
Yet have I partners in mine infamy.
'Tis wondrous, that so young a toward warriour,
Should bide the shock of such approved knights,
As he this day hath match'd, and mated too:
But virtue should not envy good desert,
Therefore, *Erastus,* happy; laud thy fortune:
But my *Lucina,* how she chang'd her colour,
When at th' encounter I did lose a stirrop;
Hanging her head, as partner of my shame.
Therefore now will I go visit her,
And please her with this carcanet of worth,
Which by good fortune I have found to-day;
When valour fails, then must gold make the way. [*Exit.*

Enter Basilisco *riding of a mule.*
Basilisco.
O cursed fortune, enemy to fame,
Thus to disgrace thy honoured name,
By overthrowing him that far hath spread thy praise,
Beyond the course of *Titan's* burning rays.—

Enter Piston.

Page, set aside the gesture of my enemy;
Give him a fidler's fee, and send him packing.
Piston.
Ho, God save you, sir; have you burst your shin?
Basilisco.
Ay, villain; I have broken my shin bone,
My back bone, my channel bone, and my thigh bone,
Beside two dozen of small inferiour bones.
Piston.
A shrewd loss, by my faith, sir:
But where's your courser's tail?
Basilisco.
He lost the same in service.
Piston.
There was a hot piece of service where he lost his tail;
But how chance, his nose is slit?
Basilisco.
For presumption, for covering the emperor's mare.
Piston.
Marry, a foul fault; but why are his ears cut?
Basilisco.
For neighing in the emperor's court.
Piston.
Why then, thy horse hath been a colt in his time.
Basilisco.
True, thou hast said.
O, touch not the cheek of my palfrey,
Lest he dismount me while my wounds are green;
Page,

Page, run, bid the furgeon bring his incifion:
Yet ftay, I'll ride along with thee myfelf.   [*Exit*,
    Pifton.
And I'll bear you company.
    [Pifton *getteth up on his afs, and rideth with him*
       to the door, and meeteth the Crier.

Enter the Crier.

Come, firra, let me fee how finely you'll cry this chain.
    Crier.
Why, what was it worth?
    Pifton.
It was worth more than thou and all thy kin are worth.
    Crier.
It may be fo; but what muft he have that finds it?
    Pifton.
Why, a hundred crowns.
    Crier.
Why then, I'll have ten for the crying of it.
    Pifton.
Ten crowns! and had but fixpence
For crying a little wench of thirty years old and upwards,
That had loft herfelf betwixt a tavern and a baudy houfe.
    Crier.
Ay, that was a wench, and this is gold,
She was poor, but this is rich.
    Pifton.
Why then, by this reck'ning, a hackney-man
Should have ten fhillings for horfing a gentlewoman,
Where he hath but ten pence of a beggar.
    Crier.
Why, and reafon good;
Let them pay, that beft may,
As the lawyers ufe their rich clients,
When they let the poor go under *forma pauperis.*

                                          Pifton.

Piston.
Why then, I pray thee, cry the chain for me
Sub forma pauperis:
For money goes very low with me at this time.
Crier.
Ay, sir, but your master is, though you be not.
Piston.
Ay, but he must not know, that thou cry'st the chain
   for me:
I do but use thee to save me a labour,
That am to make inquiry after it.
Crier.
Well, sir, you'll see me consider'd, will you not?
Piston.
Ay, marry, will I; why, what lighter payment
Can there be, than consideration?
Crier.
O yes.

Enter Erastus.

Erastus.
How now, sirra? what are you crying?
Crier.
A chain, sir, a chain, that your man bad me cry.
Erastus.
Get you away, sirra, I advise you,
Meddle with no chains of mine. —   [*Exit* Crier.
You paltry knave, how durst thou be so bold
To cry the chain, when I bid thou shouldst not?
Did I not bid thee only underhand,
Make privy inquiry for it through the town,
Lest publick rumour might advertise her,
Whose knowledge were to me a second death?
Piston.
Why, would you have me run up and down the town,
And my shoes are done?
Erastus.
What you want in shoes, I'll give you in blows.
Piston.

Piston.
I pray you, sir, hold your hands,
And as I am an honest man,
I'll do the best I can to find your chain. [*Exit* Piston.
Erastus.
Ah treacherous *Fortune*, enemy to *Love*,
Didst thou advance me for my greater fall?
In dallying war I lost my chiefest peace;
In hunting after praise I lost my love,
And in love's shipwreck will my life miscarry:
Take thou the honour, and give me the chain,
Wherein was link'd the sum of my delight.
When she deliver'd me the carcanet,
Keep it, quoth she, as thou wouldst keep myself.
I kept it not, and therefore she is lost;
And lost with her is all my happiness;
And loss of happiness is worse than death.
Come therefore, gentle *Death*, and ease my grief,
Cut short what malice *Fortune* misintends;
But stay awhile, good *Death*, and let me live;
Time may restore what *Fortune* took from me:
Ah, no; great losses seldom are restored.
What, if my chain shall never be restored?
My innocence shall clear my negligence.
Ah, but my love is ceremonious,
And looks for justice at her lover's hand:
Within forc'd furrows of her clouding brow,
As storms that fall amid a sunshine day,
I read her just desires, and my decay. [*Exit.*

Enter Soliman, Haleb, Amurath, *and Janisaries.*
Soliman.
I long, till *Brusor* be return'd from *Rhodes*,
To know how he hath born him 'gainst the *Christians*,
That are assembled there to try their valour;
But more, to be well assured by him,
How *Rhodes* is fenc'd, and how I best may lay
My never failing siege to win that plot: For,

For, by the holy alcoran I swear,
I'll call my soldiers home from *Persia*,
And let the sophy breathe, and from the *Russian* broils
Call home my hardy dauntless janisaries,
And from the other skirts of christendom,
Call home my bashaws, and my men of war,
And so beleaguer *Rhodes* by sea and land.
That key will serve to open all the gates;
Through which our passage cannot find a stop,
Till it have prick'd the heart of christendom,
Which now that paltry island keeps from scath. —
Say, brother *Amurath*, — and, *Haleb*, say,
What think you of our resolution?
                Amurath.
  Great *Soliman*, heav'n's only substitute,
And earth's commander under *Mahomet*,
So counsel I, as thou thyself hast said.
                Haleb.
  Pardon me, dread sov'reign, I hold it not
Good policy, to call your forces home
From *Persia* and *Polonia*, bending them
Upon a paltry isle of small defence:
A common press of base superfluous *Turks*
May soon be levied for so slight a task.
Ah, *Soliman*, whose name hath shak'd thy foes,
As wither'd leaves with autumn thrown down,
Fog not thy glory with so foul eclipse;
Let not thy soldiers found a base retire,
Till *Persia* stoop and thou be conqueror.
What scandal were it to thy mightiness,
After so many valiant bashaws slain,
Whose blood hath been manured to their earth,
Whose bones hath made their deep ways passable,
To found a homeward, dull, and harsh retreat,
Without a conquest, or a mean revenge?
Strive not for *Rhodes*, by letting *Persia* slip;
The one's a lion almost brought to death,
Whose skin will countervail the hunter's toil:

The other is a wasp with threat'ning sting,
Whose honey is not worth the taking up.
　　　　　Amurath.
　Why, *Haleb*, didst thou not hear our brother swear
Upon the alcoran religiously,
That he would make an universal camp
Of all his scatter'd legions? and darest thou
Infer a reason, why it is not meet,
After his highness swears it shall be so?
Were it not, thou art my father's son,
And striving kindness wrestled not with ire,
I would not hence, till I had let thee know,
What 'twere to thwart a monarch's holy oath.
　　　　　Haleb.
　Why, his highness gave me leave to speak my will;
And, far from flattery, I spoke my mind,
And did discharge a faithful subject's love:
Thou, *Aristippus* like, didst flatter him,
Not like my brother, or a man of worth.
And for his highness' vow, I cross'd it not;
But gave my censure, as his highness bad.
Now for thy chastisement know, *Amurath*,
I scorn them, as a reckless lion scorns
The humming of a gnat in summer's night.
　　　　　Amurath.
　I take it, *Haleb*, thou art friend to *Rhodes*.
　　　　　Haleb.
　Not half so much am I a friend to *Rhodes*,
As thou art enemy to thy sovereign.
　　　　　Amurath.
　I charge thee, say wherein; or else, by *Mahomet*,
I'll hazard duty in my sovereign's presence.
　　　　　Haleb.
　Not for thy threats, but for myself I say,
It is not meet, that one so base as thou
Shouldst come about the person of a king.
　　　　　Soliman.
　Must I give aim to this presumption?
　　　　　　　　　　　　Amurath.

Amurath.
Your highnefs knows, I fpake in duteous love.
Haleb.
Your highnefs knows, I fpake at your command,
And to the purpofe, far from flattery.
Amurath.
Think'ft thou, I flatter? now I flatter not.
[*He kills* Haleb.
Soliman.
What difmal planet guides this fatal hour?
Villain, thy brother's groans do call for thee,
[Soliman *kills* Amurath,
To wander with them through eternal night.
Amurath.
O *Soliman*, for loving thee I die.
Soliman.
No, *Amurath*, for murdering him thou dieft.
O *Haleb*, how fhall I begin to mourn,
Or how fhall I begin to fhed falt tears,
For whom no words, nor tears, can well fuffice?
Ah, that my rich imperial diadem
Could fatisfy thy cruel deftiny!
Or that a thoufand of our *Turkifh* fouls,
Or twenty thoufand millions of our foes,
Could ranfome thee from fell death's tyranny!
To win thy life would *Soliman* be poor,
And live in fervile bondage all my days.
Accurfed *Amurath*, that for a worthlefs caufe
In blood hath fhorten'd our fweet *Haleb's* days!
Ah, what is dearer bond than brotherhood?
Yet, *Amurath*, thou wert my brother too,
If wilful folly did not blind mine eyes;
Ay, ay, and thou as virtuous as *Haleb*,
And I as dear to thee as unto *Haleb*,
And thou as near to me as *Haleb* was.
Ah, *Amurath*, why wert thou fo unkind to him,
For uttering but a thwarting word?
And, *Haleb*, why did not thy heart's counfel

Bridle

Bridle the fond intemperance of thy tongue?
Nay, wretched *Soliman*, why didſt not thou
Withhold thy hand from heaping blood on blood?
Might I not better ſpare one joy than both?
If love of *Haleb* forc'd me on to wrath,
Curs'd be that wrath that is the way to death!
If juſtice forc'd me on, curs'd be that juſtice
That makes the brother, butcher of his brother!—
Come, *Janiſaries*, and help me to lament,
And bear my joys on either ſide of me;
Ay, late my joys, but now my laſting ſorrow.
Thus, thus, let *Soliman* paſs on his way,
Bearing in either hand his heart's decay. [*Exeunt.*

Enter Chorus.

Love.
Now, *Death*, and *Fortune*, which of all us three,
Hath in the actors ſhown the greateſt power?
Have not I taught *Eraſtus* and *Perſeda*,
By mutual tokens to ſeal up their loves?

Fortune.
Ay, but thoſe tokens the ring and carcanet,
Were *Fortune's* gifts; *Love* gives no gold, or jewels.

Love.
Why, what is jewels, or what is gold but earth;
An humour knit together by compreſſion,
And by the world's bright eye, firſt brought to light,
Only to feed men's eyes with vain delight?
Love's works are more than of a mortal temper,
I couple minds together by conſent:
Who gave *Rhodes'* princeſs to the *Cyprian* prince,
But *Love*?

Fortune.
Fortune, that firſt by chance brought them together;
For till by *Fortune* perſons meet each other,
Thou canſt not teach their eyes to wound their hearts.

Love.

Love.
I made those knights of several sect and countries,
Each one by arms to honour his beloved.
Fortune.
Nay, one alone to honour his beloved,
The rest by turning of my tickle wheel,
Came short in reaching of fair honour's mark:
I gave *Erastus* only that day's prize,
A sweet renown, but mix'd with bitter sorrow;
For, in conclusion of his happiness,
I made him lose the precious carcanet,
Whereon depended all his hope and joy.
Death.
And more than so; for he that found the chain,
Even for that chain shall be depriv'd of life.
Love.
Besides, *Love* hath enforc'd a fool,
The fond braggardo to presume to arms.
Fortune.
Ay, but thou see'st how he was overthrown
By *Fortune's* high displeasure.
Death.
Ay, and by *Death* had been surpriz'd,
If fates had giv'n me leave;
But what I miss'd in him, and in the rest,
I did accomplish on *Haleb* and *Amurath*,
The worthy brethren of great *Soliman:*
But wherefore stay we? let the sequel prove,
Who is the greatest, *Fortune, Death,* or *Love.* [*Exeunt.*

A C T

ACT II.

Enter Ferdinando, *and* Lucina.

Ferdinando.

AS fits the time, so now well fits the place,
To cool affection with our words and looks,
If in our thoughts be semblance sympathy.
Lucina.
My words, my looks, my thoughts, are all on thee:
Ferdinando is *Lucina's* only joy.
Ferdinando.
What pledge thereof?
Lucina.
An oath, a hand, a kiss.
Ferdinando.
O holy oath, fair hand, and sugar'd kiss!
O, never may *Ferdinando* lack such bliss!
But say, my dear, when shall the gates of heaven
Stand all wide open for celestial gods,
With gladsome looks to gaze at *Hymen's* robes?
When shall the graces, or *Lucina's* hand,
With rosy chaplets deck my golden tresses;
And *Cupid* bring me to thy nuptial bed,
Where thou in joy and pleasure must attend
A blissful war with me thy chiefest friend?
Lucina.
Full fraught with love, and burning with desire,
I long have long'd for light of *Hymen's* lights.
Ferdinando.
Then that same day, whose warm and pleasant sight,
Brings in the spring with many gladsome flowers,
Be our first day of joy, and perfect peace:
Till when, receive this precious carcanet,

In sign, that as the links are interlaced,
So both our hearts are still combin'd in one,
Which never can be parted but by death.

Enter Basilisco, *and* Perseda.
Lucina.
And if I live, this shall not be forgot:
But see, *Ferdinando*, where *Perseda* comes,
Whom women love for virtue, men for beauty;
All the world loves, none hates but envy.
Basilisco.
All hail, brave cavalier : — Good morrow, madam,
The fairest shine that shall this day be seen,
Except *Perseda's* beauteous excellence,
Shame to love's queen, and empress of my thoughts.
Ferdinando.
Marry, thrice happy is *Perseda's* chance,
To have so brave a champion to her 'squire.
Basilisco.
Her 'squire! her knight: and whoso else denies
Shall feel the rigour of my sword and lance.
Ferdinando.
O, sir, not I.
Lucina.
Here is none but friends; yet let me challenge you,
For gracing me with a malignant style,
That I was fairest, and yet *Perseda* fairer:
We ladies stand upon our beauties much.
Perseda.
Herein, *Lucina*, let me buckler him.
Basilisco.
Not *Mars* himself had e'er so fair a buckler.
Perseda.
Love makes him blind; and blind can judge no colour.
Lucina.
Why then, the mends is made, and we still friends.

Perseda.
Still friends! still foes: she wears my carcanet.
Ah, false *Erastus*, how am I betray'd! [*aside.*
Lucina.
What ails you, madam, that your colour changes?
Perseda.
A sudden qualm; I therefore take my leave.
Lucina.
We'll bring you home.
Perseda.
No; I shall soon get home.
Lucina.
Why then, farewel: — *Ferdinando*, let's away.
[*Exeunt* Ferdinando *and* Lucina.
Basilisco.
Say, world's bright star, whence springs this sudden change;
Is it unkindness at the little praise
I gave *Lucina* with my glosing style?
Perseda.
No, no; her beauty far surpasseth mine,
And from my neck her neck hath won the praise.
Basilisco.
What is it then? if love of this my person,
By favour and by justice of the heavens,
At last have pierc'd through thy tranflucent breast,
And thou misdoubst, perhaps, that I'll prove coy;
O, be assur'd, 'tis far from noble thoughts
To tyrannize over a yielding foe.
Therefore be blithe, sweet love, abandon fear,
I will forget thy former cruelty.
Perseda.
Ah, false *Erastus*, full of treachery.
Basilisco.
I always told you, that such coward knights
Were faithless swains, and worthy no respect.
But tell me, sweet love, what is his offence?

That

That I with words and stripes may chastise him,
And bring him bound for thee to tread upon.
    Perseda.
 Now must I find the means to rid him hence.—
Go thou forthwith, arm thee from top to toe,
And come an hour hence unto my lodging;
Then will I tell thee this offence at large,
And thou in my behalf shalt work revenge.
    Basilisco.
 Ay, thus should men of valour be employ'd;
This is good argument of thy true love:
I go; make reck'ning, that *Erastus* dies,
Unless, forewarn'd, the weakling coward flies.
         [*Exit* Basilisco.
    Perseda.
 Thou foolish coward! flies? *Erastus* lives,
The fairest shape, but foulest minded man,
That ere sun saw within our hemisphere:
My tongue, to tell my woes is all too weak,
I must unclasp me, or my heart will break;
But inward cares are most pent in with grief,
Unclasping therefore yields me no relief.
Ah, that my moist and cloud-compacted brain,
Could spend my cares in showers of weeping rain!
But scalding sighs, like blasts of boist'rous winds,
Hinder my tears from falling on the ground,
And I must die by closure of my wound.
Ah, false *Erastus*, how had I misdone,
That thou shouldst quit my love with such a scorn!

    Enter Erastus.

Here comes the *Sinon* of my heart:
I'll frame myself to his dissembling art.
    Erastus.
 Desire persuades me on, fear pulls me back:
Tush! I will to her; innocence is bold.—
How fares *Perseda*, my sweet second self?
             Perseda.

THE TRAGEDY OF

Perseda.
Well, now *Erastus*, my heart's only joy,
Is come to join both hearts in union.

Erastus.
And till I came whereas my love did dwell,
My pleasure was but pain, my solace wo.

Perseda.
What love means my *Erastus*? pray thee, tell.

Erastus.
Matchless *Perseda*, she that gave me strength,
To win late conquests from many victors hands,
Thy name was conqueror, not my chivalry;
Thy looks did arm me, not my coat of steel;
Thy beauty did defend me, not my force;
Thy favours bore me, not my light-foot steed;
Therefore to thee I owe both love and life:
But wherefore makes *Perseda* such a doubt,
As if *Erastus* could forget himself;
Which if I do, all vengeance light on me!

Perseda.
Aye me, how graceless are these wicked men!
I can no longer hold my patience.
Ah, how thine eyes can forge alluring looks,
And feign deep oaths, to wound poor silly maids!
Are there no honest drops in all thy cheeks,
To check thy fraudful countenance with a blush?
Call'st thou me love, and lov'st another better?
If heav'ns were just, thy teeth would tear thy tongue,
For this thy perjur'd false disloyalty:
If heav'ns were just, men should have open breasts,
That we therein might read their guileful thoughts:
If heav'ns were just, that power that forceth love,
Would never couple wolves and lambs together:
Yes, heav'ns are just, but thou art so corrupt,
That in thee all their influence doth change,
As in the spider, good things turn to poison.
Ah, false *Erastus*, how had I misdone,
That thou shouldst pawn my true affection's pledge
To her whose worth will never equal mine? What

What, is *Lucina's* wealth exceeding mine?
Yet mine sufficient to encounter thine:
Is she more fair than I? that's not my fault,
Nor her desert: what's beauty but a blast,
Soon crop'd with age, or with infirmities?
Is she more wise? her years are more than mine:
Whate'er she be, my love was more than hers;
And for her chastity let others judge.
But what talk I of her? the fault is thine:
If I were so disgracious in thine eye,
That she must needs enjoy my interest,
Why didst thou deck her with my ornament?
Could nothing serve her but the carcanet,
Which, as my life, I gave to thee in charge?
Couldst thou abuse my true simplicity,
Whose greatest fault was, overloving thee?
I'll keep no tokens of thy perjury:
Here, give her this; *Perseda* now is free,
And all my former love is turn'd to hate.
    Erastus.
Ah, stay, my sweet *Perseda*; hear me speak.
    Perseda.
What are thy words, but *Sirens* guileful songs,
That please the ear, but seek to spoil the heart.
    Erastus.
Then view my tears that plead for innocence.
    Perseda.
What are thy tears? but *Circe's* magick seas,
Where none scape wreck'd, but blindfold mariners.
    Erastus.
If words and tears displease, then view my looks,
That plead for mercy at thy rigorous hands.
    Perseda.
What are thy looks? but like the cockatrice
That seeks to wound poor silly passengers.
    Erastus.
If words, nor tears, nor looks, may win remorse,
What then remains? for my perplexed heart,
Hath no interpreters but words, or tears, or looks,

Perseda.
And they are all as false, as thou thyself. *Exit.*
Erastus.
Hard doom of death, before my case be known;
My judge unjust, and yet I cannot blame her,
Since love and jealousy misled her thus,
Myself in fault, and yet not worthy blame,
Because that fortune made the fault, not love.
The ground of her unkindness grows, because I lost
The precious carcanet she gave to me:
Lucina hath it, as her words import;
But how she got it, heav'n knows, not I:
Yet this is some aleavement to my sorrow,
That, if I can but get the chain again,
I boldly then shall let *Perseda* know,
That she hath wrong'd *Erastus*, and her friend.
Ah, love, and if thou be'st of heav'nly power,
Inspire me with some present stratagem:
It must be so; *Lucina's* a frank gamester,
And, like it is, in play she'll hazard it;
For if report but blazon her aright,
She's a frank gamester, and inclin'd to play.—
Ho! *Piston!*

Enter Piston.

Piston.
Here, sir, what would you with me?
Erastus.
Desire *Guelpio*, and signior *Julio*, come speak with me,
And bid them bring some store of crowns with them:
And, sirra, provide me four vizards,
Four gowns, a box, and a drum;
For I intend to go in mummery.
Piston.
I will, sir. [*Exit* Piston.]
Erastus.
Ah, virtuous lamps of ever-turning heavens,
Incline her mind to play, and mine to win!
Nor do I covet but what is mine own: Then

Then shall I let *Perseda* understand,
How jealousy had arm'd her tongue with malice.
Ah, were she not *Perseda*, whom my heart
No more can fly, than iron can adamant,
Her late unkindness would have chang'd my mind.

Enter Guelpio, *and* Julio, *with* Piston.
Guelpio.
How now, *Erastus?* wherein may we pleasure thee?
Erastus.
Sirs, thus it is: we must in mummery
Unto *Lucina*, neither for love nor hate;
But, if we can, to win the chain she wears:
For, though I have some interest therein,
Fortune may make me master of mine own,
Rather than I'll seek justice 'gainst the dame.
But this assure yourselves, it must be mine,
By game, or change, by one devise or other:
The rest I'll tell you, when our sport is done.
Julio.
Why then, let's make us ready, and about it.
Erastus.
What store of crowns have you brought?
Guelpio.
Fear not for money, man, I'll bear the box.
Julio.
I have some little reply, if need require.
Piston.
Ay, but hear you, master, was not he a fool
That went to shoot, and left his arrows behind him?
Erastus.
Yes, but what of that?
Piston.
Marry, that you may lose your money,
And go without the chain, unless you carry false dice.
Guelpio.
'Mass, the fool says true; let's have some got.
Piston,

THE TRAGEDY OF

Piston.
Nay, I use not to go without a pair of false dice;
Here are tall men, and little men.
Julio.
High men, and low men,* thou wouldst say.
Erastus.
Come, sirs, let's go: — Drumsler, pray for me,
And I'll reward thee: — And, sirra, *Piston,*
Mar not our sport with your foolery.
Piston.
I warrant you, sir, they get not one wise word of me.
[*Sound up the drum to* Lucina's *door.*

Enter Lucina.
Lucina.
Ay, marry, this shows that *Charleman* is come:
What, shall we play here? content,
Since signior *Ferdinand* will have it so.
[*Then they play; and, when she hath lost her gold,*
Erastus *pointeth to her chain, and then
she says:*
Ay, were it *Cleopatra's* union.
[*Then* Erastus *winneth the chain, and loseth his
gold.*
Lucina.
Signior *Ferdinando*, I am sure, 'tis you: —
And, gentlemen, unmask ere you depart,
That I may know to whom my thanks are due
For this so courteous, and unlook'd-for sport.
No? will't not be? then sup with me to-morrow:
Well, then I'll look for you; till then, farewel.
[*Exit* Lucina.
Erastus.
Gentlemen, each thing hath sorted to our wish;
She took me for *Ferdinando*, mark'd you that?
Your gold shall be repair'd with double thanks; —
And, fellow drumsler, I'll reward you well.

* So Shakes. *Mer. Wiv. of Wind.* A. I. S. 8. *Pist.* — And *high* and *low* beguiles the rich and poor. i. e. *High and low men*, false dice so called.

Piston.
But is there no reward for my false dice?
Eraſtus.
Yes, sir, a garded suit, from top to toe.

Enter Ferdinando.
Dazzle mine eyes, or is't *Lucina's* chain?—
False treacher, lay down the chain that thou haſt ſtole.
Eraſtus.
He lewdly lies that calls me treacherous.
Ferdinando.
That lie my weapon ſhall put down thy throat.
[*Then* Eraſtus *ſlays* Ferdinando*.*
Julio.
Fly, *Eraſtus*, ere the governor have any news,
Whoſe near ally he was and chief delight.
Eraſtus.
Nay, gentlemen, fly you and ſave yourſelves,
Leſt you partake the hardneſs of my fortune.
[*Exeunt* Guelpio, *and* Julio.
Ah, fickle and blind guidreſs of the world,
What pleaſure haſt thou in my miſery?
Was't not enough, when I had loſt the chain,
Thou didſt bereave me of my deareſt love;
But now, when I ſhould repoſſeſs the ſame,
To croſs me with this hapleſs accident?
Ah, if but time and place would give me leave,
Great eaſe it were for me to purge myſelf,
And to accuſe fell *Fortune*, *Love*, and *Death*;
For all theſe three conſpire my tragedy:
But danger waits upon my words and ſteps;
I dare not ſtay, for if the governor
Surprize me here, I die my marſhal law,
Therefore I go: but whither ſhall I go?
If into any ſtay adjoining *Rhodes*,
They will betray me to *Philippo's* hands,
For love, or gain, or flattery.

To

To *Turkey* must I go; the passage short,
The people warlike, and the king renown'd
For all heroical and kingly virtues.
Ah, hard attempt, to tempt a foe for aid!
Necessity yet says, it must be so,
Or suffer death for *Ferdinando*'s death;
Whom honour's title forc'd me to misdo,
By checking his outrageous insolence. —
Piston, here take this chain, and give it to *Perseda*;
And let her know what hath befallen me:
When thou'st deliver'd it, take ship and follow me,
I will be in *Constantinople*. —
Farewel, my country, dearer than my life;
Farewel, dear friends, dearer than country soil;
Farewel, *Perseda*, dearest of them all,
Dearer to me than all the world besides. [*Exit* Eraſtus.
     Piston.
Now am I growing into a doubtful agony,
What I were best to do; to run away with this chain,
Or deliver it, and follow my master:
If I deliver it, and follow my master, I shall have thanks;
But they will make me never the fatter:
If I run away with it, I may live upon credit,
All the while I wear this chain;
Or domineer with the money, when I have sold it:
Hitherto all goes well; but, if I be taken, —
Ay, marry, sir, then the case is alter'd; ay, and halter'd
  too:
Of all things I do not love to preach
With a halter about my neck:
Therefore, for this once, I'll be honest against my will;
Perseda shall have it: but, before I go, I'll be so bold
As to dive into the gentleman's pocket, for good luck sake,
If he deny me not: — How say you, sir? are you con‑
  tent? —
A plain case: *Qui tacet consſiliri* * *videtur*.

   * He means to say, *consentiri*.

            Enter

SOLIMAN AND PERSEDA. 235

Enter Philippo, *and* Julio.

See, where his body lies.
Philippo.
Ay, ay; I see his body all too soon:
What barb'rous villain is't that rifles him?
Ah, *Ferdinando*, the stay of my old age,
And chief remainder of our progeny!
Ah, loving cousin, how art thou misdone!
By false *Erastus?* ah, no; by treachery:
For well thy valour hath been often tried.
But whilst I stand, and weep, and spend the time
In fruitless plaints, the murd'rer will escape
Without revenge, sole salve for such a sore.—
Say, villain, wherefore didst thou rifle him?
Piston.
'Faith, sir, for pure good will;
Seeing he was going towards heaven,
I thought to see, if he had a passport to saint *Nicholas,*
or no.
Philippo.
Some sot he seems to be, 'twere pity to hurt him.—
Sirra, canst thou tell who slew this man?
Piston.
Ay, sir, very well; it was my master *Erastus.*
Philippo.
Thy master? and whither is he gone now?
Piston.
To fetch the sexton to bury him, I think.
Philippo.
'Twere pity to imprison such a sot.
Piston.
Now it fits my wisdom to counterfeit the fool. [*aside.*
Philippo.
Come hither, sirra; thou knowest me
For the governor of the city, dost thou not?
Piston.
Ay, forsooth, sir.

Philippo.

Philippo.
Thou art a bondman, and wouldſt fain be free?
Piſton.
Ay, forſooth, ſir,
Philippo.
Then do but this, and I will make thee free,
And rich withal; learn where *Eraſtus* is,
And bring me word, and I'll reward thee well.
Piſton.
That I will, ſir; I ſhall find you at the caſtle, ſhall
I not?
Philippo.
Yes.
Piſton.
Why, I'll be here, as ſoon as ever I come again.
[*Exit* Piſton.
Philippo.
But for aſſurance that he may not ſcape,
We'll lay the ports, and havens round about;
And let proclamation ſtraight be made,
That he that can bring forth the murderer,
Shall have three thouſand ducats for his pain:
Myſelf will ſee the body born from hence,
And honoured with balm and funeral. [*Exeunt.*

Enter Piſton.

God ſends fortune to fools;
Did you ever ſee wiſe men eſcape, as I have done?
I muſt betray my maſter! Ay, but when? can you tell?

Enter Perſeda.

See, where *Perſeda* comes, to ſave me a labour.—
After my moſt hearty commendations,
This is to let you underſtand, that my maſter
Was in good health at the ſending hereof:

Yours

Yours for ever, and ever, and ever,
In moſt humble wife, *Piſton.*
 [*Then he delivers her the chain.*
 Perſeda.
This makes me think, that I have been too cruel:—
How got he this from off *Lucina's* arm?
 Piſton.
'Faith, in a mummery, and a pair of falſe dice;
I was one of the mummers myſelf, ſimple as I ſtand here.
 Perſeda.
I rather think, it coſt him very dear.
 Piſton.
Ay, ſo it did; for it coſt *Ferdinando* his life.
 Perſeda.
How ſo?
 Piſton.
After we had got the chain in mummery,
And loſt our box in counter cambio,
My maſter wore the chain about his neck;
Then *Ferdinando* met us on the way,
And revil'd my maſter, ſaying, he ſtole the chain:
With that they drew; and there *Ferdinando* had the
 prickado.
 Perſeda.
And whither fled my poor *Eraſtus* then?
 Piſton.
To *Conſtantinople*, whither I muſt follow him:
But ere he went, with many ſighs and tears,
He deliver'd me the chain; and bad me give it you,
For perfect argument that he was true,
And you too credulous.
 Perſeda.
Ah, ſtay, no more; for I can hear no more.
 Piſton.
And I can ſing no more.
 Perſeda.
My heart had arm'd my tongue with injury,

To

To wrong my friend whofe thoughts were ever true.
Ah, poor *Eraftus*, how thy ftars malign!—
Thou great commander of the fwift-wing'd winds,
And dreadful *Neptune*, bring him back again:
But, *Æolus*, and *Neptune*, let him go;
For here is nothing but revenge and death:
Then, let him go; I'll fhortly follow him,
Not with flow fails, but with love's golden wings:
My fhip fhall be born with tears, and blown with fighs;
So will I foar about the *Turkifh* land,
Until I meet *Eraftus*, my fweet friend:
And then and there fall down amid his arms,
And in his bofom there pour forth my foul,
For fatisfaction of my trefpafs paft.

Enter Bafilifco *armed*.
Bafilifco.
Fair love, according unto thy command,
I feek *Eraftus*, and will combat him.
Perfeda.
Ay, feek him, find him, bring him to my fight;
For till we meet, my heart fhall want delight.
[*Exit* Perfeda.
Bafilifco.
My pretty fellow, where haft thou hid thy mafter?
Pifton.
Marry, fir, in an armourer's fhop,
Where you had not beft go to him.
Bafilifco.
Why fo? I am in honour bound to combat him.
Pifton.
Ay, fir; but he, knowing your fierce conditions,
Hath planted a double cannon in the door,
Ready to difcharge it upon you, when you go by:
I tell you, for pure good will.

Bafilifco.

Basilisco.
In knightly courtesy, I thank thee:
But hopes the coystrel to escape me so?
Thinks he, bare cannon-shot can keep me back?
Why, wherefore serves my targe of proof, but for the bullet,
That, once put by, I roughly come upon him,
Like to the wings of lightning from above;
I with a martial look astonish him,
Then falls he down poor wretch! upon his knee,
And all too late repents his surquedry:
Then do I take him on my finger's point,
And thus I bear him thorough every street,
To be a laughing-stock to all the town:
That done, I lay him at my mistress' feet,
For her to give him doom of life or death.
Piston.
Ay, but hear you, sir; I am bound,
In pain of my master's displeasure,
To have a bout at cuffs, afore you and I part.
Basilisco.
Ha, ha, ha! Eagles are calleng'd by paltry flies:
Thy folly gives thee privilege; be gone, be gone.
Piston.
No, no, sir: I must have a bout with you sir, that's flat;
Lest my master turn me out of service.
Basilisco.
Why, art thou weary of thy life?
Piston.
No, by my faith, sir.
Basilisco.
Then fetch thy weapons; and with my single fist
I'll combat thee, my body all unarm'd.
Piston.
Why, lend me thine, and save me a labour.
Basilisco.
I tell thee, if *Alcides* liv'd this day,
He could not wield my weapons.
Piston.

THE TRAGEDY OF

Piston.
Why, wilt thou stay till I come again?
Basilisco.
Ay, upon my honour.
Piston.
That shall be, when I come from *Turkey*.
[*Exit* Piston.
Basilisco.
Is this little desperate fellow gone?
Doubtless, he is a very tall fellow;
And yet it were a disgrace to all my chivalry,
To combat one so base:
I'll send some crane to combat with the pigmy;
Not that I fear, but that I scorn to fight.
[*Exit* Basilisco.

Enter Chorus.

Love.
Fortune, thou madest *Ferdinando* find the chain;
But yet by *Love's* instruction he was taught,
To make a present of it to his mistress.
Fortune.
But *Fortune* would not let her keep it long.
Love.
Nay, rather, *Love*, by whose suggested power
Erastus us'd such dice, as, being false,
Ran not by *Fortune*, but necessity.
Fortune.
Meantime, I brought *Ferdinando* on the way,
To see and challenge what *Lucina* lost.
Death.
And by that challenge I abridg'd his life,
And forc'd *Erastus* into banishment,
Parting him from his love, in spite of *Love*.
Love.
But with my golden wings I'll follow him,
And give him aid and succour in distress.
Fortune.

SOLIMAN AND PERSEDA.

Fortune.
And doubt not too, but *Fortune* will be there,
And crofs him too, and fometimes flatter him,
And lift him up, and throw him down again.
Death.
And here and there in ambufh *Death* will ftand,
To mar what *Love*, or *Fortune* takes in hand. [*Exeunt.*

ACT III.

Enter Soliman, *and* Brufor, *with Janifaries.*

Soliman.

HOW long fhall *Soliman* fpend his time,
And wafte his days in fruitlefs obfequies?
Perhaps, my grief, and long continual moan,
Adds but a trouble to my brother's ghoft;
Which, but for me, would now have took their reft:
Then, farewel, forrow; and now, revenge, draw near.
In controverfy touching the ifle of *Rhodes*,
My brothers died; on *Rhodes* I'll be reveng'd:—
Now tell me, *Brufor*, what's the news at *Rhodes*?
Hath the young prince of *Ciprus* married
Cornelia, daughter to the governour?
Brufor.
He hath, my lord, with the greateft pomp
That ere I faw at fuch a feftival.
Soliman.
What, greater than at our coronation?
Brufor.
Inferiour to that only.
Soliman.
At tilt, who won the honour of the day?

Brusor.
A worthy knight of *Rhodes*, a matchless man,
His name *Erastus*, not twenty years of age,
Not tall, but well proportion'd in his limbs:
I never saw, except your excellence,
A man whose presence more delighted me;
And, had he worship'd *Mahomet* for *Christ*,
He might have born me throughout all the world:
So well I lov'd, and honoured the man.

Soliman.
These praises, *Brusor*, touch me to the heart;
And make me wish, that I had been at *Rhodes*,
Under the habit of some errant knight,
Both to have seen and try'd his valour.

Brusor.
You should have seen him foil, and overthrow
All the knights that there encountered him.

Soliman.
Whate'er he be, ev'n for his virtue's sake,
I wish, that fortune of our holy wars
Would yield him prisoner unto *Soliman*;
That for retaining one so virtuous
We may ourselves be fam'd for virtues.
But let him pass; and, *Brusor*, tell me now,
How did the *Christians* use our knights?

Brusor.
As if that we and they had been one sect.

Soliman.
What think'st thou of their valour and demeanour?

Brusor.
Brave men at arms, and friendly out of arms;
Courteous in peace, in battle dangerous;
Kind to their foes, and liberal to their friends;
And, all in all, their deeds heroical.

Soliman.
Then tell me, *Brusor*, how is *Rhodes* fenced?
For either *Rhodes* shall be brave *Soliman's*,
Or cost me more brave soldiers
Than all that isle will bear.

Brusor.

SOLIMAN AND PERSEDA.

Brusor.
Their fleet is weak;
Their horse, I deem them fifty thousand strong;
Their footmen more, well exercis'd in war;
And, as it seems, they want no needful victual.
Soliman.
However *Rhodes* be fenc'd by sea or land,
It either shall be mine or bury me.

Enter Erastus.

What's he that thus boldly enters in?
His habit argues him a *Christian*.
Erastus.
Ay, worthy lord, a forlorn *Christian*.
Soliman.
Tell me, man, what madness brought thee hither?
Erastus.
Thy virtuous fame, and mine own misery.
Soliman.
What misery? speak; for though you *Christians*
Account our *Turkish* race but barbarous,
Yet have we ears to hear a just complaint,
And justice to defend the innocent,
And pity to such as are in poverty,
And liberal hands to such as merit bounty.
Brusor.
My gracious sov'reign, as this knight
Seems by grief tied to silence,
So his deserts bind me to speak for him:
This is *Erastus*, the *Rhodian* worthy,
The flow'r of chivalry and courtesy.
Soliman.
Is this the man that thou hast so described?
Stand up, fair knight, that what my heart desires
Mine eyes may view with pleasure and delight:
This face of thine should harbour no deceit.
Erastus, I'll not yet urge to know the cause

That

That brought thee hither, left
With the discourse thou shouldst afflict thyself,
And cross the fulness of my joyful passion.
But that we are assur'd,
Heav'ns brought thee hither for our benefit,
Know thou, that *Rhodes*, nor all that *Rhodes* contains,
Shall win thee from the side of *Soliman*,
If we but find thee well inclin'd to us.
     Erastus.
 If any ignoble, or dishonourable thoughts,
Should dare attempt, or but creep near my heart,
Honour should force disdain to root it out:
As air-bred eagles, * if they once perceive,
That any of their brood but close their sight,
When they should gaze against the glorious sun,
They straightway seize upon him with their talents,
That on the earth it may untimely die,
For looking but askew at heav'n's bright eye.
     Soliman.
 Erastus, to make thee well assured,
How well thy speech, and presence liketh us,
Ask what thou wilt, it shall be granted thee.
     Erastus
 Then this, my gracious lord, is all I crave,
That, being banish'd from my native soil,
I may have liberty to live a *Christian.*
     Soliman.
 Ay, that, or any thing thou shalt desire;
Thou shalt be captain of our janisaries,
And in our council shalt thou sit with us,
And be great *Soliman's* adopted friend.
     Erastus.
 The least of these surpass my best desert,
Unless true loyalty may seem desert.

---

* *Naturalists tell us, the eagle holds up its brood, as soon as 'tis hatched, to the sun, to prove whether they are genuine or not. To this* Shakespeare *alludes,* Hen. 6. 3d pt. *Act II. S. 1.*
 Rich. *Nay, if thou be that princely eagle's bird,*
  Show thy descent by gazing 'gainst the sun.

     Soliman.

SOLIMAN AND PERSEDA.

Soliman.
Eraſtus, now thou haſt obtain'd thy boon,
Deny not *Soliman* this one requeſt;
A virtuous envy pricks me with deſire,
To try thy valour: ſay, art thou content?
Eraſtus.
Ay, if my ſov'reign ſay, content, I yield.
Soliman.
Then give us ſwords and targets:
And now, *Eraſtus,* think thee mine enemy,
But ever after, thy continual friend;
And ſpare me not, for then thou wrong'ſt my honour.
 [*Then they fight, and* Eraſtus *overcomes* Soliman.
Nay, nay, *Eraſtus,* throw not down thy weapons,
As if thy force did fail; it is enough,
That thou haſt conquer'd *Soliman* by ſtrength:
By courteſy let *Soliman* conquer thee.
And now from arms, to council ſit thee down;
Before thy coming, I vow'd to conquer *Rhodes:*
Say, wilt thou be our lieutenant there,
And further us in manage of theſe wars?
Eraſtus.
My gracious ſovereign, without preſumption,
If poor *Eraſtus* may once more entreat,
Let not great *Soliman's* command,
To whoſe beheſt I vow obedience,
Enforce me ſheathe my ſlaught'ring blade
In the dear bowels of my countrymen:
And, were it not that *Solimàn* hath ſworn,
My tears ſhould plead for pardon in that place.
I ſpeak not this, to ſhrink away for fear,
Or hide my head in time of dangerous ſtorms;
Employ me elſewhere in thy foreign wars,
Againſt the *Perſians,* or the barbarous *Moor,*
Eraſtus will be foremoſt in the battle.
Soliman.
Why favour'ſt thou thy countrymen ſo much,
By whoſe cruelty thou art exil'd?

Eraſtus.

THE TRAGEDY OF

Eraſtus.
'Tis not my country, but *Philippo's* wrath,
(It muſt be told,) for *Ferdinando's* death,
Whom I in honour's cauſe have reft of life.

Soliman.
Nor ſuffer this or that to trouble thee:
Thou ſhalt not need *Philippo,* nor his iſle;
Nor ſhalt thou war againſt thy countrymen:
I like thy virtue in refuſing it. —
But, that our oath may have his current courſe,
Bruſor, go levy men;
Prepare a fleet, t' aſſault and conquer *Rhodes.*
Meantime, *Eraſtus* and I will ſtrive
By mutual kindneſs to excel each other.
Bruſor, be gone; and ſee not *Soliman,*
Till thou haſt brought *Rhodes* in ſubjection. —
                                    [*Exit* Bruſor.
And now, *Eraſtus,* come and follow me,
Where thou ſhalt ſee what pleaſures and what ſports
My minions, and my eunuchs, can deviſe,
To drive away this melancholy mood. [*Exit* Soliman.

Enter Piſton.

Piſton.
O maſter, ſee where I am.

Eraſtus.
Say, *Piſton,* what's the news at *Rhodes?*

Piſton.
Cold, and comfortleſs for you:
Will you have them all at once?

Eraſtus.
Ay.

Piſton.
Why the governour will hang you, and he catch you:
Ferdinando is buried; your friends commend them to you;
Perſeda hath the chain, and is like to die for ſorrow.

Eraſtus.

Eraftus.
Ay, that's the grief, that we are parted thus:
Come follow me, and I will hear the reft;
For now I muft attend the emperour. [*Exeunt.*

Enter Perfeda, Lucina, *and* Bafilifco.
Perfeda.
Accurfed chain! unfortunate *Perfeda!*
Lucina.
Accurfed chain! unfortunate *Lucina!*
My friend is gone, and I am defolate.
Perfeda.
My friend is gone, and I am defolate:—
Return him back, fair ftars, or let me die.
Lucina.
Return him back, fair heav'ns, or let me die;
For, what was he but comfort of my life?
Perfeda.
For, what was he but comfort of my life?
But why was I fo careful of the chain?
Lucina.
But why was I fo carelefs of the chain?
Had I not loft it, my friend had not been flain.
Perfeda.
Had I not afk'd it, my friend had not departed;
His parting is my death.
Lucina.
His death's my life's departing;
And here my tongue doth ftay, with fwoln heart's grief.
Perfeda.
And here my fwoln heart's grief doth ftay my tongue.
Bafilifco.
For whom weep you?
Lucina.
Ah, for *Ferdinando's* dying.
Bafilifco.
For whom mourn you?
Perfeda.

Perseda.
Ah, for *Erastus'* flying.
Basilisco.
Why, lady, is not *Basilisco* here?
Why, lady, doth not *Basilisco* live?
Am not I worth both these for whom you mourn?
Then take each one half of me, and cease to weep;
Or if you gladly would enjoy me both,
I'll serve the one by day, the other by night:
And I will pay you both your found delight.
Lucina.
Ah, how unpleasant is mirth to melancholy!
Perseda.
My heart is full, I cannot laugh at folly.
[*Exeunt Ladies.*
Basilisco.
See, see; *Lucina* hates me, like a toad,
Because that when *Erastus* spake my name,
Her love *Ferdinando* died at the same:
So dreadful is our name to cowardise.
On the other side, *Perseda* takes it unkindly,
That, ere he went, I brought not bound unto her
Erastus, that faint-hearted runaway.
Alass! how could I? for his man no sooner
Inform'd him, that I sought him up and down,
But he was gone in twinkling of an eye:
But I will after my delicious love;
For, well I wot, though she dissemble thus,
And cloak affection with her modesty,
With love of me her thoughts are over-gone,
More than was *Phillis* with her *Demophon.* [*Exit.*

Enter

SOLIMAN AND PERSEDA.

Enter Philippo, *the Prince of* Ciprus,
with other soldiers.

Philippo.
Brave prince of *Ciprus*, and our son-in-law,
Now there is little time to stand and talk;
The *Turks* have pass'd our gallies, and are landed:
You with some men at arms shall take the tower;
I with the rest will down unto the strand : [1]
If we be beaten back, we'll come to you;
And here, in spite of damned *Turks*, we'll gain
A glorious death, or famous victory.
     Ciprus.
About it then.   [*Exeunt.*

Enter Brusor, *and his soldiers.*
     Brusor.
Drum, sound a parley to the citizens.
    [*The Prince of* Ciprus *on the walls.*
     Ciprus.
What parley craves the *Turkish* at our hands?
     Brusor.
We come with mighty *Soliman's* command,
Monarch, and mighty emperour of the world,
From east to west, from south to septentrion;
If you resist, expect what war affords,
Mischief, murder, blood, and extremity:
What, wilt thou yield, and try our clemency?
Say ay, or no; for we are peremptory.
     Ciprus.
Your lord usurps in all that he possesseth;
And that great God which we do truly worship,
Shall strengthen us against your insolence.

    1 *strand.*

          Brusor.

THE TRAGEDY OF

Brusor.
Now if you plead for mercy, 'tis too late.—
Come, fellow soldiers, let us to the breach,
That's made already on the other side.
  [*Exeunt to the battle.* Philippo, *and* Ciprus *are
  both slain.*

Enter Brusor, *with soldiers, having* Guelpio *and* Julio,
and Basilisco, *with* Perseda, *and* Lucina, *prisoners.*

Brusor.
Now, *Rhodes* is yok'd, and stoops to *Soliman*;
There lies the governour, and there his son:
Now let their souls tell sorry tidings to their ancestors,
What millions of men oppress'd with ruin and scath,
The *Turkish* armies did in *Christendom.* —
What say these pris'ners? will they turn *Turk,* or no?

Julio.
First, *Julio* will die ten thousand deaths.

Guelpio.
And *Guelpio,* rather than deny his *Christ.*

Brusor.
Then stab the slaves, and send their souls to hell.
  [*They stab* Julio, *and* Guelpio.

Basilisco.
I turn, I turn; o, save my life, I turn.

Brusor.
Forbear to hurt him: when we land in *Turkey,*
He shall be circumcis'd and have his rites.

Basilisco.
Think you, I turn *Turk,* for fear of servile death?
That's but a sport: i'faith, sir, no;
'Tis for *Perseda,* whom I love so well,
That I would follow her though she went to hell.

Brusor.
Now for these ladies: their lives privilege
Hangs on their beauty; they shall be preserv'd
To be presented to great *Soliman,*
The greatest honour fortune could afford, *Perseda.*

Perseda.
The moſt diſhonour that could e'er befall. [*Exeunt.*

Enter Chorus.
Love.
Now, *Fortune,* what haſt thou done in this latter paſſage?
Fortune.
I plac'd *Eraſtus* in the favour
Of *Soliman* the *Turkiſh* emperour.
Love.
Nay, that was *Love,* for I couched myſelf
In poor *Eraſtus*' eye, and with a look,
O'erſpread with tears, bewitched *Soliman:*
Beſide, I ſat on valiant *Bruſor's* tongue,
To guide the praiſes of the *Rhodian* 1 knight;
Then in the ladies paſſions I ſhow'd my power:
And laſtly, *Love* made *Baſiliſco's* tongue,
To countercheck his heart by turning *Turk,*
And ſave his life, in ſpite of *Death's* deſpite.
Death.
How chance it then, that *Love,* and *Fortune's* power,
Could neither ſave *Philippo,* nor his ſon,
Nor *Guelpio,* nor ſignior *Julio,*
Nor reſcue *Rhodes,* from out the hands of *Death?*
Fortune.
Why, *Bruſor's* victory was *Fortune's* gift.
Death.
But had I ſlept, his conqueſt had been ſmall.
Love.
Wherefore ſtay we? there's more behind which proves,
That, though *Love* wink, *Love's* not ſtark blind.
[*Exeunt.*

1 *herodian.*

A C T

ACT IV.

Enter Eraftus, *and* Pifton.

Pifton.

'FAITH, mafter, methinks you are unwife,
That you wear not the high fugar-loaf hat,
And the gilded gown the emperour gave you.

Eraftus.

Peace, fool! a fable weed fits difcontent:
Away, be gone.

Pifton.

I'll go provide your fupper,
A fhoulder of mutton and never a fallad. [*Exit* Pifton.

Eraftus.

I muft confefs, that *Soliman* is kind,
Paft all compare, and more than my defert:
But what helps gay garments, when the mind's opprefs'd?
What pleafeth the eye, when the fenfe is alter'd?
My heart is overwhelm'd with thoufand woes,
And melancholy leads my foul in triumph;
No marvel then, if I have little mind
Of rich embroidery, or coftly ornaments,
Of honour's titles, or of wealth, or gain,
Of mufick, viands, or of dainty dames.
No, no; my hope full long ago was loft,
And *Rhodes* itfelf is loft, or elfe deftroy'd:
If not deftroy'd, yet bound and captivate;
If captivate, then forc'd from holy faith;
If forc'd from faith, for ever miferable:
For what is mifery, but want of God?
And God is loft, if faith be overthrown.

Enter

Enter Soliman.

Soliman.
Why how now, *Eraſtus*, always in thy dumps?
Still in black habit, fitting funeral?
Cannot my love perſuade thee from this mood,
Nor all my fair entreats and blandiſhments?
Wert thou my friend, thy mind would jump with mine;
For what are friends, but one mind in two bodies?
Perhaps, thou doubt'ſt my friendſhip's conſtancy;
Then doſt thou wrong the meaſure of my love,
Which hath no meaſure, and ſhall never end.
Come, *Eraſtus*, ſit thee down by me,
And I'll impart to thee our *Bruſor's* news;
News to our honour, and to thy content:
The governour is ſlain that fought thy death.
Eraſtus.
A worthy man, though not *Eraſtus*' friend.
Soliman.
The prince of *Ciprus* too is likewiſe ſlain.
Eraſtus.
Fair bloſſom, likely to have prov'd good fruit.
Soliman.
Rhodes is taken, and all the men are ſlain,
Except ſome few that turn to *Mahomet*.
Eraſtus.
Ay, there it is; now all my friends are ſlain,
And fair *Perſeda*, murder'd or deflowr'd:
Ah, gracious *Soliman*, now ſhow thy love
In not denying thy poor ſuppliant;
Suffer me not to ſtay here in thy preſence,
But by myſelf lament me once for all:
Here if I ſtay, I muſt ſuppreſs my tears,
And tears ſuppreſs'd, will but increaſe my ſorrow.
Soliman.
Go then, go ſpend thy mournings all at once,
That in thy preſence *Soliman* may joy;
For hitherto have I reap'd little pleaſure.
[*Exit* Eraſtus.

THE TRAGEDY OF

Well, well, *Eraſtus*, *Rhodes* may bleſs thy birth:
For his ſake only will I ſpare them more,
From ſpoil, pillage, and oppreſſion,
Than *Alexander* ſpared warlike *Thebes*
For *Pindarus*; or than *Auguſtus*
Spared rich *Alexander* for *Arias'* ſake.

Enter Bruſor, Perſeda, *and* Lucina.

Bruſor.
My gracious lord, rejoice in happineſs:
All *Rhodes* is yok'd, and ſtoops to *Soliman*.

Soliman.
Firſt, thanks to heav'n; and next, to *Bruſor's* valour,
Which I'll not guerdon with large promiſes;
But ſtraight reward thee with a bounteous largeſs:
But what two *Chriſtian* virgins have we here?

Bruſor.
Part of the ſpoil of *Rhodes*, which were preſerved
To be preſented to your mightineſs.

Soliman.
This preſent pleaſeth more than all the reſt;
And, were their garments turn'd from black to white,
I ſhould have deem'd them *Juno's* goodly ſwans,
Or *Venus'* milkwhite doves: ſo mild they are,
And ſo adorn'd with beauty's miracle.—
Here, *Bruſor*, this kind turtle ſhall be thine;
Take her, and uſe her at thy pleaſure:
But this kind turtle is for *Soliman*,
That her captivity may turn to bliſs.
Fair looks, reſembling *Phœbus'* radiant beams,
Smooth forehead, like the table of high *Jove*,
Small penſil'd eyebrows, like two glorious rainbows,
Quick lamplike eyes, like heav'n's two brighteſt orbs,
Lips of pure coral, breathing ambroſie,

SOLIMAN AND PERSEDA.

Cheeks, where the rose and lily are in combat,
Neck, whiter than the snowy *Apenines,*
Breasts, like two overflowing fountains,
'Twixt which a vale leads to th' *Elysian* shades,
Where under covert lies the fount of pleasure,
Which thoughts may guess, but tongue must not profane;
A sweeter creature nature never made:
Love never tainted *Soliman* till now. —
Now, fair virgin, let me hear thee speak.
          Perseda.
What can my tongue utter, but grief and death?
          Soliman.
The sound is honey, but the sense is gall:
Then, sweeting, bless me with a cheerful look.
          Perseda.
How can mine eyes dart forth a pleasant look,
When they are stop'd with floods of flowing tears?
          Soliman.
If tongue with grief, and eyes with tears be fill'd,
Say, virgin, how doth thy heart admit,
The pure affection of great *Soliman?*
          Perseda.
My thoughts are like pillars of adamant,
Too hard to take an new impression.
          Soliman.
Nay, then, I see, my stooping makes her proud;
She is my vassal, and I will command: —
Coy virgin, know'st thou what offence it is,
To thwart the will, and pleasure of a king?
Why, thy life is done, if I but say the word.
          Perseda.
Why, that's the period that my heart desires.
          Soliman.
And die thou shalt unless thou change thy mind.
          Perseda.
Nay then, *Perseda* grows resolute :
Soliman's thoughts and mine resemble

Lines parallel,[1] that never can be join'd.
Soliman.
Then kneel thee down,
And at my hands receive the stroke of death
Doom'd to thyself by thine own wilfulness.
Perseda.
Strike, strike; thy words pierce deeper that thy blows.
Soliman.
Brusor, hide her; for her looks withhold me.
[*Then* Brusor *hides her with a lawn.*
O *Brusor*, thou hast not hid her lips;
For there sits *Venus* with *Cupid* on her knee,
And all the *Graces* smiling round about her,
So craving pardon, that I cannot strike.
Brusor.
Her face is cover'd over quite, my lord.
Soliman.
Why, so: O *Brusor*, seest thou not
Her milkwhite neck, that alabaster tower?
'Twill break the edge of my keen scimitar,
And pieces, flying back, will wound myself.
Brusor.
Now she is all covered, my lord.
Soliman.
Why now at last she dies.
Perseda.
O *Christ*, receive my soul.
Soliman.
Hark, *Brusor*; she calls on *Christ*:
I will not send her to him. Her words are musick;
The selfsame musick that in ancient days
Brought *Alexander* from war to banqueting,
And made him fall from skirmishing to kissing.—
No, my dear love would not let me kill thee,
Though majesty would turn desire to wrath:
There lies my sword, humbled at thy feet;
And I myself, that govern many kings,
Entreat a pardon for my rash misdeed.

[1] *Lives paralize,*

Perseda.

Perseda.
Now *Soliman* wrongs his imperial state;
But if thou love me, and have hope to win,
Grant me one boon that I shall crave of thee.
Soliman.
Whate'er it be, *Perseda*, I grant it thee.
Perseda.
Then let me live a *Christian* virgin still,
Unless my state shall alter by my will.
Soliman.
My word is past, and I recall my passions:
What should he do with crowns and empery,
That cannot govern private fond affections?
Yet give me leave, in honest sort to court thee,
To ease, though not to cure, my malady:
Come, sit thee down upon my right hand here;
This seat I keep void for another friend. —
Go, *Janisaries*, call in your governour;
So shall I joy between two captive friends,
And yet myself be captive to them both,
If friendship's yoke were not at liberty: —
See where he comes my other best beloved.

Enter Eraſtus.

Perseda.
My sweet, and best beloved.
Eraſtus.
My sweet, and best beloved.
Perseda.
For thee, my dear *Eraſtus*, have I liv'd.
Eraſtus.
And I for thee, or else I had not liv'd.
Soliman.
What words in affection do I see?
Eraſtus.
Ah, pardon me, great *Soliman*; for this is she,

THE TRAGEDY OF

For whom I mourn'd more than for all *Rhodes*,
And from whose absence I deriv'd my sorrow.
Perseda.
And pardon me, my lord; for this is he,
For whom I thwarted *Soliman's* entreats,
And for whose exile I lamented thus.
Erastus.
Ev'n from my childhood have I tender'd thee;
Witness the heavens, of my unfeigned love.
Soliman.
By this one accident I well perceive,
That heav'ns, and heav'nly powers do manage love.
I love them both, I know not which the better:
They love each other best, what then should follow,
But that I conquer both by my deserts,
And join their hands whose hearts are knit already? —
Erastus, and *Perseda*, come you hither,
And both give me your hands. —
Erastus, none but thou couldst win *Perseda*: —
Perseda, none but thou couldst win *Erastus*,
From great *Soliman*; so well I love you both.
And now, to turn late promises to good effect,
Be thou, *Erastus*, governour of *Rhodes*:
By this thou shalt dismiss my garrison.
Brusor.
Must he reap that, for which I took the toil?
Come, envy, then, and fit in friendship's seat;
How can I love him that enjoys my right? [*Aside.*
Soliman.
Give me a crown, to crown the bride withal. —
[*Then he crowns* Perseda.
Perseda, for my sake, wear this crown. —
Now is she fairer than she was before;
This title so augments her beauty, as the fire
That lay with honour's hand rak'd up in ashes
Revives again to flames, the force is such:
Remove the cause, and then the effect will die;
They must depart, or I shall not be quiet. —

Erastus,

Eraſtus, and *Perſeda*, marvel not,
That all in haſte I wiſh you to depart;
There is an urgent cauſe, but privy to myſelf:
Command my ſhipping for to waft you over.
                Eraſtus.
My gracious lord, when *Eraſtus* doth forget
This favour, then let him live abandon'd and forlorn.
                Perſeda.
Nor will *Perſeda* ſlack, ev'n in her prayers;
But ſtill ſolicit God for *Soliman*,
Whoſe mind hath prov'd ſo good and gracious.
                                    [*Exeunt.*
                Soliman.
Farewel, *Eraſtus*;—*Perſeda*, farewel too.—
Methinks, I ſhould not part with two ſuch friends,
The one ſo renown'd for arms, and courteſy,
The other ſo adorn'd with grace and modeſty:
Yet of the two *Perſeda* moves me moſt,
Ay, and ſo moves me, that I now repent
That e'er I gave away my heart's deſire;
What was it, but abuſe of fortune's gift?
And therefore fortune now will be reveng'd:
What was it, but abuſe of love's command?
And therefore mighty love will be reveng'd:
What was it but abuſe of heav'ns that gave her me?
And therefore angry heav'ns will be reveng'd:
Heav'ns, love, and fortune, all three have decreed
That I ſhall love her ſtill, and lack her ſtill;
Like ever-thirſting wretched *Tantalus*.
Fooliſh *Soliman*, why did I ſtrive
To do him kindneſs, and undo myſelf?
Well govern'd friends do firſt regard themſelves.
                Bruſor.
Ay, now occaſion ſerves to ſtumble him,
That thruſt his ſickle in my harveſt corn:—   [*Aſide.*
Pleaſeth your majeſty, to hear *Bruſor* ſpeak?

Soliman.
To one paſt cure good counſel comes too late;
Yet ſay thy mind.
Bruſor.
With ſecret letters woo her, and with gifts.
Soliman.
My lines and gifts will but return my ſhame.
Lucina.
Hear me, my lord; let me go over to *Rhodes*,
That I may plead in your affection's cauſe:
One woman may do much to win another.
Soliman.
Indeed, *Lucina*, were her huſband from her,
She happily might be won by thy perſuades;
But, whilſt he lives, there is no hope in her.
Bruſor.
Why lives he then to grieve great *Soliman?*
This only remains, that you conſider
In two extremes the leaſt is to be choſen:
If ſo your life depend upon her love,
And that her love depends upon his life,
Is it not better, that *Eraſtus* die
Ten thouſand deaths, than *Soliman* ſhould periſh?
Soliman.
Ay, ſay'ſt thou ſo? why then, it ſhall be ſo:
But by what means ſhall poor *Eraſtus* die?
Bruſor.
This ſhall be the means: I'll fetch him back again,
Under colour of great conſequence;
No ſooner ſhall he land upon our ſhore,
But witneſs ſhall be ready to accuſe him
Of treaſon done againſt your mightineſs,
And then he ſhall be doom'd by marſhal law.
Solimau.
O, fine device! *Bruſor*, get thee gone:
Come thou again; but let the lady ſtay
To win *Perſeda* to my will: meanwhile,

Will

SOLIMAN AND PERSEDA.

Will I prepare the judge and witnesses;
And if this take effect, thou shalt be viceroy,
And fair *Lucina* queen of *Tripoli*:
Brusor, be gone; for till thou come I languish.
       [*Exeunt* Brusor, *and Lucina.*
And now, to ease my troubled thoughts at last,
I will go sit among my learned eunuchs,
And hear them play, and see my minions dance;
For till that *Brusor* bring me my desire,
I may assuage, but never quench love's fire.   [*Exit.*

    Enter Basilisco.

     Basilisco.
Since the expugnation of the *Rhodian* isle,
Methinks, a thousand years are overpass'd,
More for the lack of my *Perseda's* presence,
Than for the loss of *Rhodes*, that paltry isle,
Or for my friends that there were murdered:
My valour every where shall purchase friends;
And where a man lives well, there is his country.
Alas! the *Christians* are but very shallow
In giving judgment of a man at arms,
A man of my desert and excellence:
The *Turks*, whom they account for barbarous,
Having foreheard of *Basilisco's* worth,
A number underprop me with their shoulders,
And in procession bare me to the church,
As I had been a second *Mahomet*;
I, fearing they would adore me for a God,
Wisely inform'd them that I was but man,
Although in time, perhaps, I might aspire,
To purchase godhead as did *Hercules*;
I mean, by doing wonders in the world.
Amidst their church they bound me to a pillar,
And to make trial of my valiancy,
They lop'd a collop of my tenderest member;

      R 3   But

THE TRAGEDY OF

But think you *Basilisco* squicht for that
Ev'n as a cow for tickling in the horn?
That done, they set me on a milkwhite ass,
Compassing me with goodly ceremonies:
That day, methought, I sat in *Pompey's* chair,
And view'd the capitol, and was *Rome's* greatest glory.

Enter Piston.

Piston.
I would, my master had left
Some other to be his agent here:
'Faith, I am weary of the office already.—
What, signior *Tremomundo*,
That rid a pilgrimage to beg cake-bread?
  Basilisco.
O, take me not unprovided; let me fetch my weapon.
  Piston.
Why, I meant nothing but a *basolus manus*.*
  Basilisco.
No? didst thou not mean to give me the privy stab?
  Piston.
No, by my troth, sir.
  Basilisco.
Nay, if thou hadst, I had not fear'd thee, I;
I tell thee, my skin holds out pistol-proof.
  Piston.
Pistol-proof? I'll try, if it will hold out pin-proof.
  [*Then he pricks him with a pin.*
  Basilisco.
O, shoot no more; great god, I yield to thee.
  Piston.
I see, his skin is but pistol-proof from
The girdle upward:—What sudden agony was that?
  Basilisco.
Why, saw'st thou not, how *Cupid* god of love,
Not daring look me in the marshal face,

* He means to say, *baissez les mains*.

Came

Came like a coward, stealing after me,
And with his pointed dart prick'd my posteriors?
Piston.
Then hear my opinion concerning that point:
The ladies of *Rhodes*, hearing that you have lost
A capital part of your lady-ware,
Have made their petition to *Cupid*,
To plague you above all other,
As one prejudicial to their muliebrity:
Now, sir, *Cupid*, seeing you already hurt before,
Thinks it a greater punishment to hurt you behind;
Therefore I would wish you to have an eye to the back
    door.
Basilisco.
'Sooth, thou say'st, I must be fenc'd behind;
I'll hang my target there.
Piston.
Indeed, that will serve to bear off some blows,
When you run away in a fray.
Basilisco.
Sirra, sirra, what art thou,
That thus encroachest upon my familiarity,
Without special admittance?
Piston.
Why, do you not know me? I am *Erastus'* man.
Basilisco.
What, art thou that petty pigmy,
That challeng'd me at *Rhodes*,
Whom I refus'd to combat for his minority?
Where is *Erastus*? I owe him chastisement in *Perseda*'s
    quarrel.
Piston.
Do not you know, that they are all friends,
And *Erastus* married to *Perseda*,
And *Erastus* made governour of *Rhodes*,
And I left here to be their agent?

Basilisco.

THE TRAGEDY OF

Basilisco.
O *cœlum, o terra, o maria,* Neptune!
Did I turn *Turk* to follow her so far?
Piston.
The more shame for you.
Basilisco.
And is she link'd in liking with my foe?
Piston.
That's because you were out of the way.
Basilisco.
O wicked *Turk* for to steal her hence.
Piston.
O wicked turn-coat that would have her stay.
Basilisco.
The truth is, I will be a *Turk* no more.
Piston.
And, I fear, thou wilt never prove good *Christian.*
Basilisco.
I will after to take revenge.
Piston.
And I'll stay here about my master's business.
Basilisco.
Farewel, *Constantinople*; I will to *Rhodes.* [*Exit.*
Piston.
Farewel, counterfeit fool! —
God send him good shipping: 'tis nois'd about, that
 Brusor
Is sent to fetch my master back again;
I cannot be well, till I hear the rest of the news,
Therefore I'll about it straight. [*Exit.*

Enter Chorus.

Love.
Now, *Fortune*, what haft thou done in this latter act?
Fortune.
I brought *Perseda* to the prefence
Of *Soliman*, the *Turkish* emperour,
And gave *Lucina* into *Brusor's* hands.
Love.
And firft I ftung them with confenting love;
And made great *Soliman*, fweet beauty's thrall,
Humble himfelf at fair *Perseda's* feet,
And made him praife love, and captive's beauty:
Again I made him to recall his paffions,
And give *Perseda* to *Eraftus'* hands,
And, after, make repentance of the deed.
Fortune.
Meantime, I fill'd *Eraftus'* fails with wind,
And brought him home unto his native land.
Death.
And I fuborn'd *Brusor*, with envious rage,
To counfel *Soliman* to flay his friend:
Brusor is fent to fetch him back again:
Mark well what follows; for the hiftory,
Proves me chief actor in this tragedy. [*Exeunt.*

ACT

ACT V.

Enter Eraſtus, *and* Perſeda.

Eraſtus.

PERSEDA, theſe days are our days of joy:
What could I more deſire than thee to wife?
And that I have: or than to govern *Rhodes?*
And that I do, thanks to great *Soliman*.

Perſeda.
And thanks to gracious heav'ns, that ſo
Brought *Soliman* from worſe to better;
For though I never told it thee till now,
His heart was purpos'd once to do thee wrong.

Eraſtus.
Ay, that was before he knew thee to be mine;
But now, *Perſeda*, let's forget old griefs,
And let our ſtudies wholly be employ'd
To work each other's bliſs and heart's delight.

Perſeda.
Our preſent joys will be ſo much the greater,
When as we call to mind forepaſſed griefs:
So ſings the mariner upon the ſhore,
When he hath paſs'd the dangerous time of ſtorms;
But if my love will have old griefs forgot,
They ſhall lay buried in *Perſeda's* breaſt.

Enter Bruſor, *and* Lucina.

Eraſtus.
Welcome, lord *Bruſor*.

Perſeda.
And, *Lucina* too.

Bruſor.

Brusor.
Thanks, lord governour.
Lucina.
And thanks to you, madam.
Erastus.
What hasty news brings you so soon to *Rhodes?*—
Although to me you never come too soon.
Brusor.
So it is, my lord, that upon great affairs,
Importuning health and wealth of *Soliman*,
His highness by me entreateth you,
As ever you respect his future love,
Or have regard unto his courtesy,
To come yourself in person, and visit him,
Without inquiry what should be the cause.
Erastus.
Were there no ships to cross the seas withal,
My arms should frame mine oars to cross the seas;
And, should the seas turn tide to force me back,
Desire should frame me wings to fly to him:
I go, *Perseda*, thou must give me leave.
Perseda.
Though loath, yet *Soliman*'s command prevails.
Lucina.
And, sweet *Perseda*, I will stay with you,
From *Brusor* my beloved; and I'll want him,
Till he bring back *Erastus* unto you.
Erastus.
Lord *Brusor*, come; 'tis time that we were gone.
Brusor.
Perseda, farewel; be not angry,
For that I carry thy beloved from thee,
We will return with all speed possible:—
And thou, *Lucina*, use *Perseda* so,
That for my carrying of *Erastus* hence,
She curse me not; and so farewel to both.
Perseda.
Come, *Lucina*, let's in; my heart is full. [*Exeunt.*

Enter

Enter Soliman, *Lord marshal, the two Witnesses, and Janisaries.*

Soliman.
Lord marshal, see you handle it cunningly:
And, when *Erastus* comes, our perjur'd friend,
See he be condemn'd by marshal law;
Here will I stand to see, and not be seen.
Marshal.
Come, fellows, see when this matter comes in question,
You stagger not: — and, *Janisaries*,
See that your strangling cords be ready.
Soliman.
Ah, that *Perseda* were not half so fair,
Or that *Soliman* were not so fond,
Or that *Perseda* had some other love,
Whose death might save my poor *Erastus*' life.

Enter Brusor, *and* Erastus.

See where he comes, whom though I dearly love,
Yet must his blood be spilt for my behoof:
Such is the force of marrow-burning [1] love.
Marshal.
Erastus, lord governour of *Rhodes*,
I arrest you in the king's name.
Erastus.
What thinks lord *Brusor* of this strange arrest?
Hast thou entrap'd me to this treachery?
Intended, well I wot, without the leave
Or licence of my lord, great *Soliman*.
Brusor.
Why then appeal to him, where thou shalt know,
And be assur'd, that I betray thee not.
Soliman.
Yes, thou, and I, and all of us betray him.

[1] *morrow burning*

Marshal.

Marshal.
No, no; in this cafe no appeal shall serve.
Erastus.
Why, then, to thee, or unto any else:
I here protest by heav'ns unto you all,
That never was there man more true or just;
Or in his deeds more loyal and upright;
Or more loving, or more innocent,
Than I have been to gracious *Soliman,*
Since first I set my feet on *Turkish* land.
Soliman.
Myself would be his witness, if I durst;
But bright *Perseda's* beauty stops my tongue.
Marshal.
Why, firs, why face to face express you not
The treasons you reveal'd to *Soliman?*
1 *Witness.*
That very day *Erastus* went from hence,
He sent for me into his cabinet,
And for that man that is of my profession.
Erastus.
I never saw them I until this day.
1 *Witness.*
His cabin door fast shut, he first began
To question us of all sorts of fireworks;
Wherein when we had fully resolved him,
What might be done, he, spreading on the board
A huge heap of our imperial coin;
All this is yours, quoth he, if you consent,
To leave great *Soliman* and serve in *Rhodes.*
Marshal.
Why, that was treason; but onward with the rest.

Enter

Enter Piston.

Piston.
What have we here? my master before the marshal?
              1 *Witness.*
We said not, ay, nor durst we say him, nay,
Because we were already in his gallies;
But seem'd content to fly with him to *Rhodes:*
With that he purs'd the gold, and gave it us.
The rest I dare not speak it is so bad.
             Erastus.
Heav'ns, hear you this, and drops not vengeance on
   them?
            2 *Witness.*
The rest, and worse will I discourse in brief:
Will you consent, quoth he, to fire the fleet,
That lies hard by us here in *Bosphoron?*
For be it spoke in secret here, quoth he,
Rhodes must no longer bear the *Turkish* yoke:
We said, the task might easily be perform'd,
But that we lack'd such drugs to mix with powder,
As were not in his gallies to be got:
At this he leap'd for joy, swearing and promising,
That our reward should be redoubled:
We came aland not minding to return,
And as our duty, and allegiance bound us,
We made all known unto great *Soliman;*
But ere we could summon him aland,
His ships were past a kenning from the shore:
Belike, he thought we had betray'd his treasons.
            Marshal.
That all is true, that here you have declar'd,
Both lay your hands upon the alcoran.
           1 *Witness.*
Foul death betide me, if I swear not true.
           2 *Witness.*
And mischief light on me, if I swear false.

                                    Soliman.

Soliman.
Mischief and death shall light upon you both.
Marshal.
Erastus, thou see'st what witness hath produc'd against thee:
What answer'st thou unto their accusation?
Erastus.
That these are *Sinons,* and myself poor *Troy.*
Marshal.
Now it resteth, I appoint thy death;
Wherein thou shalt confess, I'll favour thee,
For that thou wert belov'd of *Soliman:*
Thou shalt forthwith be bound unto that post,
And strangled as our *Turkish* order is.
Piston.
Such favour send all *Turks,* I pray God.
Erastus.
I see, this train was plotted ere I came:
What boots complaining where's no remedy?
Yet give me leave, before my life shall end,
To moan *Perseda,* and accuse my friend.
Soliman.
O unjust *Soliman!* o wicked time!
Where filthy lust must murder honest love.
Malshal.
Despatch, for our time limited is past.
Erastus.
Alas, how can he but be short, whose tongue
Is fast ty'd with galling sorrow? —
Farewel, *Perseda;* no more but that for her: —
Inconstant *Soliman,* no more but that for him: —
Unfortunate *Erastus,* no more but that for me:
Lo, this is all; and thus I leave to speak.
[*Then they strangle him.*
Piston.
Marry, sir, this is a fair warning for me to get me gone. [*Exit Piston.*

Soliman.

THE TRAGEDY OF

Soliman.
O, save his life, if it be possible;
I will not lose him for my kingdom's worth.—
Ah, poor *Erastus*, art thou dead already?
What bold presumer durst be so resolved,
For to bereave *Erastus*' life from him,
Whose life to me was dearer than mine own?
Was't thou? — and thou? — Lord marshal, bring them hither;
And at *Erastus*' hand let them receive
The stroke of death, whom they have spoil'd of life.—
What, is thy hand too weak? then mine shall help
To send them down to everlasting night,
To wait upon thee through eternal shade;
Thy soul shall not go mourning hence alone:—
Thus die, and thus; for thus you murder'd him.

[*Then he kills the two* Janisaries, *that kill'd* Erastus.

But, soft; methinks, he is not satisfied:
The breath doth murmur softly from his lips,
And bids me kill those bloody witnesses,
By whose treachery *Erastus* died:—
Lord marshal, hale them to the tower's top,
And throw them headlong down into the valley;
So let their treasons with their lives have end.

1 *Witness.*
Yourself procur'd us.

2 *Witness.*
Is this our hire?

[*Then the* Marshal *bears them to the tower top.*

Soliman.
Speak not a word; lest, in my wrathful fury,
I doom you to ten thousand direful torments:—
And, *Brusor,* see *Erastus* be inter'd
With honour in a kingly sepulchre:—
Why, when, lord *Marshal?* great *Hector's* son,
Although his age did plead for innocence,
Was sooner tumbled from the fatal tower,

Than

Than are thofe perjur'd wicked witneffes.
                    [*Then they are both tumbled down.*
Why now *Eraftus*' ghoft is fatisfied:
Ay, but yet the wicked judge furvives,
By whom *Eraftus* was condemn'd to die. —
Brufor, as thou lov'ft me ftab in the *Marfhal*,
Left he detect us unto the world,
By making known our bloody practices;
And then will thou and I hoift fail to *Rhodes*,
Where thy *Lucina*, and my *Perfeda* lives.
            Brufor.
I will, my lord: — Lord *Marfhal*, it is his highnefs'
    pleafure,
That you commend him to *Eraftus*' foul.
                [*Then he kills the* Marfhal.
            Soliman.
Here ends my dear *Eraftus*' tragedy,
And now begins my pleafant comedy;
But if *Perfeda* underftand thefe news,
Our fcene will prove but tragicomical.
            Brufor.
Fear not, my lord, *Lucina* plays her part,
And wooes apace in *Soliman's* behalf.
            Soliman.
Then, *Brufor*, come; and with fome few men
Let's fail to *Rhodes* with all convenient fpeed:
For, till I fold *Perfeda* in mine arms,
My troubled ears are deaf'd with love's alarms. [*Exeunt*.

Enter Perfeda, Lucina, *and* Bafilifco.
            Perfeda.
Now, fignior *Bafilifco*, which like you,
The *Turkifh*, or our nation beft?
            Bafilifco.
That which your ladyfhip will have me like.
            Lucina.
I am deceiv'd, but you were circumcifed.
VOL. II.   S   *Bafilifco*.

Basilisco.
Indeed, I was a little cut in the porpuse.[1]
Perseda.
What means made you to steal back to *Rhodes?*
Basilisco.
The mighty pinck-an-ey'd, brand-bearing god,
To whom I am so long true servitour,
When he espy'd my weeping floods of tears
For your depart, he bad me follow him:
I follow'd him; he with his firebrand
Parted the seas, and we came over dryshod.
Lucina.
A matter not unlikely: but how chance,
Your *Turkish* bonnet is not on your head?
Basilisco.
Because I now am *Christian* again,
And that by natural means; for, as
The old canon says very prettily,
Nihil est tam naturale, quod eo modo colligatum est,
And so forth: so I became a *Turk* to follow her,
To follow her, am now return'd a *Christian.*

Enter Piston.

Piston.
O lady, and mistress, weep and lament,
And wring your hands; for my master
Is condemn'd, and executed.
Lucina.
Be patient, sweet *Perseda*; the fool but jests.
Perseda.
Ah, no; my nightly dreams foretold me this,
Which, foolish woman! fondly I neglected.—
But say, what death died my poor *Erastus?*
Piston.
Nay, God be prais'd, his death was reasonable;
He was but strangled.

[1] *porpuse.* sic.   *Perseda.*

SOLIMAN AND PERSEDA.

Perseda.
But strangled! ah, double death to me:
But say, wherefore was he condemn'd to die?
Piston.
For nothing but high treason.
Perseda.
What treason, or by whom was he condemn'd?
Piston.
'Faith, two great knights of the post swore upon
The alcoran that he would have fir'd the *Turks* fleet.
Perseda.
Was *Brusor* by?
Piston.
Ay.
Perseda.
And *Soliman*?
Piston.
No; but I saw where he stood,
To hear, and see the matter well convey'd.
Perseda.
Accursed *Soliman!* profane alcoran!—
Lucina, came thy husband to this end,
To lead a lamb unto the slaughter-house?
Hast thou for this in *Soliman's* behalf,
With cunning words tempted my chastity?
Thou shalt abie for both your treacheries.—
It must be so,— *Basilisco*, dost thou love me? speak.
Basilisco.
Ay, more than I love either life or soul:
What, shall I stab the emperour for thy sake?
Perseda.
No, but *Lucina*; if thou lov'st me, kill her.
[Then Basilisco *takes a dagger, and feels upon the point of it.*
Basilisco.
The point will mar her skin.

Perseda.

THE TRAGEDY OF

Perseda.
What, dar'st thou not? give me the dagger then.
There's a reward for all thy treasons past.
　　　　　　　[*Then* Perseda *kills* Lucina.
Basilisco.
Yet dare I bear her hence, to do thee good.
Perseda.
No; let her lie, a prey to rav'ning birds;
Nor shall her death alone suffice for his,
Rhodes now shall be no longer *Soliman's*:
We'll fortify our walls, and keep the town,
In spite of proud, insulting *Soliman*.
I know the lecher hopes to have my love;
And first, *Perseda* shall with this hand die,
Than yield to him, and live in infamy.
　　　　　　　[*Exeunt.* Manet Basilisco
Basilisco.
I will ruminate: Death, which the poets
Feign to be pale and meagre, hath depriv'd
Erastus' trunk from breathing vitality,
A brave cavalier, but my approved foeman.
Let me see: where is that *Alcides*, surnam'd *Hercules*,
The only club-man of his time? dead.
Where is the eldest son of *Priam*,
That *Abraham-*colour'd *Trojan?* dead.
Where is the leader of the myrmidons,
That well-knit *Achilles?* dead.
Where is that furious *Ajax*, the son of *Telamon*,
Or that fraudful 'squire of *Ithaca*, yclep'd *Ulysses?* dead,
Where is tipsy *Alexander*, that great cup-conqueror,
Or *Pompey*, that brave warrior? dead.
I am myself strong, but I confess
Death to be stronger: I am valiant, but mortal;
I am adorned with nature's gifts,
A giddy goddess, that now giveth and anon taketh;
I am wise, but quiddits will not answer death.
To conclude in a word; to be captious, virtuous, in
　　genious,
　　　　　　　　　　　　　　　　　　　　Or

Or to be nothing when it pleafeth death to be envious.
The great *Turk*, whofe feat is *Conftantinople*,
Hath beleaguer'd *Rhodes*, whofe chieftain is a woman:
I could take the rule upon me;
But the fhrub is fafe, when the cedar fhaketh:
I love *Perfeda*, as one worthy;
But I love *Bafilifco*, as one I hold more worthy,
My father's fon, my mother's folace, my proper felf.
'Faith, he can do little, that cannot fpeak;
And he can do lefs, that cannot run away:
Then fith man's life is as a glafs, and a fillip may crack it,
Mine is no more, and a bullet may pierce it;
Therefore I will play leaft in fight. [*Exit.*

Enter Soliman, Brufor, *with Janifaries.*

Soliman.
The gates are fhut; which proves, that *Rhodes* revolts,
And that *Perfeda* is not *Soliman's*.—
Ah, *Brufor*, fee where thy *Lucina* lies,
Butcher'd defpitefully without the walls.

Brufor.
Unkind *Perfeda*, couldft thou ufe her fo?
And yet we us'd *Perfeda* little better.

Soliman.
Nay, gentle *Brufor*, ftay thy tears a while,
Left with thy woes thou fpoil my comedy,
And all too foon be turn'd to tragedies.
Go, *Brufor*, bear her to thy private tent,
Where we at leifure will lament her death,
And with our [1] tears bewail her obfequies;
For yet *Perfeda* lives for *Soliman*.—
Drum, found a parley:—Were it not for her
I would fack the town, ere I would found a parley.
[*The drum founds a parley.*
[*Perfeda comes upon the walls in man's apparel.*
Bafilifco, and Pifton, upon the walls.

1 *her*   *Perfeda.*

Perseda.
At whose entreaty is this parley founded?
Soliman.
At our entreaty, therefore yield the town.
Perseda.
Why, what art thou, that boldly bid'st me yield?
Soliman.
Great *Soliman*, lord of all the world.
Perseda.
Thou art not lord of all, *Rhodes* is not thine.
Soliman.
It was, and shall be, maugre who says no.
Perseda.
I that say no, will never see it thine.
Soliman.
Why, what art thou that dar'st resist my force?
Perseda.
A gentleman, and thy mortal enemy,
And one that dares thee to the single combat.
Soliman.
First tell me, doth *Perseda* live, or no?
Perseda.
She lives to see the wreck of *Soliman*.
Soliman.
Then I will combat thee, whate'er thou art.
Perseda.
And in *Erastus*' name I'll combat thee;
And here I promise thee on my *Christian* faith,
Then will I yield *Perseda* to thy hands,
That, if thy strength shall overmatch my right,
To use, as to thy liking it shall seem best:
But ere I come to enter single fight,
First, let my tongue utter my heart's despite;
And thus my tale begins: Thou wicked tyrant!
Thou murderer! accursed homicide!
For whom hell gapes, and all the ugly fiends
Do wait for to receive thee in their jaws!
Ah, perjur'd, and inhuman *Soliman!*
How could thy heart harbour a wicked thought,

Againſt the ſpotleſs life of poor *Eraſtus*?
Was he not true? 'would thou hadſt been as juſt!
Was he not valiant? 'would thou hadſt been as virtuous!
Was he not loyal? 'would thou hadſt been as loving!
Ah, wicked tyrant! in that one man's death
Thou haſt betray'd the flower of *Chriſtendom*.
Dy'd he, becauſe his worth obſcured thine?
In ſlaught'ring him thy virtues are defam'd:
Didſt thou miſdo him, in hope to win *Perſeda*?
Ah, fooliſh man, therein thou art deceiv'd:
For though ſhe live, yet will ſhe ne'er live thine;
Which to approve, I'll come to combat thee.
　　　　　　Soliman.
Injurious, foul-mouth'd knight, my wrathful arm
Shall chaſtiſe, and rebuke theſe injuries.
　[*Then* Perſeda *comes down to* Soliman, *and* Baſiliſco
　and Piſton.
　　　　　　Piſton.
Ay, but hear you, are you ſo fooliſh to fight with him?
　　　　　　Baſiliſco.
Ay, ſirra; why not, as long as I ſtand by?
　　　　　　Soliman.
I'll not defend *Eraſtus*' innocence,
But thee in maintaining *Perſeda*'s beauty.
　　[*Then they fight,* Soliman *kills* Perſeda.
　　　　　　Perſeda.
Ay, now I lay *Perſeda* at thy feet;
But with thy hand firſt wounded to the death:
Now ſhall the world report, that *Soliman*
Slew *Eraſtus* in hope to win *Perſeda*,
And murder'd her for loving of her huſband.
　　　　　　Soliman.
What, my *Perſeda*! all that have I done:
Yet kiſs me, gentle love, before thou die.
　　　　　　Perſeda.
A kiſs I grant thee, though I hate thee deadly.
　　　　　　Soliman.
I lov'd thee dearly, and accept thy kiſs;
Why didſt thou love *Eraſtus* more than me?　　　Or

Or, why didst thou not give *Soliman* a kiss
Ere this unhappy time? then hadst thou liv'd.
            Basilisco.
Ah, let me kiss thee too before I die.
                    [*Then* Soliman *kills* Basilisco.
            Soliman.
Nay, die thou shalt for thy presumption,
For kissing her whom I do hold so dear.
            Piston.
I will not kiss her, sir, but give me leave
To weep over her; for, while she lived,
She lov'd me dearly, and I loved her.
            Soliman.
If thou didst love her, villain, as thou said'st,
Then wait on her thorough eternal night.—
                    [*Then* Soliman *kills* Piston.
Ah, *Perseda*, how shall I mourn for thee?
Fair springing rose, ill-pluck'd before thy time!
Ah, heav'ns that hitherto have smil'd on me,
Why do you unkindly lower on *Soliman?*
The loss of half my realms, nay crown's decay
Could not have prick'd so near unto my heart,
As doth the loss of my *Perseda's* life:
And with her life I likewise lose my love;
And with her love my heart's felicity:
Ev'n for *Erastus'* death the heav'ns have plagued me;
Ah, no, the heav'ns did never more accurse me,
Than when they made me butcher of my love:
Yet justly how can I condemn myself,
When *Brusor* lives that was the cause of all?—
Come, *Brusor,* help to lift her body up:
Is she not fair?
            Brusor.
Ev'n in the hour of death.
            Soliman.
Was she not constant?
            Brusor.
As firm as are the poles whereon heav'n lies.
            Soliman.

Soliman.
Was she not chaste?
Brusor.
As is *Pandora*, or *Diana's* thoughts.
Soliman.
Then tell me, (his treasons set aside,)
What was *Erastus* in thy opinion?
Brusor.
Fair-spoken, wise, courteous, and liberal;
Kind, even to his foes, gentle and affable;
And, all in all, his deeds heroical.
Soliman.
Ah! was he so? how durst thou then, ungracious counsellor,
First cause me murder such a worthy man,
And after tempt so virtuous a woman?
Be this therefore the last that e'er thou speak.—
Janisaries, take him straight unto the block;
Off with his head, and suffer him not to speak.
[*Exit* Brusor.
And now, *Perseda*, here I lay me down,
And on thy beauty still contemplate,
Until mine eyes shall surfeit by my gazing:
But stay, let me see what paper is this.
[*Then he takes up a paper, and reads in it as followeth.*
Tyrant, my lips were sauc'd [1] with deadly poison,
To plague thy heart that is so full of poison.
What, am I poison'd? — Then, *Janisaries*,
Let me see *Rhodes* recover'd ere I die:—
Soldiers, assault the town on ev'ry side;
Spoil all, kill all; let none escape your fury.—
[*Sound an alarum to the fight.*
Say, *Captain*, is *Rhodes* recovered again?
Captain.
It is, my lord, and stoops to *Soliman*.
Soliman.
Yet that alays the fury of my pain

I sawst   Before

Before I die, for doubtlefs die I muft;
Ay, fates, injurious fates have fo decreed:
For now I feel the poifon 'gins to work,
And I am weak, ev'n to the very death;
Yet fomething more contentedly I die,
For that my death was wrought by her devife,
Who, living, was my joy, whofe death my wo.—
Ah, *Janifaries*, now dies your emperour,
Before his age hath feen his mellow'd years;
And, if you ever lov'd your emperour,
Affright me not with forrows and laments:
And, when my foul from body fhall depart,
Trouble me not; but let me pafs in peace,
And in your filence let your love be fhown:
My laft requeft, for I command no more,
Is, that my body with *Perfeda's* be
Inter'd, where my *Eraftus* lies intomb'd,
And let one epitaph contain us all. —
Ah, now I feel, the paper told me true;
The poifon is difpers'd through ev'ry vein,
And boils, like *Ætna*, in my fryifig guts.—
Forgive me, dear *Eraftus*, my unkindnefs;
I have reveng'd thy death with many deaths:
And, fweet *Perfeda*, fly not *Soliman*,
When as my gliding ghoft fhall follow thee
With eager mood thorough eternal night.—
And now pale death fits on my panting foul,
And with revenging ire doth tyrannize,
And fays, — For *Soliman's* too much amifs,
This day fhall be the period of my blifs.

[*Then* Soliman *dies, and they carry him forth with filence.* [*Exeunt omnes*,

Enter Chorus.

Fortune.

I gave *Eraftus* wo and mifery
Amidft his greateft joy and jollity.

Love.

Love.
But I that have power in earth and heav'n above,
Stung them both with never-failing love.
Death.
But I bereft them both of love and life.
Love.
Of life, but not of love; for ev'n in death
Their souls are knit, though bodies be disjoin'd:
Thou didst but wound their flesh, their minds are free,
Their bodies buried, yet they honour me.
Death.
Hence, foolish *Fortune,* and thou, wanton *Love*;
Your deeds are trifles, mine of consequence.
Fortune.
I give world's happiness, and wo's increase.
Love.
By joining persons, I increase the world.
Death.
By wasting all, I conquer all the world:
And now to end our difference at last,
In this last act note but the deeds of *Death.*
Where is *Erastus* now, but in my triumph?
Where are the murderers, but in my triumph?
Where's judge, and witness, but in my triumph?
Where's false *Lucina,* but in my triumph?
Where's fair *Perseda,* but in my triumph?
Where's *Basilisco,* but in my triumph?
Where's faithful *Piston,* but in my triumph?
Where's valiant *Brusor,* but in my triumph?
And where's great *Soliman,* but in my triumph?
Their loves and fortune ended with their lives,
And they must wait upon the car of death.
Alack, *Love,* and *Fortune,* play in comedies;
For powerful *Death* best fitteth tragedies.
Love.
I go, yet *Love* shall never yield to *Death.*
[*Exit* Love.

Death.

Death.
But *Fortune* shall; for when I waste the world,
Then times and kingdoms *Fortunes* shall decay.
Fortune.
Meantime will *Fortune* govern as she may.
[*Exit* Fortune.

Death.
Ay, now will *Death* in his most haughty pride,
Fetch his imperial car from deepest hell,
And ride in triumph through the wicked world:
Sparing none but sacred *Cynthia's* friend,
Whom *Death* did fear before her life began;
For holy fates have grav'n it in their tables,
That *Death* shall die, if he attempt her end,
Whose life is heav'n's delight, and *Cynthia's* friend.
[*Exit.*

THE
TRAGEDY
OF
FERREX AND PORREX,

SET FORTH WITHOUT
ADDITION OR ALTERATION
BUT ALTOGETHER AS THE SAME WAS
SHOWED ON STAGE
BEFORE THE QUEEN'S MAJESTY,
ABOUT NINE YEARS PAST,

VIZ.

THE 18. DAY OF JANUARY. 1561.

BY THE GENTLEMEN OF THE INNER-TEMPLE.

THE
TRAGEDY
OF
FERREX AND PORREX

SET FORTH WITHOUT
ADDITION OR ALTERATION
BUT ALTOGETHER AS THE SAME WAS
SHOWED ON STAGE
BEFORE THE QUEEN'S MAJESTY,
ABOUT NINE YEAR'S PAST,
VIZ.
THE 18. DAY OF JANUARY. 1561.
BY THE GENTLEMEN OF THE INNER-TEMPLE.

THE TRAGEDY OF FERREX AND PORREX,
Or, as it is usually called,
GORBODUC,

—in point of antiquity, claims precedence of any in this volume: the omission of it in its proper place was owing to an unforeseen accident. To suppress entirely a play, that was esteemed by the wits of the age in which it was written the best of its time, would be unpardonable. There needs no other testimony of its merit than that of Sir Philip Sydney: "Our Tragedies "and comedies," says that noble author in his Defence of Poesie, "not without cause cried out against, observing rules "neither of honest civilitie, nor skilfull poetrie. Excepting "Gorboduck, which notwithstanding, as it is full of stately "speeches, and well sounding phrases, climing to the height "of Seneca his stile, and as full of notable moralitie, which "it doth most delightfully teach, and so obtaine the very end "of Poesie: Yet in truth, it is verie defectious in the cir- "cumstances, which grieves me, because it might not remaine "as an exact model of all tragedies. For it is faultie both in "place and time, the two necessary companions of all corporall "actions." It is here to be observed, that few authors of later ages have strictly conformed themselves to the unities. After him, Mr. Rymer in his Short View of Tragedy, page 84, "says, Gorboduc is a fable, doubtless better turned for tra- "gedy than any on this side the Alps in his time; and might "have been a better direction to Shakespeare and Ben Jonson "than any guide they have had the luck to follow. Mr. Pope, extracting the sense of both these criticks, dispenses it in the following words: "The writers of the succeeding age might "have improved as much in other respects, by copying from "him a propriety in the sentiments, and dignity in the sen- "tences, and an unaffected perspicuity of style, which are so "essential to tragedy, and which all the succeeding poets, not "excepting Shakespeare himself, either little understood, or "perpetually neglected." To which Mr. Spence adds, that "'tis no wonder, if the language of kings and statesmen should "be less happily imitated by a poet than a privy-counsellor.

Notwithstanding

Notwithstanding the concurrent testimony of these writers, Gorboduc has welnigh sunk into oblivion, owing, no doubt, to the inaccuracies, and capital blunders of spurious copies. Though the authors themselves gave a correct edition of this play in 1571, yet every subsequent editor printed from the spurious copy of 1565; of which the authors make heavy complaint in the advertisement prefixed to their own edition: which is preserved in the Bodleian library, and is here presented to the reader.

THE P. TO THE READER.

WHERE this tragedy was for furniture of part of the grand *Chriſtmas* in the *Inner-Temple* firſt written about nine years ago by the right honourable *Thomas*, now lord *Buckhurſt*, and by *T. Norton*, and after ſhowed before her majeſty, and never intended by the authors thereof to be publiſhed: yet one *W. G.* getting a copy thereof at ſome young man's hand that lacked a little money and much diſcretion, in the laſt great plague, *an.* 1565. about five years paſt, while the ſaid Lord was out of *England*, and *T. Norton* far out of *London*, and neither of them both made privy, put it forth exceedingly corrupted: even as if by means of a broker or hire, he ſhould have enticed into his houſe a fair maid and done her villany, and after all to beſcratched her face, torn her apparel, berayed and disfigured her, and then thruſt her out of doors diſhoneſted. In ſuch plight after long wandering ſhe came at length home to the ſight of her friends, who ſcant knew her but by a few tokens and marks remaining. They, the authors I mean, though they were very much diſpleaſed that ſhe ſo ran abroad without leave, whereby ſhe caught her ſhame, as many wantons do, yet ſeeing the caſe as it is remedileſs, have for common honeſty and ſhamefacedneſs new apparelled, trimmed and attired her in ſuch form as ſhe was before. In which better form ſince ſhe hath come to me, I have harboured her for her friends ſake and her own; and I do not doubt, her parents the authors will not now be diſcontent that ſhe go abroad among you, good readers, ſo it be in honeſt company. For ſhe is by my encouragement and others ſomewhat leſs aſhamed of the diſhoneſty done to her becauſe it was by fraud and force. If ſhe be welcome among you, and gently entertained, in favour of the houſe from whence ſhe is deſcended, and of her own nature courteouſly diſpoſed to offend no man, her friends will thank you for it. If not, but that ſhe ſhall be ſtill reproached with her former miſhap, or quarrelled at by envious perſons, ſhe, poor

poor gentlewoman, will surely play *Lucrece's* part, and of herself die for shame; and I shall wish, that she had tarried still at home with me, where she was welcome: for she did never put me to more charge, but this one poor black gown lined with white that I have now given her to go abroad among you withal.

The ARGUMENT of the TRAGEDY.

GORBODUC, king of Britain, *divided his realm in his life time to his sons,* FERREX *and* PORREX: *the sons fell to dissention: the younger killed the elder: the mother that more dearly loved the elder, for revenge killed the younger: the people, moved with the cruelty of the fact, rose in rebellion and slew both father and mother: the nobility assembled, and most terribly destroyed the rebels: and afterwards, for want of issue of the prince whereby the succession of the crown became uncertain, they fell to civil war, in which both they and many of their issues were slain, and the land for a long time almost desolate and miserably wasted.*

The Order of the Dumb Show before the First Act, *and the Signification thereof.*

FIRST the mufick of violins began to play, during which came in upon the stage six wild men clothed in leaves; of whom the first bare in his neck a faggot of small sticks, which they all, both severally and together, assayed with all their strengths to break, but it could not be broken by them. At the length one of them plucked out one of the sticks and brake it; and the rest plucking out all the other sticks one after another, did easily break them, the same being severed; which, being conjoined, they had before attempted in vain. After they had this done, they departed the stage, and the mufick ceased. Hereby was signified, that a state knit in unity, doth continue strong against all force; but being divided, is easily destroyed. As befell upon duke *Gorboduc* dividing his land to his two sons, which he before held in monarchy, and upon the dissention of the brethren to whom it was divided.

The NAMES of the SPEAKERS.

GORBODUC, *King of* Great Britain.
VIDENA, *Queen, and Wife to King* GORBODUC.
FERREX, *Elder Son to King* GORBODUC.
PORREX, *Younger Son to King* GORBODUC.
CLOYTON, *Duke of* Cornwall.
FERGUS, *Duke of* Albany.
MANDUD, *Duke of* Loegris.
GWENARD, *Duke of* Cumberland.
EUBULUS, *Secretary to the King.*
AROSTUS, *a Counsellor to the King.*
DORDAN, *a Counsellor assigned by the King to his Eldest Son* FERREX.
PHILANDER, *A Counsellor assigned by the King to his Youngest Son* PORREX. *Both being of the Old King's Council before.*
HERMON, *a Parasite, remaining with* FERREX.
TYNDAR, *a Parasite, remaining with* PORREX.
NUNTIUS, *a Messenger of the Elder Brother's Death.*
NUNTIUS, *a Messenger of Duke* FERGUS' *rising in Arms.*

MARCELLA, *a Lady, of the Queen's Privy Chamber.*

CHORUS, *Four Ancient and Sage Men of* Britain.

THE
TRAGEDY
OF
FERREX AND PORREX.

ACT I. SCENE I.

Viden. Ferrex.

Viden.

THE filent night that brings the quiet paufe,
From painful travels of the weary day,
Prolongs my careful thoughts, and makes me blame
The flow *Aurore*, that fo for love or fhame
Doth long delay to fhow her blufhing face;
And now the day renews my grieful plaint.

Ferrex.

My gracious lady and my mother dear,
Pardon my grief for your fo grieved mind,
To afk what caufe tormenteth fo your heart.

Viden.

So great a wrong, and fo unjuft defpite,
Without all caufe, againft all courfe of kind!

Ferrex.
Such causeless wrong and so unjust despite,
May have redress, or at the least, revenge.
Viden.
Neither, my son; such is the froward will,
The person such, such my mishap and thine.
Ferrex.
Mine know I none, but grief for your distress.
Viden.
Yes; mine for thine, my son: a father? no:
In kind a father, not in kindliness.
Ferrex.
My father? why? I know nothing at all,
Wherein I have misdone unto his grace.
Viden.
Therefore, the more unkind to thee and me:
For, knowing well, my son, the tender love
That I have ever born and bear to thee,
He, griev'd thereat, is not content alone
To spoil thee of my sight, my chiefest joy,
But thee, of thy birthright, and heritage,
Causeless, unkindly, and in wrongful wise,
Against all law and right he will bereave:
Half of his kingdom he will give away.
Ferrex.
To whom?
Viden.
Ev'n to *Porrex* his younger son;
Whose growing pride I do so sore suspect,
That being rais'd to equal rule with thee,
Methinks I see his envious heart to swell,
Fill'd with disdain and with ambitious hope.
The end the gods do know, whose altars I
Full oft have made in vain, of cattle slain
To send the sacred smoke to heaven's throne,
For thee my son; if things do so succeed,
As now my jealous mind misdeemeth sore.

Ferrex.

Ferrex.
Madam, leave care and careful plaint for me!
Juſt hath my father been to every wight:
His firſt injuſtice he will not extend
To me, I truſt, that give no cauſe thereof;
My brother's pride ſhall hurt himſelf, not me.
Viden.
So grant the gods! But yet thy father ſo
Hath firmly fixed his unmoved mind,
That plaints and prayers can no whit avail;
For thoſe have I aſſay'd, but even this day,
He will endeavour to procure aſſent
Of all his council to his fond deviſe.
Ferrex.
Their anceſtors from race to race have born
True faith to my forefathers and their feed:
I truſt, they eke will bear the like to me.
Viden.
There reſteth all; but if they fail thereof,
And if the end bring forth an ill ſucceſs,
On them and theirs the miſchief ſhall befall,
And ſo I pray the gods requite it them!
And ſo they will, for ſo is wont to be.
When lords and truſted rulers under kings,
To pleaſe the preſent fancy of the prince,
With wrong tranſpoſe the courſe of governance,
Murders, miſchief, or civil ſword at length,
Or mutual treaſon, or a juſt revenge,
When right-ſucceeding line returns again,
By *Jove's* juſt judgment and deſerved wrath,
Brings them to cruel and reproachful death,
And roots their names and kindreds from the earth.
Ferrex.
Mother, content you, you ſhall ſee the end.
Viden.
The end? thy end I fear, *Jove* end me firſt!

ACT

THE TRAGEDY OF

ACT I. SCENE II.

Gorboduc, Aroſtus, Philander, Eubulus.

Gorboduc.
My lords, whoſe grave advice and faithful aid
Have long upheld my honour and my realm,
And brought me to this age from tender years,
Guiding ſo great eſtate with great renown,
Now more importeth me, than erſt, to uſe
Your faith and wiſdom, whereby yet I reign;
That when by death my life and rule ſhall ceaſe,
The kingdom yet may with unbroken courſe,
Have certain prince, by whoſe undoubted right,
Your wealth and peace may ſtand in quiet ſtay:
And eke that they, whom nature hath prepar'd
In time to take my place in princely ſeat,
While in their father's time their pliant youth
Yields to the frame of ſkilful governance,
May ſo be taught and train'd in noble arts,
As what their fathers which have reign'd before
Have with great fame derived down to them,
With honour they may leave unto their ſeed;
And not be thought for their unworthy life,
And for their lawleſs ſwerving out of kind,
Worthy to loſe what law and kind them gave:
But that they may preſerve the common peace,
The cauſe that firſt began and ſtill maintains
The lineal courſe of kings inheritance.
For me, for mine, for you, and for the ſtate,
Whereof both I and you have charge and care,
Thus do I mean to uſe your wonted faith
To mē and mine, and to your native land.
My lords, be plain, without all wry reſpect,
Or poiſonous craft to ſpeak in pleaſing wiſe,
Leſt as the blame of ill ſucceeding things
Shall light on you, ſo light the harms alſo.

Aroſtus.

Aroſtus.
Your good acceptance ſo, moſt noble king,
Of ſuch our faithfulneſs, as heretofore
We have employ'd in duties to your grace,
And to this realm whoſe worthy head you are,
Well proves that neither you miſtruſt at all,
Nor we ſhall need in boaſting wiſe to ſhow
Our truth to you, nor yet our wakeful care
For you, for yours, and for our native land.
Wherefore, o king, I ſpeak as one for all,
Sith all as one do bear you egal faith:
Doubt not to uſe our counſels and our aids
Whoſe honours, goods, and lives, are whole avow'd
To ſerve, to aid, and to defend your grace.
     Gorboduc.
 My lords, I thank you all. This is the caſe:
Ye know, the gods, who have the ſovereign care
For kings, for kingdoms, and for commonweals,
Gave me two ſons in my more luſty age,
Who now in my decaying years are grown
Well towards riper ſtate of mind and ſtrength,
To take in hand ſome greater princely charge.
As yet they live, and ſpend their hopeful days,
With me and with their mother here in court:
Their age now aſketh other place and trade,
And mine alſo doth aſk another change;
Theirs to more travail, mine to greater eaſe.
When fatal death ſhall end my mortal life,
My purpoſe is to leave unto them twain
The realm divided in two ſundry parts:
The one, *Ferrex* mine elder ſon ſhall have,
The other, ſhall the younger *Porrex* rule.
That both my purpoſe may more firmly ſtand,
And eke that they may better rule their charge,
I mean forthwith to place them in the ſame:
That in my life they may both learn to rule,
And I may joy to ſee their ruling well.
This is in ſum, what I would have ye weigh:

             Firſt,

First, whether ye allow my whole devife,
And think it good for me, for them, for you,
And for our country, mother of us all:
And if ye like it, and allow it well,
Then for their guiding and their governance,
Show forth such means of circumftance,
As ye think meet to be both known and kept.
Lo, this is all; now tell me your advice.

Aroftus.

And this is much, and afketh great advice;
But for my part, my fovereign lord and king,
This do I think: Your majefty doth know,
How under you in juftice and in peace,
Great wealth and honour long we have enjoy'd;
So as we can not feem with greedy minds
To wifh for change of prince or governance:
But if we like your purpofe and devife,
Our liking muft be deemed to proceed
Of rightful reafon, and of heedful care,
Not for ourfelves, but for the common ftate,
Sith our own ftate doth need no better change:
I think in all as erft your grace hath faid.
Firft, when you fhall unload your aged mind
Of heavy care and troubles manifold,
And lay the fame upon my lords your fons,
Whofe growing years may bear the burden long,
(And long I pray the gods to grant it fo)
And in your life while you fhall fo behold
Their rule, their virtues, and their noble deeds,
Such as their kind behighteth to us all;
Great be the profits that fhall grow thereof,
Your age in quiet fhall the longer laft,
Your lafting age fhall be their longer ftay:
For cares of kings, that rule as you have rul'd
For publick wealth and not for private joy,
Do wafte man's life, and haften crooked age
With furrow'd face and with enfeebled limbs,
To draw on creeping death a fwifter pace.

FERREX AND PORREX.

They two yet young, shall bear the parted reign
With greater eafe, than one, now old, alone,
Can wield the whole, for whom much harder is
With leffen'd ftrength the double weight to bear.
Your eye, your counfel, and the grave regard
Of father, yea of fuch a father's name,
Now at beginning of their funder'd reign
When is the hazard of their whole fuccefs,
Shall bridle fo their force of youthful heats,
And fo reftrain the rage of infolence
Which moft affails the young and noble minds,
And fo fhall guide and train in temper'd ftay
Their yet green bending wits with reverent awe,
As now inur'd with virtues at the firft,
Cuftom, o king, fhall bring delightfulnefs.
By ufe of virtue, vice fhall grow in hate;
But if you fo difpofe it, that the day
Which ends your life, fhall firft begin their reign,
Great is the peril, what will be the end,
When fuch beginning of fuch liberties
Void of fuch ftays as in your life do lye,
Shall leave them free to random of their will,
An open prey to traiterous flattery,
The greateft peftilence of noble youth:
Which peril fhall be paft, if in your life,
Their temper'd youth with aged father's awe
Be brought in ure of fkilful ftayednefs;
And in your life, their lives difpofed fo,
Shall length your noble life in joyfulnefs.
Thus think I that your grace hath wifely thought,
And that your tender care of common weal,
Hath bred this thought, 'fo to divide your land,
And plant your fons to bear the prefent rule,
While you yet live to fee their ruling well,
That you may longer live by joy therein.
What further means behooveful are and meet,
At greater leifure may your grace devife,
When all have faid; and when we be agreed

If this be best to part the realm in twain,
And place your sons in present government:
Whereof as I have plainly said my mind,
So would I hear the rest of all my lords.

Philander.

In part I think as hath been said before,
In part again my mind is otherwise.
As for dividing of this realm in twain,
And lotting out the same in egal parts,
To either of my lords your grace's sons,
That think I best for this your realm's behoof,
For profit and advancement of your sons,
And for your comfort and your honour eke:
But so to place them while your life do last,
To yield to them your royal governance,
To be above them only in the name
Of father, not in kingly state also,
I think not good for you, for them, nor us.
This kingdom since the bloody civil field,
Where *Morgan* slain did yield his conquer'd part
Unto his cousin's sword in *Cumberland*,
Containeth all that whilome did suffice
Three noble sons of your forefather *Brute:*
So your two sons, it may suffice also;
The moe the stronger, if they gree in one:
The smaller compass that the realm doth hold
The easier is the sway thereof to wield;
The nearer justice to the wronged poor,
The smaller charge, and yet enough for one.
And when the region is divided so
That brethren be the lords of either part,
Such strength doth nature knit between them both,
In sundry bodies by conjoined love,
That not as two, but one of doubled force,
Each is to other as a sure defence;
The nobleness and glory of the one,
Doth sharp the courage of the other's mind
With virtuous envy to contend for praise:

And

And such an egalness hath nature made,
Between the brethren of one father's seed,
As an unkindly wrong it seems to be,
To throw the brother subject under feet
Of him, whose peer he is by course of kind:
And nature that did make this egalness,
Oft so repineth at so great a wrong,
That oft she raiseth up a grudging grief
In younger brethren at the elder's state:
Whereby both towns and kingdoms have been rased,
And famous stocks of royal blood destroyed:
The brother, that should be the brother's aid,
And have a wakeful care for his defence,
Gapes for his death, and blames the ling'ring years
That draw not forth his end with faster course;
And oft impatient of so long delays,
With hateful slaughter he prevents the fates,
And heaps a just reward for brother's blood,
With endless vengeance on his stock for aye.
Such mischiefs here are wisely met withal;
If egal state may nourish egal love,
Where none hath cause to grudge at other's good.
But now the head to stoop beneath them both,
Ne kind, ne reason, ne good order bears.
And oft it hath been seen, where nature's course
Hath been perverted in disorder'd wise,
When fathers cease to know that they should rule,
The children cease to know they should obey:
And often over-kindly tenderness,
Is mother of unkindly stubbornness.
I speak not this in envy or reproach,
As if I grudg'd the glory of your sons,
Whose honour I beseech the gods increase:
Nor yet as if I thought there did remain
So filthy cankers in their noble breasts,
Whom I esteem (which is their greatest praise)
Undoubted children of so good a king;
Only I mean to show by certain rules,

Which

Which kind hath graft within the mind of man,
That nature hath her order and her courſe,
Which, being broken, doth corrupt the ſtate
Of minds and things ev'n in the beſt of all.
My lords, your ſons may learn to rule of you;
Your own example in your noble court,
Is fitteſt guider of their youthful years.
If you deſire to ſee ſome preſent joy
By ſight of their well ruling in your life,
See them obey, ſo ſhall you ſee them rule:
Whoſo obeyeth not with humbleneſs,
Will rule with outrage and with inſolence.
Long may they rule, I do beſeech the gods;
But long may they learn, ere they begin to rule.
If kind and fates would ſuffer, I would wiſh
Them aged princes and immortal kings.
Wherefore, moſt noble king, I well aſſent,
Between your ſons that you divide your realm,
And as in kind, ſo match them in degree:
But while the gods prolong your royal life,
Prolong your reign; for thereto live you here,
And therefore have the gods ſo long forborn
To join you to themſelves, that ſtill you might
Be prince and father of our common weal:
They, when they ſee your children ripe to rule,
Will make them room, and will remove you hence,
That yours in right enſuing of your life
May rightly honour your immortal name.
Eubulus.
 Your wonted true regard of faithful hearts,
Makes me, o king, the bolder to preſume
To ſpeak what I conceive within my breaſt;
Although the ſame do not agree at all
With that which other here my lords have ſaid,
Nor which yourſelf have ſeemed beſt to like.
Pardon I crave, and that my words be deem'd
To flow from hearty zeal unto your grace,
And to the ſafety of your common weal.

To part your realm unto my lords your sons,
I think not good for you, ne yet for them,
But worst of all, for this our native land:
Within one land, one single rule is best:
Divided reigns do make divided hearts;
But peace preserves the country and the prince.
Such is in man the greedy mind to reign,
So great is his desire to climb aloft,
In worldly stage the statelieſt parts to bear,
That faith and justice and all kindly love
Do yield unto desire of sovereignty.
Where egal state doth raise an egal hope
To win the thing that either would attain.
Your grace remembereth how in pasſed years,
The mighty *Brute*, first prince of all this land,
Poſſeſs'd the same and rul'd it well in one:
He, thinking that the compaſs did ſuffice,
For his three ſons three kingdoms eke to make,
Cut it in three, as you would now in twain:
But how much *British* blood hath ſince been ſpilt,
To join again the ſunder'd unity?
What princes ſlain before their timely hour?
What waſte of towns and people in the land?
What treaſons heap'd on murders and on ſpoils!
Whoſe juſt revenge ev'n yet is ſcacely ceaſed,
Ruthful remembrance is yet raw in mind.
The gods forbid the like to chance again:
And you, o king, give not the cauſe thereof.
My lord *Ferrex* your elder ſon, perhaps
Whom kind and cuſtom gives a rightful hope
To be your heir and to ſucceed your reign,
Shall think that he doth ſuffer greater wrong
Than he perchance will bear, if power ſerve.
Porrex the younger, ſo upraiſ'd in ſtate,
Perhaps in courage will be raiſ'd alſo.
If flattery then, which fails not to aſſail
The tender minds of yet unſkilful youth,
In one ſhall kindle and increaſe diſdain,

And

And envy in the other's heart inflame,
This fire shall waste their love, their lives, their land,
And ruthful ruin shall destroy them both.
I wish not this, o king, so to befall,
But fear the thing, that I do most abhor.
Give no beginning to so dreadful end;
Keep them in order and obedience;
And let them both by now obeying you,
Learn such behaviour as beseems their state;
The elder, mildness in his governance,
The younger, a yielding contentedness;
And keep them near unto your presence still,
That they, restrained by the awe of you,
May live in compass of well temper'd stay,
And pass the perils of their youthful years.
Your aged life draws on to feebler time,
Wherein you shall less able be to bear
The travails that in youth you have sustain'd,
Both in your presence and your realm's defence.
If planting now your sons in further parts,
You send them further from your present reach,
Less shall you know how they themselves demean:
Traiterous corrupters of their pliant youth,
Shall have unspied a much more free access;
And if ambition and inflam'd disdain
Shall arm the one, the other, or them both,
To civil war, or to usurping pride,
Late shall you rue that you ne reck'd before.
Good is, I grant, of all to hope the best,
But not to live still dreadless of the worst.
So trust the one, that th' other be foreseen.
Arm not unskilfulness with princely power;
But you that long have wisely rul'd the reins
Of royalty within your noble realm,
So hold them, while the gods for our avails
Shall stretch the thread of your prolonged days.
Too soon he clamb, into the flaming car,
Whose want of skill did set the earth on fire.

Time

Time and example of your noble grace
Shall teach your fons both to obey and rule;
When time hath taught them, time shall make them place,
The place that now is full: and fo I pray
Long it remain, to comfort of us all.
     Gorloduc.
 I take your faithful hearts in thankful part:
But fith I fee no caufe to draw my mind,
To fear the nature of my loving fons,
Or to mifdeem that envy or difdain
Can there work hate, where nature planteth love;
In one felf purpofe do I ftill abide:
My love extendeth egally to both,
My land fufficeth for them both alfo.
Humber fhall part the marches of their realms:
The fouthern part the elder fhall poffefs,
The northern fhall *Porrex* the younger rule.
In quiet I will pafs mine aged days,
Free from the travail and the painful cares
That haften age upon the worthieft kings.
But left the fraud that ye do feem to fear
Of flattering tongues, corrupt their tender youth,
And writhe them to the ways of youthful luft,
To climbing pride, or to revenging hate,
Or to neglecting of their careful charge,
Lewdly to live in wanton recklefsnefs,
Or to oppreffing of the rightful caufe,
Or not to wreak the wrongs done to the poor,
To tread down truth, or favour falfe deceit;
I mean to join to either of my fons
Some one of thofe whofe long approved faith
And wifdom tried, may well affure my heart:
That mining fraud fhall find no way to creep
Into their fenfed ears with grave advife.
This is the end; and fo I pray you all,
To bear my fons the love and loyalty
That I have found within your faithful breafts.

Aroftus.

Aroſtus.
You, nor your ſons, our ſovereign lord, ſhall want
Our faith and ſervice while our lives do laſt.

CHORUS.

When ſettled ſtay doth hold the royal throne
In ſtedfaſt place by known and doubtleſs right,
And chiefly when deſcent on one alone
Makes ſingle and unparted reign to light;
Each change of courſe unjoints the whole eſtate,
And yields it thrall to ruin by debate.
 The ſtrength that knit by faſt accord in one,
Againſt all foreign power of mighty foes,
Could of itſelf defend itſelf alone,
Disjoined once, the former force doth loſe.
The ſticks, that ſunder'd brake ſo ſoon in twain,
In faggot bound attempted were in vain.
 Oft tender mind that leads the partial eye
Of erring parents in their children's love,
Deſtroys the wrongly loved child thereby:
This doth the proud ſon of *Apollo* prove,
Who, raſhly ſet in chariot of his ſire,
Inflam'd the parched earth with heaven's fire.
 And this great king, that doth divide his land,
And change the courſe of his deſcending crown,
And yields the reign into his childrens hand;
From bliſsful ſtate of joy and great renown,
A mirror ſhall become to princes all,
To learn to ſhun the cauſe of ſuch a fall.

The Order and Signification of the Dumb Show before the Second Act.

FIRST the mufick of cornets began to play, during which came in upon the ftage a king accompanied with a number of his nobility and gentlemen. And after he had placed himfelf in a chair of eftate prepared for him, there came and kneeled before him a grave and aged gentleman and offered up a cup unto him of wine in a glafs, which the king refufed. After him comes a brave and lufty young gentleman and prefents the king with a cup of gold filled with poifon, which the king accepted, and drinking the fame, immediately fell down dead upon the ftage, and fo was carried thence away by his lords and gentlemen, and then the mufick ceafed. Hereby was fignified, that as glafs by nature holdeth no poifon, but is clear and may eafily be feen through, ne boweth by any art: fo a faithful counfellor holdeth no treafon, but is plain and open, ne yieldeth to any undifcreet affection, but giveth wholefome counfel, which the ill-advifed prince refufeth. The delightful gold filled with poifon betokeneth flattery, which under fair feeming of pleafant words beareth deadly poifon, which deftroyeth the prince that receiveth it. As befell in the two brethren *Ferrex* and *Porrex*, who, refufing the wholefome advice of grave counfellors, credited thefe young parafites, and brought to themfelves death and deftruction thereby.

ACT II. SCENE I.

Ferrex, Hermon, Dordan.

Ferrex.

I Marvel much what reason led the king
My father, thus without all my desert,
To reave me half the kingdom, which by course
Of law and nature should remain to me.

Hermon.

If you with stubborn and untamed pride
Had stood against him in rebelling wise,
Or if with grudging mind you had envied
So slow a sliding of his aged years,
Or sought before your time to haste the course
Of fatal death upon his royal head,
Or stain'd your stock with murder of your kin;
Some face of reason might perhaps have seem'd
To yield some likely cause to spoil ye thus.

Ferrex.

The wreakful gods pour on my cursed head
Eternal plagues and never dying woes,
The hellish prince adjudge my damned ghost
To *Tantale's* thirst, or proud *Ixion's* wheel,
Or cruel gripe ¹ to gnaw my growing heart,
To during torments and unquenched flames;
If ever I conceiv'd so foul a thought,
To wish his end of life, or yet of reign.

Dordan.

Ne yet your father, o most noble prince,
Did ever think so foul a thing of you:
For he, with more than father's tender love,
While yet the fates do lend him life to rule,

---

¹ *gripe,* sic. Quære, *grife* for *griffin,* or *vulture.*

(Who long might live to fee your ruling well)
To you, my lord, and to his other fon,
Lo, he refigns his realm and royalty;
Which never would fo wife a prince have done,
If he had once mifdeem'd, that in your heart
There ever lodged fo unkind a thought.
But tender love, my lord, and fettled truft
Of your good nature; and your noble mind,
Made him to place you thus in royal throne,
And now to give you half his realm to guide;
Yea, and that half which in abounding ftore
Of things that ferve to make a wealthy realm,
In ftately cities, and in fruitful foil,
In temperate breathing of the milder heaven,
In things of needful ufe, which friendly fea
Tranfports by traffick from the foreign parts,
In flowing wealth, in honour and in force,
Doth pafs the double value of the part
That *Porrex* hath allotted to his reign.
Such is your cafe, fuch is your father's love.
     Ferrex.
 Ah love, my friends? love wrongs not whom he loves.
     Dordan.
 Ne yet he wrongeth you, that giveth you
So large a reign, ere that the courfe of time
Bring you to kingdom by defcended right,
Which time perhaps might end your time before.
     Ferrex.
 Is this no wrong, fay you, to reave from me
My native right of half fo great a realm?
And thus to match his younger fon with me
In egal pow'r, and in as great degree?
Yea, and what fon? the fon whofe fwelling pride
Would never yield one point of reverence,
When I the elder and apparent heir
Stood in the likelihood to poffefs the whole;
Yea, and that fon which from his childifh age
Envieth mine honour, and doth hate my life.
What will he now do, when his pride, his rage,

The mindful malice of his grudging heart,
Is arm'd with force, with wealth, and kingly state?
    Hermon.
 Was this not wrong? Yea ill-advised wrong,
To give so mad a man so sharp a sword,
To so great peril of so great mishap,
Wide open thus to set so large a way?
    Dordan.
 Alas, my lord, what grieful thing is this,
That of your brother you can think so ill?
I never saw him utter likely sign ·
Whereby a man might see or once misdeem
Such hate of you, ne such unyielding pride:
Ill is their counsel, shameful be their end,
That, raising such mistrustful fear in you,
Sowing the seed of such unkindly hate,
Travail by treason to destroy you both.
Wise is your brother and of noble hope,
Worthy to wield a large and mighty realm;
So much a stronger friend have you thereby,
Whose strength is your strength, if you gree in one.
    Hermon.
 If nature and the gods had pinched so
Their flowing bounty, and their noble gifts
Of princely qualities from you, my lord,
And pour'd them all at once in wasteful wise
Upon your father's younger son alone;
Perhaps there be, that in your prejudice
Would say that birth should yield to worthiness:
But sith in each good gift and princely art
Ye are his match, and in the chief of all
In mildness and in sober governance
Ye far surmount; and sith there is in you
Sufficing skill and hopeful towardness
To wield the whole, and match your elder's praise;
I see no cause why ye should lose the half,
Ne would I wish you yield to such a loss:
Lest your mild sufferance of so great a wrong

          Be

Be deemed cowardifhe and fimple dread,
Which fhall give courage to the fiery head
Of your young brother to invade the whole.
While yet therefore fticks in the people's mind
The loathed wrong of your difheritance;
And ere your brother have by fettled power,
By guileful cloak of an alluring fhow,
Got him fome force and favour in the realm;
And while the noble queen your mother lives,
To work and practice all for your avail;
Attempt redrefs by arms, and wreak yourfelf
Upon his life that gaineth by your lofs,
Who now to fhame of you, and grief of us,
In your own kingdom triumphs over you:
Show now your courage meet for kingly ftate,
That they which have avow'd to fpend their goods,
Their lands, their lives, and honours in your caufe,
May be the bolder to maintain your part
When they do fee that coward fear in you
Shall not betray ne fail their faithful hearts.
If once the death of *Porrex* end the ftrife,
And pay the price of his ufurped reign,
Your mother fhall perfuade the angry king,
The lords your friends eke fhall appeafe his rage;
For they be wife, and well they can forefee
That ere long time your aged father's death
Will bring a time when you fhall well requite
Their friendly favour, or their hateful fpite,
Yea, or their flacknefs to avaunce your caufe.
" Wife men do not fo hang on paffing ftate
" Of prefent princes, chiefly in their age,
" But they will further caft their reaching eye,
" To view and weigh the times and reigns to come.
Ne is it likely, though the king be wroth,
That he yet will, or that the realm will bear
Extreme revenge upon his only fon:
Or if he would, what one is he that dare
Be minifter to fuch an enterprife?

And

And here you be now placed in your own,
Amid your friends, your vaffals and your ftrength:
We fhall defend and keep your perfon fafe;
Till either counfel turn his tender mind,
Or age, or forrow end his weary days.
But if the fear of gods, and fecret grudge
Of nature's law, repining at the fact,
Withhold your courage from fo great attempt,
Know ye, that luft of kingdoms hath no law,
The gods do bear and well allow in kings
The things that they abhor in rafcal routs.
" When kings on flender quarrels run to wars,
" And then in cruel and unkindly wife,
" Command thefts, rapes, murders of innocents,
" The fpoil of towns, ruins of mighty realms;
" Think you fuch princes do fuppofe themfelves
" Subject to laws of kind, and fear of gods?
Murders, and violent thefts in private men,
Are heinous crimes and full of foul reproach:
Yet none offence, but deck'd with glorious name
Of noble conquefts in the hands of kings.
But if you like not yet fo hot devife,
Ne lift to take fuch vantage of the time,
But, though with peril of your own eftate,
You will not be the firft that fhall invade;
Affemble yet your force for your defence,
And for your fafety ftand upon your guard.
            Dordan.
O heaven! was there ever heard or known
So wicked counfel to a noble prince?
Let me, my lord, difclofe unto your grace
This heinous tale, what mifchief it contains;
Your father's death, your brother's, and your own,
Your prefent murder, and eternal fhame.
Hear me, o king, and fuffer not to fink
So high a treafon in your princely breaft.

                                        Ferrex.

Ferrex.
The mighty gods forbid, that ever I
Should once conceive such mischief in my heart.
Although my brother hath bereft my realm,
And bear perhaps to me an hateful mind,
Shall I revenge it with his death therefore?
Or shall I so destroy my father's life
That gave me life? the gods forbid, I say;
Cease you to speak so any more to me.
Ne you, my friend, with answer once repeat
So foul a tale: in silence let it die.
What lord or subject shall have hope at all
That under me they safely shall enjoy
Their goods, their honours, lands, and liberties,
With whom, neither one only brother dear,
Ne father dearer, could enjoy their lives?
But sith I fear my younger brother's rage,
And sith perhaps some other man may give
Some like advice, to move his grudging head
At mine estate, which counsel may perchance
Take greater force with him, than this with me;
I will in secret so prepare myself,
As, if his malice or his lust to reign
Break forth in arms or sudden violence,
I may withstand his rage, and keep mine own.
Dordan.
I fear the fatal time now draweth on
When civil hate shall end the noble line
Of famous *Brute*, and of his royal seed:—
Great *Jove*, defend the mischiefs now at hand!
O that the secretary's wife advice
Had erst been heard, when he besought the king
Not to divide his land, nor send his sons
To further parts from presence of his court,
Ne yet to yield to them his governance.
Lo, such are they now in the royal throne
As was rash *Phaeton* in *Phœbus'* car;
Ne then the fiery steeds did draw the flame

With

With wilder random through the kindled skies,
Than traiterous counsel now will whirl about
The youthful heads of these unskilful kings.
But I hereof their father will inform;
The reverence of him perhaps shall stay
The growing mischiefs, while they yet are green:
If this help not, then wo unto themselves,
The prince, the people, the divided land!

ACT II.   SCENE II.

Porrex, Tindar, Philander.

Porrex.
And is it thus? and doth he so prepare
Against his brother as his mortal foe?
And now while yet his aged father lives?
Neither regards he him? nor fears he me?
War would he have? and he shall have it so.
Tyndar.
I saw myself the great prepared store
Of horse, of armour, and of weapon there;
Ne bring I to my lord reported tales,
Without the ground of seen and searched truth.
Lo, secret quarrels run about his court
To bring the name of you, my lord, in hate.
Each man almost can now debate the cause
And ask a reason of so great a wrong,
Why he so noble and so wise a prince
Is, as unworthy, reft his heritage?
And why the king, misled by crafty means,
Divided thus his land from course of right?
The wiser sort hold down their grieful heads;
Each man withdraws from talk and company

Of thofe that have been known to favour you:
To hide the mifchief of their meaning there,
Rumours are fpread of your preparing here.
The rafcal numbers of unfkilful fort,
Are fill'd with monftrous tales of you and yours.
In fecret I was counfell'd by my friends,
To hafte me thence, and brought you, as you know,
Letters from thofe that both can truly tell,
And would not write unlefs they knew it well.
Philander.
My lord, yet ere you move unkindly war,
Send to your brother to demand the caufe:
Perhaps fome traiterous tales have fill'd his ears
With falfe reports againft your noble grace;
Which once difclos'd, fhall end the growing ftrife,
That elfe not ftay'd with wife forefight in time,
Shall hazard both your kingdoms and your lives:
Send to your father eke, he fhall appeafe
Your kindled minds, and rid you of this fear.
Porrex.
Rid me of fear? I fear him not at all;
Ne will to him, ne to my father fend.
If danger were for one to tarry there,
Think ye it fafety to return again?
In mifchiefs, fuch as *Ferrex* now intends,
The wonted courteous laws to meffengers
Are not obferv'd, which in juft war they ufe.
Shall I fo hazard any one of mine?
Shall I betray my trufty friends to him,
That have difclos'd his treafon unto me?
Let him entreat that fears, I fear him not:
Or fhall I to the king my father fend?
Yea, and fend now while fuch a mother lives
That loves my brother and that hateth me?
Shall I give leifure, by my fond delays,
To *Ferrex* to opprefs me all unware?

I will

I will not; but I will invade his realm,
And feek the traitor-prince within his court.
Mifchief for mifchief is a due reward.
His wretched head fhall pay the worthy price
Of this his treafon and his hate to me.
Shall I abide, and treat, and fend, and pray,
And hold my yielden throat to traitor's knife,
While I with valiant mind and conquering force
Might rid myfelf of foes, and win a realm?
Yet rather, when I have the wretch's head,
Then to the king my father will I fend.
The bootlefs cafe may yet appeafe his wrath:
If not, I will defend me as I may.
 Philander.
 Lo, here the end of thefe two youthful kings!
The father's death! the ruin of their realms!
" O moft unhappy ftate of counfellors
" That light on fo unhappy lords and times,
" That neither can their good advice be heard,
" Yet muft they bear the blames of ill fuccefs.
But I will to the king their father hafte,
Ere this mifchief come to the likely end,
That if the mindful wrath of wreakful gods
Since mighty *Ilion's* fall, not yet appeafed
With thefe poor remnants of the *Trojan* name,
Have not determin'd by unmoved fate
Out of this realm to raze the *Britifh* line;
By good advice, by awe of father's name,
By force of wifer lords, this kindled hate
May yet be quench'd, ere it confume us all.

CHORUS.

CHORUS.

When youth not bridled with a guiding ſtay,
Is left to random of their own delight,
And wields whole realms, by force of ſovereign ſway,
Great is the danger of unmaſter'd might,
Left ſkilleſs rage throw down with headlong fall
Their lands, their ſtates, their lives, themſelves and all.
    When growing pride doth fill the ſwelling breaſt,
And greedy luſt doth raiſe the climbing mind,
O, hardly may the peril be repreſs'd;
Ne fear of angry gods, ne laws of kind,
Ne country's care can fired hearts reſtrain,
When force hath armed envy and diſdain.
    When kings of foreſet will neglect the rede
Of beſt advice, and yield to pleaſing tales,
That do their fancy's noiſome humour feed,
Ne reaſon, nor regard of right avails:
Succeeding heaps of plagues ſhall teach too late,
To learn the miſchiefs of miſguided ſtate.
    Foul fall the traitor falſe, that undermines
The love of brethren, to deſtroy them both!
Wo to the prince that pliant ear inclines,
And yields his mind to poiſonous tale that floweth
From flattering mouth! and wo to wretched land,
That waſtes itſelf with civil ſword in hand!
    Lo thus it is, poiſon in gold to take,
And wholeſome drink in homely cup forſake.

The Order and Signification of the Dumb Show before the Third Act.

FIRST the musick of flutes began to play, during which came in upon the stage a company of mourners all clad in black, betokening death and sorrow to ensue upon the ill-advised misgovernment and dissention of brethren, as befell upon the murder of *Ferrex* by his younger brother. After the mourners had passed thrice about the stage, they departed, and then the musick ceased.

ACT III. SCENE I.

Gorboduc, Eubulus, Aroſtus, Philander, Nuntius.

Gorboduc.

O Cruel fates, o mindful wrath of gods,
Whoſe vengeance neither *Simois'* ſtained ſtreams
Flowing with blood of *Trojan* princes ſlain,
Nor *Phrygian* fields made rank with corpſes dead
Of *Aſian* kings and lords, can yet appeaſe;
Ne ſlaughter of unhappy *Priam's* race,
Nor *Ilion's* fall made level with the ſoil,
Can yet ſuffice: but ſtill continued rage
Purſues our lines, and from the fartheſt ſeas
Doth chaſe the iſſues of deſtroyed *Troy*.
" O, no man happy till his end be ſeen."
If any flowing wealth and ſeeming joy
In preſent years might make a happy wight,
Happy was *Hecuba*, the wofulleſt wretch
That ever liv'd to make a mirror of;
And happy *Priam* with his noble ſons;
And happy I, till now alas, I ſee
And feel my moſt unhappy wretchedneſs.
Behold, my lords, read ye this letter here;
Lo, it contains the ruin of our realm,
If timely ſpeed provide not haſty help.
Yet, o ye gods, if ever woful king
Might move ye kings of kings, wreak it on me
And on my ſons, not on this guiltleſs realm:
Send down your waſting flames from wrathful ſkies,
To reave me and my ſons the hateful breath.
Read, read, my lords; this is the matter why
I call'd ye now to have your good advice.

The

The Letter from Dordan *the Counsellor of the Elder Prince.*

[Eubulus *readeth the letter.*

MY sovereign lord, what I am loath to write
But loathest am to see, that I am forced
By letters now to make you understand.
My lord *Ferrex*, your eldest son, misled
By traitorous fraud of young untemper'd wits,
Assembleth force against your younger son;
Ne can my counsel yet withdraw the heat
And furious pangs of his inflamed head.
Disdain, saith he, of his disheritance,
Arms him to wreak the great pretended wrong
With civil sword upon his brother's life.
If present help do not restrain this rage,
This flame will waste your sons, your land, and you.

Your Majesty's faithful and most humble Subject,

Dordan.

Arostus.

O king, appease your grief and stay your plaint:
Great is the matter and a woful case;
But timely knowledge may bring timely help.
Send for them both unto your presence here:
The reverence of your honour, age, and state,
Your grave advice, the awe of father's name,
Shall quickly knit again this broken peace.
And if in either of my lords your sons
Be such untamed and unyielding pride,
As will not bend unto your noble hests;
If *Ferrex* the elder son can bear no peer,
Or *Porrex* not content, aspires to more
Than you him gave, above his native right;
Join with the juster side, so shall you force
Them to agree, and hold the land in stay.

Eubulus.

FERREX AND PORREX.

Eubulus.
What meaneth this? Lo, yonder comes in haste
Philander from my lord your younger son.
Gorboduc.
The gods send joyful news!
Philander.
                    The mighty *Jove*
Preserve your majesty, o noble king.
Gorboduc.
Philander, welcome; but how doth my son?
Philander.
Your son, sir, lives; and healthy I him left:
But yet, o king, the want of lustful health
Could not be half so griefeful to your grace,
As these most wretched tidings that I bring.
Gorboduc.
O heavens, yet more? not end of woes to me?
Philander.
Tyndar, o king, came lately from the court
Of *Ferrex,* to my lord your younger son,
And made report of great prepared store
For war, and faith that it is wholly meant
Against *Porrex,* for high disdain that he
Lives now a king, and egal in degree
With him that claimeth to succeed the whole,
As by due title of descending right.
Porrex is now so set on flaming fire,
Partly with kindled rage of cruel wrath,
Partly with hope to gain a realm thereby,
That he in haste prepareth to invade
His brother's land, and with unkindly war
Threatens the murder of your elder son;
Ne could I him persuade, that first he should
Send to his brother to demand the cause;
Nor yet to you, to stay this hateful strife.
Wherefore, sith there no more I can be heard,
I come myself now to inform your grace,

Vol. II.   X   And

And to beseech you, as you love the life
And safety of your children and your realm,
Now to employ your wisdom and your force,
To stay this mischief ere it be too late.
                Gorboduc.
   Are they in arms? would he not send to me?
Is this the honour of a father's name?
In vain we travail to assuage their minds:
As if their hearts, whom neither brother's love,
Nor father's awe, nor kingdom's cares, can move,
Our councils could withdraw from raging heat.
Jove slay them both, and end the cursed line!
For though, perhaps, fear of such mighty force
As I, my lords, joined with your noble aids,
May yet raise, shall repress their present heat;
The secret grudge and malice will remain,
The fire not quench'd, but kept in close restraint,
Fed still within, breaks forth with double flame:
Their death and mine must 'pease the angry gods.
                Philander.
   Yield not, o king, so much to weak despair:
Your sons yet live; and long, I trust, they shall.
If fates had taken you from earthly life,
Before beginning of this civil strife,
Perhaps your sons in their unmaster'd youth,
Loose from regard of any living wight,
Would run on headlong, with unbridled race,
To their own death, and ruin of this realm.
But sith the gods, that have the care for kings,
Of things and times dispose the order so,
That in your life this kindled flame breaks forth,
While yet your life, your wisdom, and your pow'r,
May stay the growing mischief, and repress
The fiery blaze of their unkindled heat;
It seems, and so ye ought to deem thereof,
That loving *Jove* hath temper'd so the time

Of this debate to happen in your days,
That you yet living may the fame appeafe,
And add it to the glory of your latter age,
And they your fons may learn to live in peace.
Beware, o king, the greateft harm of all,
Left by your wailful plaints your haftened death
Yield larger room unto their growing rage:
Preferve your life, the only hope of ftay.
And if your highnefs herein lift to ufe
Wifdom or force, council or knightly aid,
Lo we, our perfons, pow'rs, and lives are yours:
Ufe us till death; o king, we are your own.
     Eubulus.
 Lo here the peril that was erft forefeen,
When you, o king, did firft divide your land,
And yield your prefent reign unto your fons.
But now, o noble prince, now is no time
To wail and plain, and wafte your woful life;
Now is the time for prefent good advice.
Sorrow doth dark the judgment of the wit.
" The heart unbroken, and the courage free
" From feeble faintnefs of bootlefs defpair,
" Doth either rife to fafety or renown
" By noble valour of unvanquifh'd mind;
" Or yet doth perifh in more happy fort.
Your grace may fend to either of your fons
Some one both wife and noble perfonage,
Which with good counfel, and with weighty name
Of father, fhall prefent before their eyes
Your heft, your life, your fafety and their own,
The prefent mifchief of their deadly ftrife:
And in the while, affemble you the force
Which your commandment, and the fpeedy hafte
Of all my lords here prefent can prepare.
The terrour of your mighty pow'r fhall ftay
The rage of both, or yet of one at leaft.

            Nuntius.

Nuntius.

O king, the greatest grief that ever prince did hear,
That ever woful messenger did tell,
That ever wretched land hath seen before,
I bring to you: *Porrex* your younger son,
With sudden force invaded hath the land
That you to *Ferrex* did allot to rule;
And with his own most bloody hand he hath
His brother slain, and doth possess his realm.

Gorboduc.

O heav'ns! send down the flames of your revenge,
Destroy, I say, with flash of wreakful fire,
The traitor son, and then the wretched sire!
But let us go, that yet perhaps I may
Die with revenge, and pease the hateful gods.

CHORUS.

The lust of kingdom knows no sacred faith,
No rule of reason, no regard of right,
No kindly love, no fear of heaven's wrath:
But with contempt of gods, and man's despite,
Through bloody slaughter doth prepare the ways
To fatal sceptre, and accursed reign:
The son so loaths the father's ling'ring days,
Ne dreads his hand in brother's blood to stain.
O wretched prince, ne dost thou yet record
The yet fresh murders done within the land
Of thy forefathers, when the cruel sword
Bereft *Morgan* his life with cousin's hand?
Thus fatal plagues pursue the guilty race,
Whose murderous hand, imbru'd with guiltless blood,
Asks vengeance still before the heaven's face,
With endless mischiefs on the cursed brood.

The

FERREX AND PORREX.

The wicked child thus brings to woful fire
The mournful plaints to wafte his very life;
Thus do the cruel flames of civil fire
Deftroy the parted reign with hateful ftrife:
And hence doth fpring the well from which doth flow
The dead, black ftreams of mourning, plaints, and wo.

THE TRAGEDY OF

The Order and Signification of the Dumb Show before the Fourth Act.

FIRST the mufick of hautboys began to play, during which there came from under the ftage, as though out of hell, three furies, *Alecto, Megera,* and *Ctefiphone,* clad in black garments fprinkled with blood and flames, their bodies girt with fnakes, their heads fpread with ferpents inftead of hair, the one bearing in her hand a fnake, the other a whip, and the third a burning firebrand, each driving before them a king and a queen, which, moved by furies, unnaturally had flain their own children. The Names of the kings and queens were thefe, *Tantalus, Medea, Athamas, Ino, Cambyfes, Althea;* after that the furies and thefe had paffed about the ftage thrice, they departed, and then the mufick ceafed. Hereby was fignified the unnatural murders to follow; that is to fay, *Porrex* flain by his own mother, and of king *Gorboduc* and queen *Viden* killed by their own fubjects.

ACT

ACT IV.   SCENE I.

Viden *sola*.

Viden.

WHY should I live, and linger forth my time
In longer life to double my distress?
O me most woful wight, whom no mishap,
Long ere this day could have bereaved hence.
Mought not these hands by fortune or by fate,
Have pierc'd this breast, and life with iron reft?
Or in this palace here, where I so long
Have spent my days, could not that happy hour
Once, once have hap'd, in which these hugy frames
With death by fall might have oppressed me?
Or should not this most hard and cruel soil,
So oft where I have press'd my wretched steps,
Sometime had ruth of mine accursed life,
To rend in twain and swallow me therein?
So had my bones possessed now in peace
Their happy grave within the closed ground,
And greedy worms had gnawn this pined heart
Without my feeling pain: so should not now
This living breast remain the ruthful tomb
Wherein my heart yielden to death is graved:
Nor dreary thoughts with pangs of pining grief,
My doleful mind had not afflicted thus.
O my beloved son! o my sweet child!
My dear *Ferrex*, my joy, my life's delight!
Is my beloved son, is my sweet child,
My dear *Ferrex*, my joy, my life's delight
Murder'd with cruel death? O hateful wretch!
O heinous traitor both to heaven and earth!
Thou, *Porrex*, thou this damned deed hast wrought;

Thou,

Thou, *Porrex*, thou shalt dearly bye the same:
Traitor to kin and kind, to sire and me,
To thine own flesh, and traitor to thyself:
The gods on thee in hell shall wreak their wrath,
And here in earth this hand shall take revenge
On thee, *Porrex*, thou false and caitif wight:
If after blood so eager were thy thirst,
And murd'rous mind had so possessed thee;
If such hard heart of rock and stony flint
Liv'd in thy breast, that nothing else could like
Thy cruel tyrant's thought but death and blood:
Wild savage beasts, might not their slaughter serve
To feed thy greedy will, and in the midst
Of their entrails to stain thy deadly hands
With blood deserv'd, and drink thereof thy fill?
Or if nought else but death and blood of man
Mought please thy lust, could none in *Britain* land
Whose heart betorn out of his panting breast
With thine own hand, or work what death thou wouldst,
Suffice to make a sacrifice to 'pease
That deadly mind and murderous thought in thee?
But he who in the selfsame womb was wrapp'd
Where thou in dismal hour receivedst life?
Or if needs, needs, thy hand must slaughter make,
Moughtest thou not have reach'd a mortal wound,
And with thy sword have pierc'd this cursed womb
That the accursed *Porrex* brought to light,
And given me a just reward therefore?
So *Ferrex*, yet sweet life mought have enjoyed,
And to his aged father comfort brought,
With some young son in whom they both might live.
But whereunto waste I this ruthful speech,
To thee that hast thy brother's blood thus shed?
Shall I still think that from this womb thou sprung?
That I thee bare? or take thee for my son?
No, traitor, no: I thee refuse for mine;
Murderer, I thee renounce, thou are not mine:
Never, o wretch, this womb conceived thee,

Nor

Nor never bode I painful throws for thee.
Changeling to me thou art, and not my child,
Nor to no wight that spark of pity knew:
Ruthless, unkind, monster of nature's work,
Thou never suck'd the milk of woman's breast,
But from thy birth the cruel tiger's teats
Have nursed thee, nor yet of flesh and blood
Form'd is thy heart, but of hard iron wrought;
And wild and desert woods bred thee to life.
But canst thou hope to scape my just revenge?
Or that these hands will not be wrooke on thee?
Dost thou not know that *Ferrex*' mother lives,
That loved him more dearly than herself?
And doth she live, and is not veng'd on thee!

ACT IV. SCENE II.

Gorboduc, Arostus, Eubulus, Porrex, Marcella.

Gorboduc.
We marvel much whereto this ling'ring stay
Falls out so long: *Porrex* unto our court,
By order of our letters is returned;
And *Eubulus* receiv'd from us by hest
At his arrival here, to give him charge
Before our presence straight to make repair,
And yet we have no word whereof he stays.
Arostus.
Lo where he comes, and *Eubulus* with him.
Eubulus.
According to your highness' hest to me,
Here have I *Porrex* brought, even in such sort
As from his wearied horse he did alight,
For that your grace did will such haste therein.
Gorboduc.
We like and praise this speedy will in you,
To work the thing that to your charge we gave.
Porrex

Porrex, if we so far should swerve from kind,
And from those bounds which law of nature sets,
As thou hast done by vile and wretched deed,
In cruel murder of thy brother's life;
Our present hand could stay no longer time,
But straight should bathe this blade in blood of thee,
As just revenge of thy detested crime.
No; we should not offend the law of kind,
If now this sword of ours did slay thee here:
For thou hast murder'd him, whose heinous death
Even nature's force doth move us to revenge
By blood again; and justice forceth us
To measure death for death, thy due desert:
Yet sithence thou art our child, and sith as yet
In this hard case what word thou canst alledge
For thy defence, by us hath not been heard,
We are content to stay our will for that
Which justice bids us presently to work;
And give thee leave to use thy speech at full,
If aught thou have to lay for thine excuse.
  Porrex.
  Neither, o king, I can or will deny,
But that this hand from *Ferrex* life hath reft:
Which fact how much my doleful heart doth wail,
O! would it mought as full appear to sight
As inward grief doth pour it forth to me.
So yet perhaps, if ever ruthful heart
Melting in tears within a manly breast,
Through deep repentance of his bloody fact,
If ever grief, if ever woful man
Might move regret with sorrow of his fault,
I think, the torment of my mournful case
Known to your grace, as I do feel the same,
Would force even wrath herself to pity me.
But as the water troubled with the mud,
Shows not the face which else the eye should see,
Even so your ireful mind with stirred thought
Cannot so perfectly discern my cause.
  But

But this unhap, amongst so many heaps
I must content me with, most wretched man,
That to myself I must reserve my wo,
In pining thoughts of mine accursed fact,
Since I may not show here my smallest grief,
Such as it is, and as my breast endures,
Which I esteem the greatest misery
Of all mishaps that fortune now can send,
Not that I rest in hope with plaint and tears
To purchase life; for to the gods I clepe
For true record of this my faithful speech;
Never this heart shall have the thoughtful dread
To die the death that by your grace's doom,
By just desert, shall be pronounc'd to me:
Nor never shall this tongue once spend the speech
Pardon to crave, or seek by suit to live.
I mean not this, as though I were not touch'd
With care of dreadful death, or that I held
Life in contempt; but that I know, the mind
Stoops to no dread, although the flesh be frail:
And for my guilt, I yield the same so great,
As in myself I find a fear to sue
For grant of life.
    Gorboduc.
  In vain, o wretch, thou show'st
A woful heart; *Ferrex* now lies in grave,
Slain by thy hand.
    Porrex.
  Yet this, o father, hear;
And then I end: Your majesty well knows,
That, when my brother *Ferrex* and myself
By your own hest were join'd in governance
Of this your grace's realm of *Britain* land,
I never sought nor travail'd for the same;
Nor by myself, nor by no friend I wrought,
But from your highness' will alone it sprung,
Of your most gracious goodness bent to me.

           But

But how my brother's heart ev'n then repin'd
With fwol'n difdain againft mine egal rule,
Seeing that realm which by defcent fhould grow
Wholly to him, allotted half to me?
Ev'n in your highnefs' court he now remains,
And with my brother then in neareft place,
Who can record what proof thereof was fhow'd,
And how my brother's envious heart appear'd.
Yet I that judged it my part to feek
His favour and good-will, and loath to make
Your highnefs know the thing which fhould have brought
Grief to your grace, and your offence to him,
Hoping my earneft fuit fhould foon have won
A loving heart within a brother's breaft,
Wrought in that fort, that for a pledge of love
And faithful heart he gave to me his hand.
This made me think that he had banifh'd quite
All rancour from his thought, and bare to me
Such hearty love, as I did owe to him:
But after once we left your grace's court,
And from your highnefs' prefence liv'd apart,
This egal rule ftill, ftill, did grudge him fo,
That now thofe envious fparks which erft lay rak'd
In living cinders of diffembling breaft,
Kindled fo far within his heart difdain,
That longer could he not refrain from proof
Of fecret practice to deprive me life
By poifon's force; and had bereft me fo,
If mine own fervant, hired to this fact,
And mov'd by trouth with hate to work the fame,
In time had not bewray'd it unto me.
When thus I faw the knot of love unknit,
All honeft league and faithful promife broke,
The law of kind and trouth thus rent in twain,
His heart on mifchief fet, and in his breaft
Black treafon hid; then, then, did I defpair

That

That ever time could win him friend to me;
Then saw I how he smil'd with slaying knife
Wrapp'd under cloak; then saw I deep deceit
Lurk in his face, and death prepar'd for me:
Even nature mov'd me then to hold my life
More dear to me than his, and bad this hand,
Since by his life my death must needs ensue,
And by his death my life to be preserv'd,
To shed his blood, and seek my safety so;
And wisdom willed me, without protract,
In speedy wise to put the same in ure.
Thus have I told the cause that moved me
To work my brother's death, and so I yield
My life, my death, to judgment of your grace.
     Gorboduc.
 O cruel wight, should any cause prevail
To make thee stain thy hands with brother's blood?
But what of thee we will resolve to do
Shall yet remain unknown: thou in the mean
Shalt from our royal presence banish'd be,
Until our princely pleasure further shall
To thee be show'd; depart therefore our sight,
Accursed child. — What cruel destiny,
What froward fate hath sorted us this chance,
That even in those where we should comfort find,
Where our delight now in our aged days
Should rest and be, even there our only grief
And deepest sorrows to abridge our life,
Most pining cares and deadly thoughts do grow.
     Arostus.
 Your grace should now, in these grave years of yours,
Have found ere this, the price of mortal joys;
How short they be; how fading here in earth;
How full of change; how brittle our estate;
Of nothing sure, save only of the death,
To whom both man and all the world doth owe
Their end at last; neither should nature's power

In other fort againſt your heart prevail,
Than as the naked hand whoſe ſtroke aſſays
The armed breaſt where force doth light in vain.
Gorboduc.
 Many can yield right ſage and grave advice
Of patient ſprite to others wrapp'd in wo;
And can in ſpeech both rule and conquer kind;
Who if by proof they might feel nature's force,
Would ſhow themſelves men as they are indeed,
Which now will needs be gods. But what doth mean
The ſorry cheer of her that here doth come?
Marcella.
 O, where is ruth? or where is pity now?
Whither is gentle heart and mercy fled?
Are they exil'd out of our ſtony breaſts,
Never to make return? Is all the world
Drowned in blood, and ſunk in cruelty?
If not in women mercy may be found,
If not, alas, within the mother's breaſt,
To her own child, to her own fleſh and blood;
If ruth be baniſh'd thence; if pity there
May have no place; if there no gentle heart
Do live and dwell, where ſhould we ſeek it then?
Gorboduc.
 Madam, alas, what means your woful tale?
Marcella.
 O ſilly woman I; why to this hour
Have kind and fortune thus deferr'd my breath,
That I ſhould live to ſee this doleful day?
Will ever wight believe that ſuch hard heart
Could reſt within the cruel mother's breaſt?
With her own hand to ſlay her only ſon?
But out alas, theſe eyes beheld the ſame:
They ſaw the dreary ſight, and are becomen
Moſt ruthful records of the bloody fact.
Porrex, alas, is by his mother ſlain,
And with her hand, a woful thing to tell,

While

While flumbering on his careful bed he refts,
His heart ftab'd in with knife is reft of life.
Gorboduc.
O *Eubulus*, o, draw this fword of ours,
And pierce this heart with fpeed. O hateful light,
O loathfome life, o fweet and welcome death!
Dear *Eubulus*, work this we thee befeech.
Eubulus.
Patient your grace, perhaps he liveth yet,
With wound receiv'd, but not of certain death.
Gorboduc.
O let us then repair unto the place,
And fee if *Porrex* live, or thus be flain.
Marcella.
Alas, he liveth not! it is too true,
That with thefe eyes, of him a peerlefs prince,
Son to a king, and in the flower of youth,
Even with a twink a fenfelefs ftock I faw.
Aroftus.
O damned deed.
Marcella.
But hear his ruthful end:
The noble prince, pierc'd with the fudden wound,
Out of his wretched flumber haftily ftart,
Whofe ftrength now failing, ftraight he overthrew,
When in the fall his eyes even new unclos'd
Beheld the queen, and cry'd to her for help.
We then, alas, the ladies which that time
Did there attend, feeing that heinous deed,
And hearing him oft call the wretched name
Of mother, and to cry to her for aid,
Whofe direful hand gave him the mortal wound,
Pitying (alas, for nought elfe could we do)
His ruthful end, ran to the woful bed,
Defpoiled ftraight his breaft, and, all we might,
Wiped in vain with napkins next at hand
The fudden ftreams of blood that flufhed faft
Out of the gaping wound. O, what a look!

O, what

THE TRAGEDY OF

O, what a ruthful, stedfast eye, methought
He fix'd upon my face, which to my death
Will never part fro me! when with a braid,
A deep fet sigh he gave, and therewithal
Clasping his hands, to heav'n he cast his sight;
And straight pale death pressing within his face,
The flying ghost his mortal corps forsook.

Arostus.
Never did age bring forth so vile a fact!

Marcella.
O hard and cruel hap, that thus assigned
Unto so worthy a wight so wretched end:
But most hard cruel heart, that could consent
To lend the hateful destinies that hand,
By which, alas, so heinous crime was wrought!
O queen of adamant! o marble breast!
If not the favour of his comely face,
If not his princely cheer and countenance,
His valiant active arms, his manly breast,
If not his fair and seemly personage,
His noble limbs, in such proportion cast
As would have wrap'd a silly woman's thought;
If this mought not have mov'd thy bloody heart,
And that most cruel hand, the wretched weapon
Ev'n to let fall, and kiss him in the face,
With tears for ruth to reave such one by death:
Should nature yet consent to slay her son?
O mother, thou to murder thus thy child?
Ev'n *Jove* with justice must with lightning flames
From heaven, send down some strange revenge on thee.
Ah, noble prince, how oft have I beheld
Thee mounted on thy fierce and trampling steed,
Shining in armour bright before the tilt,
And with thy mistress' sleeve ty'd on thy helm,
And charge thy staff to please thy lady's eye,
That bow'd the head-piece of thy friendly foe?

How

FERREX AND PORREX.

How oft in arms on horfe to bend the mace?
How oft in arms on foot to break the fword?
Which never now thefe eyes may fee again.
Aroſtus.
Madam, alas, in vain thefe plaints are fhed,
Rather with me depart, and help to fuage
The thoughtful griefs that in the aged king
Muft needs by nature grow by death of this
His only fon, whom he did hold fo dear.
Marcella.
What wight is that which faw that I did fee,
And could refrain to wail with plaint and tears?
Not I, alas! that heart is not in me:
But let us go, for I am griev'd anew,
To call to mind the wretched father's wo.

CHORUS.

When greedy luft in royal feat to reign
Hath reft all care of gods and eke of men,
And cruel heart, wrath, treafon and difdain,
Within ambitious breaft are lodged, then
Behold how mifchief wide herfelf difplays,
And with the brother's hand the brother flays.
When blood thus fhed doth ftain the heaven's face
Crying to *Jove* for vengeance of the deed,
The mighty God ev'n moveth from his place
With wrath to wreak; then fends he forth with fpeed
The dreadful furies, daughters of the night,
With ferpents girt, carrying the whip of ire,
With hair of ftinging fnakes, and fhining bright
With flames and blood, and with a brand of fire:
Thefe for revenge of wretched murder done,
Do make the mother kill her only fon.

Blood asketh blood, and death must death requite
Jove by his just and everlasting doom,
Justly hath ever so requited it;
The times before record, and times to come
Shall find it true, and so doth present proof
Present before our eyes for our behoof.

O happy wight, that suffers not the snare
Of murderous mind to tangle him in blood;
And happy he, that can in time beware
By others harms, and turn it to his good:
But wo to him, that fearing not t'offend,
Doth serve his lust, and will not see the end.

The Order and Signification of the Dumb Show before the Fifth Act.

FIRST the drums and flutes began to sound, during which there came forth upon the stage a company of harquebusiers and of armed men, all in order of battle. These, after their pieces discharged, and that the armed men had three times marched about the stage, departed, and then the drums and flutes did cease. Hereby was signified tumults, rebellions, arms and civil wars to follow, as fell in the realm of *Great Britain*, which by the space of fifty years and more, continued in civil war between the nobility after the death of king *Gorboduc* and of his issues, for want of certain limitation in succession of the crown, till the time of *Dunwallo Molmutius*, who reduced the land to monarchy.

THE TRAGEDY OF

ACT V. SCENE I.

Clotyn, Mandud, Gwenard, Fergus, Eubulus.

Clotyn.

DID ever age bring forth such tyrants hearts?
    The brother hath bereft the brother's life;
The mother she hath dy'd her cruel hands
In blood of her own son, and now at last
The people, lo, forgetting trouth and love,
Contemning quite both law and loyal heart,
Ev'n they have slain their sovereign lord, and queen.

Mandud.
Shall this their traiterous crime unpunish'd rest?
Ev'n yet they cease not, carry'd on with rage,
In their rebellious routs, to threaten still
A new bloodshed unto the prince's kin,
To slay them all, and to uproot the race
Both of the king and queen, so are they mov'd
With *Porrex'* death, wherein they falsely charge
The guiltless king without desert at all,
And trait'rously have murdered him therefore,
And eke the queen.

Gwenard.
        Shall subjects dare with force
To work revenge upon their prince's fact?
Admit the worst that may, as sure in this
The deed was foul, the queen to slay her son,
Shall yet the subject seek to take the sword,
Arise against his lord, and slay his king?
O wretched state, where those rebellious hearts
Are not rent out ev'n from their living breasts,
And with the body thrown unto the fowls
As carrion food, for terrour of the rest.

Fergus.

Fergus.
There can no punishment be thought too great
For this so grievous crime: let speed therefore
Be us'd therein, for it behoveth so.
Eubulus.
Ye all, my lords, I see, consent in one,
And I as one consent with ye in all.
I hold it more than need, with sharpest law
To punish this tumultuous bloody rage:
For nothing more may shake the common state
Than sufferance of uproars without redress;
Whereby how some kingdoms of mighty power,
After great conquests made, and flourishing
In fame and wealth, have been to ruin brought,
I pray to *Jove* that we may rather wail
Such hap in them, than witness in ourselves.
Eke fully with the duke my mind agrees, *
Though kings forget to govern as they ought,
Yet subjects must obey as they are bound.
But now, my lords, before ye farther wade,
Or spend your speech, what sharp revenge shall fall
By justice' plague on these rebellious wights;
Methinks, ye rather should first search the way
By which in time, the rage of this uproar
Mought be repress'd, and these great tumults ceased.
Even yet the life of *Britain* land doth hang
In traitors balance of unegal weight;
Think not, my lords, the death of *Gorboduc*,
Nor yet *Videna's* blood will cease their rage:
Even our own lives, our wives and children dear,

---

* *The following lines are to be found only in the spurious copy.*

That no cause serves, whereby the subject may
Call to account the doings of his prince,
Much less in blood by sword to work revenge,
No more than may the hand cut off the head;
In act nor speech, no not in secret thought
The subject may rebel against his lord,
Or judge of him that fits in *Cæsar's* seat,
With grudging mind to damn those he mislikes.

Our country, dear'st of all, in danger stands
Now to be spoil'd; now, now made desolate,
And by ourselves a conquest to ensue.
For, give once sway unto the people's lusts,
To rush forth on, and stay them not in time,
And as the stream that rolleth down the hill,
So will they headlong run with raging thoughts,
From blood to blood, from mischief unto moe,
To ruin of the realm, themselves and all:
So giddy are the common people's minds,
So glad of change, more wavering than the sea.
Ye see, my lords, what strength these rebels have;
What hugy number is assembled still:
For though the traiterous fact for which they rose
Be wrought and done, yet lodge they still in field;
So that how far their furies yet will stretch,
Great cause we have to dread. That we may seek
By present battle to repress their power,
Speed must we use to levy force therefore;
For either they forthwith will mischief work,
Or their rebellious roars forthwith will cease:
These violent things may have no lasting long.
Let us therefore use this for present help;
Persuade by gentle speech, and offer grace,
With gift of pardon, save unto the chief,
And that upon condition that forthwith
They yield the captains of their enterprise
To bear such guerdon of their traiterous fact,
As may be both due vengeance to themselves,
And wholesome terrour to posterity.
This shall, I think, scatter the greatest part
That now are holden with desire of home,
Wearied in field with cold of winter's nights,
And some, no doubt, stricken with dread of law.
When this is once proclaimed, it shall make
The captains to mistrust the multitude,
Whose safety bids them to betray their heads;
And so much more, because the rascal routs,

In things of great and perillous attempts,
Are never trusty to the noble race.
And while we treat and stand on terms of grace,
We shall both stay their fury's rage the while,
And eke gain time, whose only help sufficeth
Withouten war to vanquish rebels power.
In the mean while, make you in readiness
Such band of horsemen as ye may prepare:
Horsemen, you know, are not the commons strength,
But are the force and store of noble men,
Whereby the unchosen and unarmed sort
Of skilless rebels, whom none other power
But number makes to be of dreadful force,
With sudden brunt may quickly be opprefs'd.
And if this gentle mean of proffer'd grace,
With stubborn hearts cannot so far avail
As to assuage their desp'rate courages,
Then do I wish such slaughter to be made,
As present age and eke posterity
May be adrad with horrour of revenge,
That justly then shall on these rebels fall:
This is, my lords, the sum of mine advice.
                    Clotyn.
    Neither this case admits debate at large;
And though it did, this speech that hath been said
Hath well abridg'd the tale I would have told.
Fully with *Eubulus* do I consent
In all that he hath said: and if the same
To you, my lords, may seem for best advise,
I wish that it should straight be put in ure.
                    Mandud.
    My lords, then let us presently depart,
And follow this that liketh us so well.
                    Fergus.
    If ever time to gain a kingdom here
Were offer'd man, now it is offer'd me.
The realm is reft both of their king and queen;
The offspring of the prince is slain and dead:

N

No issue now remains; the heir unknown;
The people are in arms and mutinies;
The nobles they are busied how to cease
These great rebellious tumults and uproars;
And *Britain* land now desert left alone,
Amid these broils uncertain where to rest,
Offers herself unto that noble heart
That will or dare pursue to bear her crown.
Shall I, that am the duke of *Albany*,
Descended from that line of noble blood,
Which hath so long flourish'd in worthy fame
Of valiant hearts, such as in noble breasts
Of right should rest above the baser sort,
Refuse to venture life to win a crown?
Whom shall I find enemies that will withstand
My fact herein, if I attempt by arms
To seek the same now in these times of broil?
These dukes power can hardly well appease
The people that already are in arms:
But if perhaps my force be once in field,
Is not my strength in pow'r above the best
Of all these lords now left in *Britain* land?
And though they should match me with power of men,
Yet doubtful is the chance of battles join'd:
If victors of the field we may depart,
Ours is the sceptre then of *Great Britain*;
If slain amid the plain this body lie,
Mine enemies yet shall not deny me this,
But that I died giving the noble charge,
To hazard life for conquest of a crown.
Forthwith therefore will I in post depart
To *Albany*, and raise in armour there
All pow'r I can: and here my secret friends
By secret practise shall solicit still,
To seek to win to me the people's hearts.

ACT

ACT V.   SCENE II.

Eubulus, Clotyn, Mandud, Gwenard, Aroſtus, Nuntius.

Eubulus.

O *Jove,* how are theſe people's hearts abus'd?
What blind fury thus headlong carries them?
That though ſo many books, ſo many rolls
Of ancient time, record what grievous plagues
Light on theſe rebels aye, and though ſo oft
Their ears have heard their aged fathers tell
What juſt reward theſe traitors ſtill receive,
Yea, though themſelves have ſeen deep death and blood,
By ſtrangling cord and ſlaughter of the ſword,
To ſuch aſſign'd, yet can they not beware;
Yet can not ſtay their lewd rebellious hands:
But ſuffering, lo, foul treaſon to diſtain
Their wretched minds, forget their loyal heart,
Reject all truth, and riſe againſt their prince.
A ruthful caſe, that thoſe whom duty's bond,
Whom grafted law by nature, truth, and faith,
Bound to preſerve their country and their king,
Born to defend their commonwealth and prince;
Ev'n they ſhould give conſent thus to ſubvert
Thee, *Britain* land, and from thy womb ſhould ſpring,
O native ſoil, thoſe that will needs deſtroy
And ruin thee, and eke themſelves in fine.
For lo, when once the dukes had offer'd grace
Of pardon ſweet, the multitude, miſled
By traiterous fraud of their ungracious heads,
One ſort that ſaw the dangerous ſucceſs
Of ſtubborn ſtanding in rebellious war,
And knew the difference of prince's power
From headleſs number of tumultuous routs,

Whom

Whom common country's care, and private fear,
Taught to repent the errour of their rage,
Lay'd hands upon the captains of their band,
And brought them bound unto the mighty dukes:
And other fort, not trufting yet fo well
The truth of pardon, or miftrufting more
Their own ofence, than that they could conceive
Such hope of pardon for fo foul mifdeed;
Or for that they their captains could not yield,
Who, fearing to be yielded, fled before,
Stale home by filence of the fecret night:
The third unhappy and unraged fort
Of defp'rate hearts, who, ftain'd in princes blood,
From traiterous furour could not be withdrawn
By love, by law, by grace, ne yet by fear,
By proffer'd life, ne yet by threaten'd death;
With minds hopelefs of life, dreadlefs of death,
Carelefs of country, and awlefs of God,
Stood bent to fight as furies did them move,
With violent death to clofe their traiterous life.
Thefe all by power of horfemen were oppref's'd,
And with revenging fword flain in the field,
Or with the ftrangling cord hang'd on the trees;
Where yet their carrion carcafes do preach,
The fruits that rebels reap of their uproars,
And of the murder of their facred prince.
But lo, where do approach the noble dukes,
By whom thofe tumults have been thus appeas'd.
Clotyn.
I think the world will now at length beware,
And fear to put on arms againft their prince.
Mandud.
If not? thofe traiterous hearts that dare rebel,
Let them behold the wide and hugy fields
With blood and bodies fpread of rebels flain,
The lofty trees clothed with the corpfes dead,
That, ftrangled with the cord, do hang thereon.

Aroftus

Aroſtus.
A juſt reward, ſuch as all times before
Have ever 'lotted to thoſe wretched folks.
Gwenard.
But what means he that cometh here ſo faſt?
Nuntius.
My lords, as duty and my trouth doth move,
And of my country work a care in me,
That if the ſpending of my breath avail'd
To do the ſervice that my heart deſires,
I would not ſhun to embrace a preſent death;
So have I now in that wherein I thought
My travail mought perform ſome good effect,
Ventur'd my life to bring theſe tidings here.
Fergus, the mighty duke of *Albany*,
Is now in arms, and lodgeth in the field
With twenty thouſand men; hither he bends
His ſpeedy march, and minds to invade the crown:
Daily he gathereth ſtrength, and ſpreads abroad,
That to this realm no certain heir remains,
That *Britain* land is left without a guide,
That he the ſceptre ſeeks for nothing elſe
But to preſerve the people and the land,
Which now remain as ſhip without a ſtern.
Lo, this is that which I have here to ſay.
Clotyn.
Is this his faith? and ſhall he falſely thus
Abuſe the vantage of unhappy times?
O wretched land, if his outragious pride,
His cruel and untemper'd wilfulneſs,
His deep diſſembling ſhows of falſe pretence,
Should once attain the crown of *Britain* land!
Let us, my lords, with timely force reſiſt
The new attempt of this our common foe,
As we would quench the flames of common fire.
Mandud.
Though we remain without a certain prince
To wield the realm, or guide the wand'ring rule,

Yet

Yet now the common mother of us all,
Our native land, our country, that contains
Our wives, children, kindred, ourselves, and all
That ever is or may be dear to man,
Cries unto us to help ourselves and her.
Let us advance our powers to repress
This growing foe of all our liberties.

Gwenard.

Yea, let us so, my lords, with hasty speed.—
And ye, o gods, send us the welcome death
To shed our blood in field, and leave us not
In loathsome life to linger out our days,
To see the hugy heaps of these unhaps
That now roll down upon the wretched land,
Where empty place of princely governance,
No certain stay now left of doubtless heir,
Thus leave this guideless realm an open prey
To endless storms and waste of civil war.

Arostus.

That ye, my lords, do so agree in one,
To save your country from the violent reign
And wrongfully usurped tyranny
Of him that threatens conquest of you all,
To save your realm, and in this realm yourselves
From foreign thraldom of so proud a prince,
Much do I praise; and I beseech the gods,
With happy honour to requite it you.
But o, my lords, sith now the heaven's wrath
Hath reft this land the issue of their prince,
Sith of the body of our late sovereign lord
Remains no moe, since the young kings be slain,
And of the title of descended crown
Uncertainly the divers minds do think
Even of the learned sort, and more uncertainly
Will partial fancy and affection deem;
But most uncertainly will climbing pride,
And hope of reign, withdraw to sundry parts
The doubtful right and hopeful lust to reign.

When

When once this noble fervice is atchieved
For *Britain* land, the mother of ye all,
When once ye have with armed force reprefs'd
The proud attempts of this *Albanian* prince,
That threatens thraldom to your native land,
When ye fhall vanquifhers return from field,
And find the princely ftate an open prey
To greedy luft, and to ufurping power;
Then, then, my lords, if ever kindly care
Of ancient honour of your anceftors,
Of prefent wealth and noblefs of your ftocks,
Yea, of the lives and fafety yet to come
Of your dear wives, your children, and yourfelves,
Might move your noble hearts with gentle ruth,
Then, then, have pity on the torn eftate;
Then help to falve the wellnear hopelefs fore;
Which ye fhall do, if ye yourfelves withhold
The flaying knife from your own mother's throat:
Her fhall you fave, and you, and yours in her,
If ye fhall all with one affent forbear
Once to lay hand, or take unto yourfelves
The crown, by colour of pretended right,
Or by what other means foe'er it be,
Till firft by common counfel of you all
In parliament, the regal diadem
Be fet in certain place of governance;
In which your parliament, and in your choice,
Prefer the right, my lords, without refpect
Of ftrength or friends, or whatfoever caufe
That may fet forward any other's part;
For right will laft, and wrong can not endure:
Right, mean I his or hers, upon whofe name
The people reft by mean of native line,
Or by the virtue of fome former law
Already made their title to advance.
Such one, my lords, let be your chofen king;
Such one fo born within your native land;
Such one prefer; and in no wife admit

The

The heavy yoke of foreign governance:
Let foreign titles yield to publick wealth.
And with that heart wherewith ye now prepare
Thus to withstand the proud invading foe,
With that same heart, my lords, keep out also
Unnatural thraldom of strangers reign,
Ne suffer you, against the rules of kind,
Your mother land to serve a foreign prince.

Eubulus.

 Lo, here the end of *Brutus*' royal line,
And, lo, the entry to the woful wreck
And utter ruin of this noble realm.
The royal king, and eke his sons are slain;
No ruler rests within the regal seat;
The heir, to whom the sceptre longs, unknown;
That to each force of foreign prince's power,
Whom vantage of our wretched state may move
By sudden arms to gain so rich a realm;
And to the proud and greedy mind at home,
Whom blinded lust to reign leads to aspire.
Lo, *Britain* realm is left an open prey,
A present spoil by conquest to ensue.
Who seeth not now how many rising minds
Do feed their thoughts with hope to reach a realm?
And who will not by force attempt to win
So great a gain that hope persuades to have?
A simple colour shall for title serve.
Who wins the royal crown will want no right;
Nor such as shall display by long descent
A lineal race to prove him lawful king.
In the mean while these civil arms shall rage,
And thus a thousand mischiefs shall unfold,
And far and near spread thee, o *Britain* land;
All right and law shall cease; and he that had
Nothing to day, to morrow shall enjoy
Great heaps of gold; and he that flow'd in wealth,
Lo, he shall be bereft of life and all;
And happiest he that then possesseth least:

The

The wives shall suffer rape, the maids deflour'd,
And children fatherless shall weep and wail;
With fire and sword thy native folk shall perish:
One kinsman shall bereave another's life;
The father shall unwitting slay the son;
The son shall slay the sire, and know it not.
Women and maids the cruel soldiers swords
Shall pierce to death, and silly children, lo,
That play in the streets and fields are found,
By violent hand shall close their latter day.
Whom shall the fierce and bloody soldier
Reserve to life? whom shall he spare from death?
Ev'n thou, o wretched mother, half alive,
Thou shalt behold thy dear and only child
Slain with the sword, while he yet sucks thy breast.
Lo, guiltless blood shall thus each where be shed.
Thus shall the wasted soil yield forth no fruit,
But dearth and famine shall possess the land.
The towns shall be consum'd and burnt with fire;
The peopled cities shall wax desolate;
And thou, o *Britain*, whilom in renown,
Whilom in wealth and fame, shall thus be torn,
Dismember'd thus, and thus be rent in twain;
Thus wasted and defaced, spoiled and destroyed:
These be the fruits your civil wars will bring.
Hereto it comes, when kings will not consent
To grave advice, but follow wilful will.
This is the end, when in fond princes hearts
Flattery prevails, and sage reed hath no place.
These are the plagues, when murder is the mean
To make new heirs unto the royal crown.
Thus wreak the gods, when that the mother's wrath
Nought but the blood of her own child may suage.
These mischiefs spring, when rebels will arise
To work revenge, and judge their prince's fact.
This, this ensues, when noble men do fail
In loyal troth, and subjects will be kings:
And this doth grow, when, lo, unto the prince

Whom

Whom death or fudden hap of life bereaves,
No certain heir remains, fuch certain heir,
As not all only is the rightful heir
But to the realm is fo made known to be,
And troth thereby vefted in fubjects hearts,
To owe faith there, where right is known to reft.
Alas, in parliament what hope can be,
When is of parliament no hope at all?
Which, though it be affembled by confent,
Yet is not likely with confent to end;
While each one for himfelf, or for his friend
Againft his foe, fhall travail what he may.
While now the ftate left open to the man
That fhall with greateft force invade the fame
Shall fill ambitious minds with gaping hope,
When will they once with yielding hearts agree?
Or in the while, how fhall the realm be ufed?
No, no; then parliament fhould have been holden,
And certain heirs appointed to the crown,
To ftay the title of eftablifhed right,
And in the people plant obedience,
While yet the prince did live, whofe name and power
By lawful fummons and authority
Might make a parliament to be of force,
And might have fet the ftate in quiet ftay:
But now, o happy man, whom fpeedy death
Deprives of life, ne is enforc'd to fee
Thefe hugy mifchiefs and thefe miferies,
Thefe civil wars, thefe murders, and thefe wrongs
Of juftice, yet muft God in fine reftore
This noble crown unto the lawful heir:
For right will always live, and rife at length,
But wrong can never take deep root to laft.

THE END OF THE TRAGEDY OF
FERREX AND PORREX.

www.ingramcontent.com/pod-product-compliance
Lightning Source LLC
Chambersburg PA
CBHW030301240426
43673CB00040B/1021